HUNGARIAN CUISINE

MARISKA VIZVÁRI

HUNGARIAN CUISINE

CORVINA

Translated from the Hungarian by

GABRIELLA MOLNÁR

Cover photo by Károly Hemző
© The heirs of Mariska Vizvári

ISBN 963 13 3908 4

DTP Impala House, Szeged
Printed in Hungary, 1994
ISBN 963 13 3908 4

CONTENTS

FOREWORD

Mariska Vizvári was the Mrs. Beeton of Hungary, Mariska Vizvári was a well-known actress in her time, Mrs. Beeton a journalist, but both are remembered by their cookery books, handed down from mother to daughter, from generation to generation.

The first English edition of Mariska Vizvári's book came at a time when the numbers of English and Americans taking their holidays on the continent of Europe began to run into millions. They learnt to like foreign food; they learnt to enjoy experimenting with it at home. And as the demand grew, formerly strange and exotic condiments and ingredients became familiar sights on the shelves of the local shops.

As a result, the "Treasure Trove of Hungarian Cookery," with its comprehensive list of recipes for all occasions, and its host of special Hungarian dishes and local specialities found a ready public, and the demand for a fourth edition has made itself felt.

What is different about Hungarian cooking? In general, the preference for rich and spicy sauces, stews and sweets over rather "drier" dishes. In particular, the liberal use of a few special ingredients which give it its own inimitable and original flavour. These are:

Paprika It should be noted that dishes flavoured with paprika need not be hot. In fact the finest brands of paprika are not strong at all.

Lard and Goose-fat The use of lard or goose-fat instead of other forms of fat for cooking is certainly typical, but if you are worried about the cholesterol content of lard, other fats can be substituted, and indeed in somewhat smaller quantities than are usual in Hungary.

Sour Cream This is an essential ingredient in many Hungarian dishes, and since it is now easily procurable in England, should always be used. It is a basic ingredient of "paprikash" (any kind of meat, or just plain potatoes, braised on a foundation of onions, seasoned with paprika, to which sour cream has been added), as well as in many Hungarian vegetable dishes and casserole stews.

Fresh Green peppers and Tomatoes are frequently used to flavour dishes, as well as the cooked and preserved form (braised in lard with onions, and called lecsó (letcho). Green peppers should always be cored and the white veins removed.

Pasta The use of pastas for desserts — especially as sweets with sugared nuts, poppy seeds, fruit jellies or jam — is probably peculiar to Hungary.

Tarhonya (something similar, called farfel, is sold in the delicatessen shops) is often used for garnish instead of rice.

Goose-liver A great favourite in Hungary, though rather expensive. While chicken-liver or calf-liver can be used as a substitute, there is nothing to equal genuine goose-liver (it is exported in tins from Hungary), and should certainly be tried for some festive occasion.

Rétes (or Strudel) This is a famous Hungarian sweet, and though it probably involves too much work for the normally busy housewife, it is worth the effort for a grand party. The real test of imagination lies in the variations on the wealth of sweet and savoury fillings.

USE OF THE INDEX Where recipes call for prepared ingredients (like egg squares, aspic, mayonnaise) and you do not have them ready-made, you can find the recipe for them under the appropriate name in the Index.

The Index is arranged in alphabetical order, whenever possible under the main ingredient in the dish. Stuffed Eggplant au Gratin, for instance, will be indexed under Eggplant, Stuffed, au Gratin.

In this edition, all weights and liquid measures have been converted to suit the English and American cook. A cup always means a breakfast cup. It works out like this:

Liquids: 1/2 cup = 1/4 pint = 1 gill
         1 cup = 1/2 pint = 2 gills
         2 cups = 1 pint = 4 gills
         4 cups = 2 pints = 8 gills

Solids: 1 ounce (oz.) = 28.35 grammes = 1/5 cup of flour,
                                        3/10 cup of sugar

1 pound (lb.) = 453.6 grammes = 3 cups of flour,
                                4 1/2 cups of sugar

HINTS FOR BEGINNERS

1. The flavour of grilled or fried meat (steaks, chops, veal cutlets, etc.) is greatly enhanced if treated before cooking in the following way: cover each slice of meat with thinly sliced onions, a sprig or two of parsley and a pinch of ground black pepper. Place meat-slices on top of each other and leave them to stand for 2–3 hours. Brush the flavourings of the meat before cooking.

2. Always put a few chopped mushrooms into the stuffing used for poultry. If the stuffing is prepared with onion, fry the finely chopped onion in a little fat before adding it to the mixture.

3. In summer time, place a bunch of fresh herbs (parsley, marjoram, and sage) in the inside of poultry to be roasted. It improves the flavour.

4. Peel hard-boiled eggs and placing in stock left over from cooking ham or smoked meat, let them simmer for about 10–15 minutes. They are excellent with steamed spinach or with sorrel sauce.

5. Fried chicken should be skinned before jointing. Leave the skin only on the wings and bony parts of the chicken.

6. Sweet foods always need a grain of salt; a pinch of sugar should be added to sour dishes. Bread and butter and jam is always better with a grain of salt added to the butter; salads need a pinch of sugar.

7. For the preparation of roux always use plain flour.

8. Soak haricot beans overnight in cold water to which a pinch of bicarbonate of soda has been added.

9. If you boil marrow-bones, salt the open ends of the bone, this way you prevent the marrow from boiling away or falling out the bone.

10. Always cover the top of the cake with greaseproof-paper if there are almonds or nuts on it, to prevent burning.

11. Add a small pinch of salt to the egg whites just before whipping and a spoonful or two of cold water.

12. When you use garlic, either scrape or crush before chopping.

13. Skinning fish is easy if you first pour some boiling hot water over it.

14. Boiled puddings should be left unopened for 6–7 minutes after lifting them out of the water. They will set and will be easier to run out.

15. For best results rub joint of pork with salt and leave to stand for 1 hour before roasting, then place it in a roasting tin and pour 1/2 cup of cold water under the joint before you put it in the oven.

COLD ENTRÉES

Aspic Jelly

Ingredients: 1 lb. chopped veal bones • 1 unpeeled onion • pinch of
salt • 6 whole black peppercorns • 2 pints water.

This is often needed for cold dishes, salad and sandwich dec-
orations. Here is an easy way to make it: prepare a stock
using 1 lb. chopped veal bones, pinch of salt, 1 unpeeled
onion, 6 whole black peppercorns and 2 pints water. Simmer
for at least 2 hours, then strain through a piece of muslin.
Add powdered gelatine, and stir till it melts completely.
Rinse a mould or bowl with cold water, strain the mixture
into it, and chill.

Jellied Chicken

Ingredients: 1 medium-sized chicken • 1 pint French vegetable
salad in mayonnaise • 2 pints of melted meat jelly (aspic).
(See Aspic Jelly above.)

Cook chicken till tender. Pull off skin and take meat off the
bones taking care to keep meat in neat pieces. Take a round
deep galantine mould and pour a 2-inch layer of melted
aspic into the bottom. Let it set. Heap French salad over the
aspic in the middle of the dish and lay the pieces of meat
neatly over it. Pour over it carefully one or two spoonfuls of
liquid aspic, allow to set so as to keep the pieces of meat in
place. Pour the remainder of melted but cool aspic over it
and let it set. Chill thoroughly. Just before serving, dip mould
in hot water, turn out on a round flat dish and decorate with
sliced hard-boiled eggs, sliced cucumber and lemon.

Galantine of Chicken

Ingredients: 1 medium-sized chicken • 1 level tbsp. salt • 3 pints water • 1 medium-sized carrot • 1 small parsnip • 1 small onion • bunch of parsley • 5 oz. mushrooms • about 1/4 pint mayonnaise • 1/2 tsp. lemon juice • 2 sheets of gelatine • lettuce • hard-boiled eggs and spring radishes.

Cook chicken in water till tender together with salt, carrot, parsnip, onion and parsley. Take out chicken, pull off the skin and bone it. Strain stock and put on low heat again with the whole mushrooms added. Simmer. Mince the chicken meat and when mushrooms are cooked mince them, too, and add to chicken. Mix with mayonnaise. Reduce stock to 1 pint, add galatine. When cool enough but not yet set, mix thoroughly with the chicken and mushroom mixture and pour into a rinsed galantine mould. Chill for 5–6 hours. Dip mould in hot water and turn galantine out onto a flat dish. Decorate with sliced hard-boiled eggs, hearts of lettuces cut in four, and spring radishes.

Breast of Turkey à la Badacsony

Ingredients: the breast of a roast turkey • 3 egg yolks • 1/2 tsp. salt • 2 gills sour cream • 1 gill olive oil • 1/2 tsp. sugar • 1 tbsp. French mustard • 1 tbsp. chopped capers • 1 tsp. chopped chives • 1/2 tsp. lemon juice • 1 green pepper.

Skin the meat and cut into neat cubes. Put egg yolks, salt and sour cream in a double saucepan and beating constantly, cook for about 10–15 minutes. Take aside and beat for another 5 minutes. Allow to cool. When cold, add the olive oil drop by drop, stirring the mixture evenly in one direction only. Then add sugar, mustard, chopped capers, chopped chives and lemon juice. Mix the meat with one-third of this sauce, heap the mixture on a round dish, and cover it generously with the rest of the sauce. Chop half of the green pepper coarsely and scatter it on top. Cut the other half into rings. Decorate with sliced, hardboiled eggs and green pepper rings.

Jellied Pork

Ingredients: 1 pair of pig's trotters • 1 tail • 1 knuckle, or similar parts of a pig for the jelly • 1 level tbsp. salt • 4 1/2 pints water • 6 whole black peppercorns • 1/2 clove garlic • tarragon vinegar.

Put the meat in salt water, add peppercorns, bring to the boil, then reduce heat and simmer very slowly for 3 hours. Skim every now and then. Take out meat, bone and cut into cubes, first trimming off superfluous fat. Put meat into individual bowls. Strain stock into another saucepan, skim off fat and add 1/2 crushed garlic clove. Let it stand for 5 minutes, then strain, dividing it equally over meat in bowls. Let it set for 24 hours then serve with tarragon vinegar.

Jellied Goose-liver

Ingredients: 1 lb. fresh goose-liver • 1 1/2 oz. goose-fat • 4 oz. mushrooms • 1/2 tsp. salt • 1 cup milk • pinch of mixed herbs • 1/2 pint aspic • buttered toast • pickled gherkins.

Put goose-liver into saucepan together with salt, goose-fat, chopped mushrooms, milk and mixed herbs. Cover and cook slowly till the milk evaporates. Cool, then take out the liver and cut into cubes. Add chopped and cooked mushrooms. Line the bottom of small, individual moulds with aspic, and let it set. Arrange small heaps of goose-liver and mushroom mixture in each mould. Pour cold but still runny aspic over them, and chill. Serve on individual slices of buttered toast ringed with chopped cucumber.

Jellied Goose-liver Mould

Ingredients: 1 lb. fresh goose-liver • 1 calf's brain cooked in vegetable stock • 1 cup milk • 4 hard-boiled eggs • juice of 1/2 lemon • 1/2 lb. aspic • 4 oz. mushrooms • endive salad • sliced green pepper.

Salt and soak goose-liver in cold water, rinse, then cook it in 1 cup of milk till milk evaporates. Soak and clean brains, cook in vegetable stock. Slice mushrooms thinly, cook in boiling salt water for 10 minutes; strain. Take yolks from hard-boiled eggs, chop whites. Now pass through sieve the egg yolks, brains and 1/4 of the goose-liver, add lemon juice, chopped egg whites and 1/2 lb. aspic which is cool but still runny. Stir well and put half of this mixture in the bottom of a dish. Now comes a layer of the thinly sliced mushrooms, then the sliced goose-liver. Cover with the remaining half of the purée. Press gently, then put it to chill. Serve with endive salad.

Roast Goose-liver

Ingredients: 1 fresh goose-liver • 1 tbsp. salt • 2 tbsp. goose-fat • 1/2 pint milk.

Take a nice, large, fresh goose-liver, sprinkle with 1 tbsp. salt and put in a deep basin, cover with cold water and let it stand. After 1 hour wash liver carefully in cold water, place in a saucepan, add 2 tbsp. goose-fat and 1/2 pint milk. Cover and cook gently till milk evaporates. Take off lid and brown top in a hot oven, basting once or twice. 5 minutes is sufficient for this. It is delicious either hot or cold.

Meat Salad

Ingredients: 1 lb. veal knuckle-meat • 3 bay leaves • 1 whole celeriac • 1 lb. boiled potatoes • 1 tsp. salt • pinch of ground black pepper • 1 tbsp. French mustard • 1 tsp. grated onion • juice of 1 lemon • grated rind of 1/2 lemon • 2 anchovies • 1 tsp. finely chopped capers • 1 tsp. chopped chives • 1 tsp. chopped parsley • 2 tbsp. oil.

Cook the meat together with the salt, bay leaves and celeriac in just enough water to cover. Take the meat out when really tender, and let it cool. Cut celeriac into small cubes. Cut cold boiled potatoes into cubes, add celeriac and the meat cut into thin strips, sprinkle with pepper and mix well with the oil. Now strain 1/2 pint of the stock into the basin, add mustard, onion, lemon juice and grated lemon peel, scraped anchovies, capers, chives and parsley. Mix this dressing into the meat-potato mixture. Stir well, chill and serve with fresh, crisp lettuce.

Savoury Veal Roll

Ingredients: 1 lb. fillet of veal • 1 tsp. salt • 1/2 lb. minced lean pork • pinch of marjoram • pinch ground black pepper • 4 oz. mushrooms • 1 smoked cooked pig's tongue • 2 gherkins • 2 oz. thinly sliced ham • 3 hard-boiled eggs • wine and vegetable stock • chopped aspic and stuffed eggs for decoration.

Take a large fillet of veal. Cut it with a sharp knife in such a way that it can be opened like a book, the two slices kept together firmly with a hinge of uncut meat. Pound meat well to make it larger. Cover it with thinly sliced ham. Flavour the minced pork with ground black pepper, marjoram and salt. Chop mushrooms coarsely and fry lightly in a very little lard. Cut tongue and gherkins into slices, chop hard-boiled eggs coarsely. Now cover the layer of ham with minced pork, follow with the layer of mushrooms, then sliced tongue and gherkins, lastly the chopped eggs. The layers should be very even. Roll up the meat tightly, using greaseproof paper, wrap it into a piece of muslin or a napkin, tie firmly all around with string. Add 1/2 pint of white wine to vegetable stock, bring to the boil, put in the meat roll and simmer for about 1 1/2 hours. Take out meat to cool, but do not take off wrapping till next day. Slice thinly with a sharp knife and serve on a long flat dish. Decorate with stuffed eggs and chopped aspic. This is enough for 10 people.

Stuffed Tomatoes (Cold)

Ingredients: 12 medium-sized firm tomatoes • 5 oz. butter •
3 egg yolks • 3 oz. grated cheese • pinch of salt • lettuce •
juice of 1/4 lemon.

Cut off the tops of nice, firm tomatoes, scrape out seed and, turning them over, let surplus juice drip off. Beat butter and egg yolks till stiff, add grated cheese and a pinch of salt. Fill tomatoes with this mixture, replace the tops, and chill thoroughly. Serve on a layer of lettuce leaves sprinkled with lemon juice. Whole-meal or rye bread and butter goes with it.

Goose-liver Mould

Ingredients: 1 large fresh goose-liver • 1/2 tsp. finely chopped
parsley • 5 oz. mushrooms • pinch of ground black pepper •
2 oz. goose-fat • pinch of mixed herbs rubbed to powder •
juice of 1/4 lemon • 1 level tbsp. salt.

Sprinkle liver with salt and put it in cold water. Leave to soak for 1 hour. Slice mushrooms and fry in goose-fat, add parsley, then put aside. Rinse goose-liver, pass half through sieve, slice the remainder. Mix the goose-liver purée and mushrooms, adding fat, herbs, lemon juice, pepper, salt. Grease a medium galantine mould, put in half of the mixture. Arrange sliced goose-liver on it, cover with other half of the purée. Close mould tightly and, putting it in a large saucepan half filled with boiling water, boil slowly for 1 hour. Cool in the galantine shape without taking off the cover. Chill thoroughly before serving.

Paprika Veal Mould

Ingredients: 1 1/2 lb. boneless veal • 1 oz. lard • 1 small onion • 1 tsp. paprika • 1 tsp. salt • 6 egg yolks • 5 oz. butter • 1 tbsp. chopped chives.

Prepare pörkölt (see p. 85) from the meat, lard, grated onion, paprika and salt. Cool, then put through fine mincer. Beat the egg yolks and butter together till creamy and stiff, mix well with the minced veal. Grease a suitable mould and put the mixture in it. Chill thoroughly, then turn out onto a flat dish. Sprinkle thickly with chopped chives. Serve with mixed salad.

Jellied Beef Mould

Ingredients: 1 lb. boiled beef • 5 oz. boiled potatoes • 1 bread-roll soaked in stock and squeezed well • 1/2 tsp. salt • 1 tbsp. prepared English mustard • pinch of ground black pepper • pinch of marjoram • 3 oz. aspic • 2 eggs • 1 tbsp. sour cream.

Put the meat, potatoes and soaked bread-roll through a fine mincer. Add salt, 1/2 tbsp. mustard, pepper, marjoram, 1 tbsp. sour cream, the melted but cool aspic, and lastly, two well-beaten eggs. Pour the mixture into a greased mould and covering tightly with greaseproof paper, steam for 1 hour. Cool before turning out, brush over with the remaining mustard. Serve decorated with sliced hard-boiled eggs and sour gherkins.

Meat Galantine with Anchovy

Ingredients: 1/2 lb. veal • 1/2 lb. lean pork • 1 oz. lard • 5 oz. butter • 2 oz. anchovy paste • 4 oz. aspic • 1 egg yolk.

Braise the lean boneless meat in lard, adding a little water every now and then to prevent burning. Put through a fine mincer when tender, and leave to cool. Cream butter with anchovy paste, mix with the minced meat thoroughly, and add the melted but cool aspic and egg yolk. Press into a suitable mould and chill. This appetizer can be served sliced and decorated with chopped aspic, or as a sandwich-paste.

Hare Galantine

Ingredients: 1 hare • 3 oz. carrots • 3 oz. parsnips • 1 small onion • 1/4 cup spiced vinegar • 2 oz. lard • 1 tbsp. sugar • 1 level tsp. salt • 5 oz. streaky bacon • 2 eggs • the grated rind of 1/2 lemon • 4 oz. melted aspic • 1 tbsp. capers • rose-hip purée or cranberry sauce.

Cut the hare into 8 pieces. Slice vegetables thinly (onion, carrots, parsnips). Melt lard in a large saucepan, add the meat, vegetables and salt. Cover and simmer, adding some of the spiced vinegar and water occasionally, to prevent burning. When meat is tender, lift pieces out of saucepan, and put them aside. Add sugar to the vegetables remaining in the saucepan and, stirring constantly, fry till the colour becomes chocolate brown. Take of the heat, add 2 tbsp. water and press through a sieve. Now take the meat off the bones, put aside the fillets and leg-meat and put the rest through a fine mincer together with the bacon. Add the vegetable purée, 2 eggs, grated lemon peel, melted aspic and the finely chopped capers. Mix well. Cut the fillets and leg-meat into neat pieces. Grease a mould, put a layer of meat-purée in the bottom, then a layer of meat pieces, lastly the remainder of the meat-purée. Cover tightly and steam under lid for 1 hour. Chill thoroughly. Just before serving dip the mould into hot water and turn galantine out onto a flat dish. Decorate with slices of lemon, rose-hip purée or cranberry sauce.

HOT ENTRÉES

Artichoke Fritters

Ingredients: 1 dozen cooked artichoke hearts • batter mixture.

Dip cold, cooked artichokes in thick batter, fry in hot fat, serve hot. The stock from the artichokes can be used for soup.

Stuffed Artichokes

Ingredients: 1 dozen cooked artichokes • 1 egg • 6 oz. chopped ham or left-over roast meat • 1 oz. fine toasted breadcrumbs • 1 oz. butter.

Mix egg, minced ham or minced cold meat (if you use the latter, add a good pinch of salt). Make a small hollow in the middle of each artichoke, put a neat heap of meat mixture on each. Arrange in a fireproof dish, sprinkle with breadcrumbs, dab small pieces of butter on each and bake in a hot oven. Serve with mushroom or tomato sauce.

Cauliflower in Wine Batter

Ingredients: 2 lb. cooked cauliflower • 1/4 pint white wine • 31/2 oz. flour • good pinch of salt • 1 large tbsp. olive oil • the stiffly beaten whites of 2 eggs.

Make a thick batter from the wine, flour, salt, olive oil and stiff beaten egg whites. Break cooked and cooled cauliflower into neat sprigs. Dip in the thick batter and fry quickly in hot fat. This recipe may sound unusual, but I assure you it is excellent. It can be served as a garnish or as a savoury.

Cauliflower and Goose-liver Casserole

Ingredients: 1 lb. cooked cauliflower • 1/2 lb. fresh goose-liver • 3 eggs • 1 1/2 gills sour cream • 3 oz. butter.

Mash cauliflower with a fork while still hot. Leave to cool, then add egg yolks, sour cream and butter. Lastly fold in the stiffly whipped egg whites. Pour into a casserole. Cut the goose-liver into 6 slices, and lay on top of the mixture. Cover the dish and place in a hot oven for about 20–25 minutes.

Brussels Sprouts in Casserole

Ingredients: 1 1/2 lb. Brussels sprouts • 3 oz. flour • 3 oz. butter • 2 gills sour cream • 2 eggs • 1/2 tsp. salt • 3 oz. grated cheese.

Cook sprouts in boiling salt water. Drain. Do not overcook. Make a very light-coloured roux from butter and flour, add sour cream into which you stirred in the egg yolks and salt previously. Put the sprouts into a greased fireproof dish, pour sauce over them. Whip egg whites till stiff, spread on the top and sprinkle with the grated cheese. Cook in a hot oven for 15 minutes, then serve immediately.

Stuffed Kohlrabis au Gratin

Ingredients: 12 small young kohlrabis • 1/2 lb. cooked minced veal • 1 calf's brain • 3 oz. butter • 3 oz. flour • 1 1/4 pint white wine • 2 gills sour cream • 3 oz. grated cheese • 1 medium-sized tin of vegetable macédoine • 2 eggs • pinch of salt • pinch of grated nutmeg.

This is for 6 people. If you are serving it as a first course, use only half of the given quantities. Soak calf's brain, peel off membranes carefully. Chop and mix with minced veal, add 2 eggs, salt, grated nutmeg. Cook kohlrabis in salt water, cool, then scoop out insides well, fill them with veal–mixture. Strain macédoine, spread in the bottom of a fireproof dish, arrange stuffed kohlrabis on it. Make a light-coloured roux from butter and flour, add 1 1/4 pint white wine. Stirring constantly, put aside, add sour cream and grated cheese. Pour this mixture over the kohlrabis and the macédoine, bake in a hot oven for 20 minutes.

Kohlrabi Stuffed with Mushrooms

Ingredients: 1 dozen small young kohlrabis • 1 heaped tsp. finely chopped parsley • 1 oz. lard • 4 oz. mushrooms • 1 egg • 1 tbsp. white breadcrumbs • 1 gill sour cream • 2 oz. butter • 1 tsp. salt.

Peel kohlrabis, scoop out centers. Fry chopped mushrooms in hot lard, add parsley, 1 whole egg. 1 tbsp. sour cream and breadcrumbs. Put mixture aside, beat well, and stuff kohlrabis with it. Butter a fireproof dish, arrange the stuffed kohlrabis in it, dot with butter and sprinkle the remaining sour cream on top. Cover and cook in medium oven for 3/4–1 hour.

Vegetable Marrow au Gratin

Ingredients: 2 lb. vegetable marrow • 1 tbsp. vinegar • 1 egg yolk • 1 gill sour cream • 2 oz. butter • 2 oz. grated cheese • 1 tsp. salt.

Peel and cut vegetable marrow into 2-inch cubes. Bring water to the boil, add salt and vinegar, put in marrow and cook for 5 or 6 minutes. Strain through colander; allow to drain thoroughly. Beat well together the egg yolk, melted butter, sour cream and grated cheese. Put marrow into fireproof dish, pour sauce over it, bake in medium oven for about 20–25 minutes.

Mock Asparagus

Ingredients: 2 lb. vegetable marrow • 1/2 tsp. salt. • 1 tsp. sugar •
1 gill sour cream • 2 oz. butter • 1 oz. white breadcrumbs.

Peel and cut marrow into asparagus-shaped pieces. Put salt and sugar into the boiling water, add marrow, and boil until tender. Strain through colander, and let drain. Butter the bottom of an oval fireproof dish, and lay marrow on it lengthwise in a neat bunch. Fry the breadcrumbs in butter till nicely browned, pour sour cream, then breadcrumbs and melted butter over marrow. Bake for 15 minutes in medium oven.

Asparagus au Gratin

Ingredients: 2 lb. asparagus • 1 heaped tsp. sugar • 4 eggs •
3 1/2 oz. butter • 4 tbsp. flour • 1 1/2 gills sour cream • 1/2 cup milk •
1/2 tsp. salt.

Trim and tie asparagus loosely together, put in boiling water, add sugar, pinch of salt and cook till nearly tender. Drain. Mix well the egg yolks, melted butter, flour, sour cream, milk and a pinch of salt in a saucepan; bring to the boil, stirring constantly, then put aside and stir for another 5 minutes. Butter an oval fireproof dish, take the twine off of asparagus, arrange neatly in the dish and pour sauce over it. Bake in a hot oven for 20 minutes.

Baked Spinach Squares

Ingredients: 1 lb. spinach • 7 oz. ham • 6 eggs • 6 tbsp. flour •
1/2 tsp. salt • 1/3 tsp. ground black pepper • 1 oz. lard.

Cook spinach in boiling salt water, strain well, then put through mincer together with the ham. Add eggs, flour and black pepper, mix thoroughly. Heat lard in a baking tin, pour mixture in it and bake in a hot oven for 15 minutes. Cut up in the tin, arrange squares on a hot dish, sprinkle generously with grated cheese and serve immediately.

Springtime Vegetable Pudding

Ingredients: 1/2 lb. asparagus • 1/2 lb. green peas • 1/2 lb. young carrots • 6 oz. mushrooms • 1 cup milk • 3 1/2 oz. butter • 4 eggs • 1 tbsp. grated cheese • 1 heaped tbsp. finely chopped parsley • 4 tbsp. toasted breadcrumbs • 1 tsp. salt • 1/3 tsp. ground white pepper • 1 tsp. sugar • 1 oz. lard.

Cook asparagus, green peas and carrots separately, adding a pinch of salt and sugar to each. Drain cooked vegetables thoroughly. Heat lard, add mushrooms cut into small pieces, the parsley and 1/2 tsp. salt. Cover and let simmer till all water evaporates, then cool. Now mix the milk, melted butter, egg yolks and breadcrumbs, and add cooked vegetables and braised mushrooms. Stir well, then fold in the stiffly whipped egg whites. Put in a buttered and floured pudding dish and bake in a brisk oven for 1/2 hour. Let it stand for 4–5 minutes before turning out on a flat dish. Sprinkle grated cheese on top.

Transylvanian Spring Cabbage

Ingredients: 2 lb. spring cabbages • 1 lb. lean pork • 1/2 lb. veal •
4 oz. boiled rice • 1 tsp. salt • 1/3 tsp. ground black pepper •
1 large onion • 3 oz. lard • 2 oz. flour • 1 gill sour cream •
juice of 1/2 lemon.

First of all scald the large spring cabbage leaves, leaving
them in the hot water for 5 minutes. Put pork and veal
through mincer, fry finely chopped onion in 1 oz. lard, add
to meat together with rice, half the salt, black pepper and
egg. Knead mixture thoroughly. Cut cabbage-leaves in two,
remove thick vein from the middle of leaf. Put small heaps
of meat mixture on 12 of the leaves, roll them up loosely,
tucking the leaf well in at both ends. Cut the remainder of
cabbage into finger-wide strips, put half in the bottom of a
deep casserole. Arrange stuffed cabbages on it, then cover
with the remainder of sliced cabbage. Make a brown roux
using the remainder of lard and the flour, add 1/2 pint cold
water, bring to the boil, stirring constantly, add remaining
salt, the juice of 1/2 lemon and sour cream. Pour it over the
cabbage, cover, and cook in a medium-hot oven for 1 hour.

Mushrooms au Gratin

Ingredients: 3/4 lb. mushrooms • 2 tbsp. finely chopped parsley •
1 small onion • 1 tsp. salt • pinch of ground black pepper •
6 tbsp. grated cheese • 5 oz. butter • 2 tbsp. flour • 1 cup milk •
6 eggs.

Heat 4 oz. butter, add sliced mushrooms, parsley, grated
onion, salt and black pepper. Cover and allow to simmer
slowly till water evaporates, then add flour, stir, then take off
heat. Stir in the milk, the well-beaten egg yolks and 6 tbsp.
grated cheese. Butter a fireproof dish with the remaining

1 oz. butter, then pour in the mixture. Beat egg whites till stiff, fold in 2 tbsp. grated cheese, and spread on the top of the mushroom mixture. Cook in a medium oven for about 20–25 minutes.

Mushrooms in Paprika Sauce

Ingredients: 1 lb. mushrooms • 1 large onion • 2 oz. lard •
1 tsp. paprika • 1 level tbsp. flour • 1 1/2 gills sour cream • 1 tsp.
salt •
1 green pepper.

Cut mushrooms in four. Heat lard, add finely chopped onion, fry till golden. Add paprika, then the mushrooms and green pepper, and the salt. Cover and cook slowly till water evaporates. Add flour, stir 1 minute or 2, then pour sour cream over it. Stirring constantly, heat well but do not boil. Serve with boiled potatoes as garnish.

Stuffed Mushrooms

Ingredients: Two large mushrooms for each person • 2 oz. butter •
1 tsp. finely chopped parsley • 1 small onion • 3 eggs • 1/2 tsp. salt •
pinch of ground black pepper • 1 oz. grated cheese • thin slices
of toast.

Break off the mushroom stalks, then scoop out the mushrooms carefully so as to leave caps about the thickness of a matchstick. Chop stalks and the scooped-out bits of mushrooms. Heat 1 oz. butter, add grated onion, chopped mushroom, parsley, salt, pepper; cover and simmer slowly till the water evaporates. Cool, then add 3 whole eggs well beaten. Butter a flat oblong fireproof dish, put in the thin slices of toast, fill mushroom caps with egg mixture and arrange them on the toast. Add a dab of butter on top of each mushroom, sprinkle with grated cheese and bake in a medium oven for about 15 minutes. Serve on the toast.

Mushroom Fritters

Ingredients: 1 1/2 lb. mushrooms • batter mixture made with about 1/2 pint light ale • 1 tsp. finely chopped parsley • 1 tsp. salt • pinch of ground black pepper • fat to fry.
For sauce: 1 tsp. chopped chives • 1 1/2 cup tartar sauce.

Do not cut off mushroom stalks, only trim them. Mushrooms should be dried between cloth. Make a thick batter, using ale instead of milk. Add salt, pepper and parsley. Heat fat in deep fryer and, dipping the mushrooms one by one in the batter, throw them into the hot fat. Fry till golden-brown. Mix chives with tartar sauce and serve separately in a sauceboat.

Stuffed Tomatoes with Mushrooms

Ingredients: 12 medium-sized firm tomatoes • 3/4 lb. mushrooms • 3 eggs • 2 tbsp. white breadcrumbs • 1 tsp. chopped parsley • 1/2 tsp. salt • pinch of ground black pepper • 2 oz. butter • 1 gill sour cream.

Cut off the tops of tomatoes, and scrape out insides. Prepare the filling: chop mushrooms, add well-beaten egg yolks, breadcrumbs, parsley, salt, black pepper, and lastly the stiffly whipped egg whites. Fill tomatoes with this mixture, arrange in a fireproof dish, put a small piece of butter on top of each and pour sour cream over them. Bake in a medium oven for about 1/2–3/4 hour.

Tomatoes Stuffed with Green Peas

Ingredients: 6 large tomatoes • 1/2 lb. cooked or tinned green peas •
3 oz. butter • sprig of mint • pinch of salt • 1/2 tsp. sugar.

Cut off tops of tomatoes, and scoop out insides. Melt
1 1/2 oz. butter in saucepan, add peas, salt, sugar, sprig of
mint, heat up well, throw mint away. Fill tomatoes with peas,
arrange in a buttered fireproof dish and bake in the oven for
about 20 minutes.

Baked Tomato with Cheese

Ingredients: 6 large, firm tomatoes • 2 gills sour cream •
2 oz. butter • 3 heaped tbsp. cheese • salt and ground white pepper
to taste.

Choose nice fleshy tomatoes, and scoop out seed. Arrange in
fireproof dish; mix sour cream, melted hot butter, grated
cheese, salt, black pepper well, pour over tomatoes. Bake in
a medium oven for about 20 minutes.

Savoury Goose-liver Pie

Ingredients: 1 lb. goose-liver • 1/2 pint dry red wine •
1 lb. flaky pastry (see p. 195) • 4 oz. mushrooms •
1 tsp. finely chopped parsley • 2 oz. butter • 1 gill sour cream •
2 egg yolks • 1 heaped tbsp. flour • salt.

Cook goose-liver in wine with a pinch of salt. Put aside to
cool, then cut into thin slices. Fry chopped mushrooms in
1 oz. butter, add parsley. Cover the bottom of a medium
oblong pan with half of the flaky pastry, and bake in hot
oven. Leave the pastry in the tin, spread cooked mushrooms
on top, then arrange the goose-liver slices on top. Cover

with pastry, bake in hot oven for 15 minutes. Sauce: heat 1 oz. butter, add sour cream, egg yolks, flour. Stir, then thin with the wine in which the goose-liver was cooked. Stir, bring to the boil, simmer for 5 minutes. Cut pastry into squares, serve sauce separately.

Special Chicken Croquettes

Ingredients: 1 boiled chicken • 1 bread-roll soaked in milk and thoroughly squeezed • 4 oz. butter • 3 oz. flour • 2 gills cream • 4 eggs • 7 oz. mushrooms • 2 tbsp. capers • 1 tbsp. finely chopped parsley • grated rind of 1/2 lemon • 1 tsp. salt • pinch of nutmeg • pinch of ground black pepper • toasted bread-crumbs • fat for frying.

Skin chicken, then cut all meat off the bones, put through mincer, and together with soaked bread-roll. Beat together eggs and cream. Heat butter in a saucepan, add flour, stir a few times, then add egg-and cream mixture, cook, stirring all the while till it thickens, add minced chicken, cook 5 more minutes and put aside. Chop mushrooms and fry in 1 oz. lard. Add to chicken mixture together with finely chopped capers and parsley, grated lemon peel, salt, black pepper and nutmeg. Stir well and let cool. Shape into croquettes, and beat remaining 2 eggs. Dip croquettes first in beaten eggs, then in toasted breadcrumbs, and fry in deep-fryer. Serve hot.

Saldonette

Ingredients: 1 boiled chicken • 1 bread-roll soaked in milk • 1/3 tsp. grated onion • 1/2 tsp. salt • pinch of grated nutmeg • pinch of ground black pepper • 7 eggs • 3 oz. lard • 1 tsp. finely chopped parsley.

Skin and bone boiled chicken, put meat through mincer together with the soaked and squeezed bread-roll. Add grated onion, salt, pepper, parsley, 1 egg, 2 1/2 oz. lard. Mix well, then grease a fireproof dish and spread mixture in it, not thicker than two fingers. Make 6 hollows in the mixture and break one egg into each carefully. Bake for about 10–15 minutes in a hot oven, until eggs set.

Steamed Veal Soufflé

Ingredients: 1 1/2 lb. boneless veal (shoulder or leg) •
1 tbsp. anchovy paste • 1 large onion • 1 oz. lard • 1/2 pint white wine • 4 oz. carrots • 4 oz. parsnips • 2 bread-rolls •
7 oz. mushrooms • 3 eggs • grated peel and juice of 1 lemon •
2 oz. butter • 1 gill sour cream.

Cut meat into 2-inch cubes, slice carrots and parsnips, chop onions finely. Heat lard, add onion, the meat, vegetables, anchovy paste and lastly the wine. Cover and simmer till meat is tender, adding a spoonful of stock when gravy is getting too low. Lift out meat and vegetables, put through the mincer; soak 2 rolls in the left-over gravy, then mince these, too. Lastly put the sliced raw mushrooms through the mincer. Add 3 eggs, lemon juice and the grated lemon peel, softened butter and sour cream. Mix thoroughly, then pour into a buttered pudding mould and steam for 1 hour. Let stand for 2 minutes with the cover on, this way you can turn out the pudding easier. Serve with tartar sauce.

Roulade with Meat Filling

Ingredients: 4 eggs • 4 level tbsp. flour • 1 oz. lard • 1 medium-sized onion • 1/2 lb. left-over meat (poultry or veal) • 1 tsp. salt •
1 medium-sized onion • pinch of ground black pepper •
1 gill sour cream • 1 oz. butter • 1/2 oz. grated cheese.

Mince the meat, grate the onion. Heat lard, add the meat and onion, 1/2 tsp. salt, pinch of black pepper. Simmer slowly under lid till moisture evaporates. It will take only 10 to 15 minutes. Put aside and mix in the sour cream. Prepare the sponge mixture. Beat egg yolks with 1/2 tsp. salt till fluffy, beat whites separately, add to yolks. Lastly fold in the flour. Bake in a medium oven on a greased and floured baking sheet. Turn sponge onto a napkin, heat up the meat filling and spread evenly on the surface. Roll up tightly with the help of a napkin, brush top with melted butter, sprinkle with grated cheese and replace in the oven for 5 minutes. Serve hot.

Minced Meat Pie

Ingredients: 3/4 lb. flaky pastry (see p. 195) • 1/2 lb. cooked minced pork • 1 small onion • 1 oz. lard • 1 level tsp. salt • pinch of ground black pepper • 1 or 2 mushrooms • 3 tbsp. cooked rice • 1 egg • 2–3 tbsp. sour cream.

Divide pastry in two, roll out both pieces to the shape of an oblong baking tin. Line the tin with one piece. Spread filling on it evenly, cover with second piece of pastry. Prick the top all over with a fork, then brush with very salt water. Bake in a medium-hot oven for about 20 minutes. Filling: mince the meat together with mushrooms. Add cooked rice, egg, salt, black pepper, a very small grated onion and enough sour cream to make a pliable paste. Cut to squares and serve with green peas and some good meat gravy.

Smoked Sausage Roll

Ingredients: 1 1/2 lb. flaky pastry (see p. 195) • 2 lengths of smoked pork sausage • 1 egg yolk.

Smoked sausages can be bought either in links or in about 10-inch lengths. You need 2 pieces of long sausages. Cook them in boiling water for 20 minutes, taking care not to prick their skins. Cool, then take off skin. Roll out pastry to 1/2-inch thickness, cut in two and roll 1 sausage in each. Put rolls in a baking tin, brush tops with egg yolk, and bake in a hot oven. Serve sliced.

Hortobágy Liver Pudding

Ingredients: 1/2 lb. calf's liver • 2 oz. lard • 2 tsp. salt • pinch of ground black pepper • 2 egg whites • 1 1/2 lb. noodles.

Cut liver to strips and put through mincer, then press through sieve to remove all gristle. Heat the lard, put in the liver purée and fry quickly for 3–4 minutes, stirring all the while. Add pepper and 1/2 tsp. salt. Allow to cool. Cook noodles in boiling salt water, strain, then rinse. Now add stiffly whipped egg whites to the liver purée, and mix with the noodles. Grease a fireproof casserole, pour in the mixture and bake in a medium-hot oven for about 20–25 minutes. Tomato sauce is a good accompaniment to this dish.

Stuffed Green Pepper au Gratin

Ingredients: 6 large green peppers • 1/2 lb. minced pork • 1/4 liver • 2 oz. streaky bacon • 1 soaked bread-roll • 2 heaped tbsp. rice • 1/2 tsp. salt • pinch of ground black pepper • 1 medium-sized onion.

Core nice, large green peppers. Mix minced meat, minced liver and bacon well together with a soaked and well-squeezed bread-roll. Add cooked rice, salt and pepper, mix again, and stuff peppers loosely with the mixture. Melt lard in a fireproof dish, arrange stuffed peppers in it, add onion cut in half and, basting frequently, bake in a medium-hot oven for 25–30 minutes. Remove onion before serving and, using the fat from the peppers, make a thin gravy. Serve gravy in a separate sauceboat.

Cheese Pudding

Ingredients: 3 bread-rolls soaked in milk • 4 eggs • 4 oz. butter • 1/4 pint milk • 1 gill sour cream • 6 oz. grated cheese • pinch of salt.

Squeeze rolls well, add egg yolks, melted butter, milk, sour cream, grated cheese and salt, stir well, lastly fold in the stiffly whipped egg whites. Butter and flour a pudding basin, pour in the mixture, close tightly and steam for 1 hour. Turn carefully out onto a hot dish, sprinkle with grated cheese before serving.

Cheese Soufflé

Ingredients: 1 pint milk • 4 oz. white breadcrumbs • 3 oz. butter • 6 eggs • 6 oz. grated cheese • pinch of salt.

Heat milk and add breadcrumbs gradually to make a not too stiff paste. Cool, then add butter, stir till creamy; stirring constantly, add egg yolks, grated cheese and salt, lastly fold in the stiffly beaten egg whites. Butter and flour a deep round fireproof dish, pour in the mixture and bake in a fairly hot oven for about 1/2 hour. The dish should be sufficiently large to allow for rising.

Ham and Cheese Soufflé

Ingredients: 1/2 lb. macaroni • 6 oz. butter • 7 oz. ham • 4 level tbsp. flour • 1 cup milk • 4 eggs • pinch of salt • 4 heaped tbsp. grated cheese.

Boil macaroni in salt water, strain. Heat 2 oz. butter in a saucepan, add chopped ham and macaroni, stir, then put aside. Heat in another saucepan 4 oz. butter, add flour, then milk, well-beaten egg yolks, salt and grated cheese. Stirring constantly cook till thick and smooth, then stir in the ham and macaroni mixture. Leave to cool, then fold in the stiffly whipped egg whites. Butter and flour a deep fireproof dish, pour in the mixture and bake in a medium oven for 1/2 hour.

Cheese and Potato Soufflé

Ingredients: 10 oz. boiled potatoes • 6 tbsp. grated cheese • 4 eggs • 1 1/2 gills sour cream • 4 oz. butter • 2 tbsp. flour • pinch of salt.

Beat well together in a saucepan the egg yolks, sour cream, melted butter and flour, put on low heat and stirring constantly cook for 6–8 minutes. Put aside and keep on stirring for another 5 minutes. Grate cold boiled potatoes, add to the sauce together with grated cheese. Lastly fold in the stiffly whipped egg whites. Butter a deep round fireproof dish, pour in the mixture and bake in a medium-hot oven for 25–30 minutes. Sprinkle some grated cheese on top before serving.

Ham and Potato Pudding

Ingredients: 1 1/2 lb. potatoes • 7 oz. minced ham • 1 cup milk • 4 eggs • 5 oz. butter • 6 tbsp. grated cheese.

Boil potatoes, press through sieve while hot. Beat together the milk, egg yolks and butter, add chopped ham, grated cheese and potato purée, mix well, then fold in the stiffly whipped egg whites. Thickly butter a tin mould. When choosing the mould you must keep in mind that this pudding will rise about 3 inches while cooking. Pour mixture into mould, and bake in a medium oven for about 25–30 minutes. Turn out onto a hot round dish, serve immediately. Excellent with mixed salad.

Chambord Potato Cakes

Ingredients: 1 1/2 lb. potatoes • 2 oz. flour • 2 oz. butter • 3 gills cream • 2 egg yolks • 5 oz. minced ham • 1/2 tsp. salt • pinch of ground white pepper • flour • 1 egg and toasted breadcrumbs.

Peel and cook potatoes, then press through sieve. Mix egg yolks and cream. Heat butter, add flour and stir, add cream-and-egg-yolk mixture, and lastly the potato purée, cook till mixture is smooth and nearly stiff. Take off heat, stir in minced ham, salt, white pepper, leave to cool. Shape neat round cakes from mixture, dip them in flour, beaten egg and toasted breadcrumbs, fry in hot fat. Serve immediately.

Ham Slices au Gratin

Ingredients: 1 lb. sliced ham • 4 oz. butter • 2 gills sour cream • 3 egg yolks • 2 level tbsp. flour • pinch of salt • 1 1/2 oz. grated cheese.

Butter thickly an oval fireproof dish. Arrange sliced ham in bottom. Beat well together the sour cream, egg yolks, flour, 2 oz. melted butter and a pinch of salt. Pour this mixture over the ham and sprinkle top thickly with grated cheese. Bake in a hot oven for about 8–10 minutes. Serve immediately.

Plain Ham Roulade

Ingredients: 6 eggs • pinch of salt • 1 gill cream • 4 heaped tbsp. flour • 1/2 oz. lard • 1/2 lb. minced ham • 1 gill sour cream • 3 tbsp. grated cheese.

Beat egg yolks with a pinch of salt till fluffy. Add by degrees — stirring constantly — the cream, and 4 tbsp. flour, lastly fold in the stiffly whipped egg whites. Heat lard in an oblong baking tin, pour in the mixture and bake in a hot oven for about 10 minutes. Turn out on a warm baking-sheet, mix grated cheese, sour cream and minced ham together, and spread this mixture evenly on the sponge. Roll up and put back in the oven for 5 minutes. Serve with tomato salad.

Savoury Pancakes

Ingredients: Pancake batter (see p. 170) • pinch of salt • pinch of ground black pepper • 1/2 lb. finely chopped cabbage • 1/2 oz. lard • 1 heaped tsp. sugar • 6 oz. chopped ham • 1 tbsp. grated cheese • fat to fry.

Prepare pancake batter, adding a pinch of salt. Heat lard in a saucepan, add sugar, let it melt to a deep brown colour, add finely chopped cabbage and fry quickly till cabbage is nicely browned. Add black pepper, let cabbage cool a little, then add it to the pancake mixture. Now fry the pancakes in the usual way, fill each with chopped ham, and, rolling them up, arrange on a heated dish. Sprinkle with grated cheese just before serving.

Pancakes with Goose-liver Filling

Ingredients: 2 pancakes for each person • 1/2 lb. fresh goose-liver • 1 tbsp. goose-fat • pinch of salt • 2 oz. finely chopped mushrooms.

Prepare pancakes (see p. 170). Put the goose-liver into a small saucepan, add a pinch of salt, 1 tbsp. goose-fat and 2 tbsp. water. Cover and simmer gently till all water evaporates. Lift out goose-liver and add the finely chopped mushrooms to the fat remaining in the saucepan. Fry till all water evaporates. Chop goose-liver, then mash with fork, add to the fried chopped mushrooms in the saucepan, stir and heat up again. Lay a pancake onto a flat round fireproof dish, spread some of the filling on it evenly. Cover with another pancake and repeat procedure till stuffing is finished. Cover the top with pancake, brush it thickly with sour cream and put in a medium-hot oven for 10 minutes. Serve hot, slice in cake-like wedges.

Savoury Paprika Pancakes

Ingredients: 2 pancakes for each person • 3/4 lb. boneless veal • 1 large onion • 1/2 tsp. salt • 1 oz. lard • 1 heaped tsp. paprika • 2 gills sour cream • 1 oz. grated cheese • 1 level tsp. flour.

Prepare pancakes (see p. 170). Cut meat into small cubes, finely chop the onion. Heat lard in a saucepan, add chopped onion, stir 1 minute or 2, then add meat, paprika, salt, and 2 tbsp. water. Cover and allow to simmer till meat is tender. Lift meat out, put through mincer. Mix sour cream with 1 level tsp. flour, add to the gravy in the saucepan, boil for a minute or two, stirring constantly. Add a tablespoonful or two of this gravy to the minced meat to get the consistency of a thick purée. Put one of the pancakes in the bottom of a round, shallow fireproof dish, spread meat mixture on it; repeat process till there is no more filling. Top with a pancake brushed thickly with some of the gravy. Reheat pancakes in a hot oven; heat up the sauce as well. Serve in the fireproof dish. Serve sauce separately.

SOUPS AND GARNISHES

SOUPS

Gulyás Soup

Ingredients: 1 1/2 oz. lard • 2 medium-sized onions •
1 tbsp. paprika • 2 Ib. beef (thick flank and fillet ends) •
1/2 raw grated potato • 1 tbsp. tomato purée • 4 1/2 pints bone
and vegetable stock • 1/2 tsp. caraway seeds • 1 Ib. potatoes •
1 green pepper.
For csipetke: 6 oz. flour • 1 egg • pinch of salt.

Fry finely chopped onions in lard to a golden colour, add
paprika, the beef cut into walnut-sized cubes, caraway seeds
and the grated raw potato. Cover and simmer for about 10
minutes, stirring occasionally. Add tomato purée, half cupful
of stock; simmer till meat is nearly done. Then add the
remainder of stock, bring to the boil, add potatoes cut in
small cubes. If available add some sliced green pepper to the
gulyás; in my opinion it gives the finishing touch to an excellent dish.

Csipetke. Genuine Hungarian Gulyás Soup is garnished
with csipetke. Make them as follows: sift flour into a bowl,
add egg and salt. Knead ingredients into a stiff dough. Flatten
between your palms and pinch into small, bean-sized pieces,
add to the gulyás and boil slowly for 10 minutes before
serving.

Mock Gulyás Soup

Ingredients: 1 1/2 oz. lard • 1 large onion • 1 tbsp. paprika •
2 parsnips • 2 carrots • 1/2 tsp. caraway seed • 1 tbsp. salt •
2 1/2 lb. potatoes • 4 1/2 pints water.

Fry the finely chopped onion in lard. Add the paprika, sliced
vegetables, caraway seed, salt and sufficient water to cover.
Cook till vegetables are nearly done, add potatoes cut into
small cubes and the remaining water. When potatoes are
nearly done, add csipetke (see previous recipe).

Clear Beef Soup

Ingredients: 2 lb. beef (topside or silverside) • 1 lb. beef bone •
1 piece of marrow-bone • 1 tbsp. salt • 4 1/2 pints water • 1 lb. mixed
vegetables • 6 whole black peppercorns • 2 or 3 raw mushrooms •
1/2 tsp. paprika • 1 small tomato • 1 green pepper • 1 small onion •
1 clove garlic • 1 bunch parsley • vermicelli or semolina dumplings
(see p. 57, 58).

Buy only the best-quality beef; remember the saying "Cheap
bargains are dear". Put the meat, together with the bones,
into a large saucepan, add 4 1/2 pints cold water and salt.
Bring to the boil then reduce heat and simmer for about an
hour. Clean the vegetables: one-half of a small savoy cabbage, 2 large carrots, 1/2 celeriac (celery root), 1/2 kohlrabi
(turnip may be substituted), 2 parsnips. Cut the root vegetables in half, put aside one finger-size piece of carrot. Add
vegetables to the soup together with the black peppercorns,
paprika, tomato, green pepper, peeled onion and garlic. The
last can be omitted if you don't like the flavour. Bring to the
boil then reduce heat and allow to simmer very gently for
2 hours. Grate the left-over piece of raw carrot, fry it in a little fat till it is well browned, and add to the soup. After

another 1/2 hour put the soup aside, and let it settle for 5–10 minutes. Put finely chopped parsley in the bottom of a large tureen, strain the hot soup over it. Serve with vermicelli or semolina dumplings (see p. 58). This soup is my favourite; I hope you will like it, too.

Transylvanian Soup

Ingredients: 10 oz. beef or mutton • 2 oz. lard • 1 medium-sized onion • 1/2 tsp. paprika • 4 pints water • 1 tbsp. salt • 1/2 lb. potatoes • 1/2 lb. French beans • 1 bay leaf • 1/2 clove garlic • 1 oz. flour • 1 1/2 gills sour cream.

Prepare pörkölt according to recipe on p. 85 using 1 oz. lard, the paprika and onion. When the meat is tender, add the potatoes cut in small cubes, sliced beans, bay leaf and salt, stir and add water. Bring to the boil and allow to cook slowly for about 20 minutes. Prepare brown roux from 1 oz. lard and the flour, reduce heat and add finely chopped garlic. Add to the soup and allow to boil for another 20 minutes. Add sour cream before serving.

Veal Ragout Soup

Ingredients: 1 lb. veal bones • 4 pints water • 1 medium-sized onion • 5 whole black peppercorns • 2 oz. butter • 1/2 lb. minced veal • 1 tbsp. chopped parsley • 2 oz. carrots • 2 oz. parsnips • 1 oz. savoy cabbage • 1 oz. celeriac • 2 oz. flour • 1 tsp. lemon juice • 1 gill sour cream • 2 egg yolks • 1 tbsp. salt • 2 oz. mushrooms.

Simmer the bones together with the onion, pepper and salt. Meanwhile sauté minced veal in the butter together with parsley, sliced mushrooms and vegetables cut into small strips. When vegetables are tender, add the flour, stir, then strain stock over it. Bring to the boil and allow to simmer for about 20 minutes. Flavour with lemon juice. Mix together egg yolks and sour cream in soup tureen, pour the hot soup over it, and serve.

Lamb Ragout Soup with Tarragon

Ingredients: 2 lamb heads or equivalent weight of shoulder of lamb • 2 oz. carrots • 2 oz. parsnips • 2 oz. celeriac • 4 1/2 pints water • 2 oz. butter • 2 oz. flour • 1 tsp. finely chopped tarragon • 1/3 tsp. ground black pepper • 7 oz. mushrooms • 1 gill sour cream • 1 egg yolk • 1 tbsp. salt • butter dumplings (see p. 58).

Cook the meat together with vegetables and salt till meat comes off the bones easily. Make a yellow roux from the butter and flour, add the finely chopped tarragon and ground pepper, strain the stock over it. Slice the mushrooms, add to the soup. Make tiny balls of the dumpling mixture and add, one by one, to the moderately boiling soup. Meanwhile, take the meat off the bones and, after cutting into small squares, add to the soup when dumplings have risen. Pull the skin off the tongues before cutting them up. Mix egg yolk and sour cream in a tureen, and pour the hot soup over it.

Chicken Ragout Soup

Ingredients: 1 whole chicken • 4 pints veal bone and vegetable stock • 3 oz. butter • 1 large bunch of parsley • 1 small onion • 1 heaping tbsp. flour • 1/4 lb. green peas • 1/4 lb. mushrooms • 1/4 lb. asparagus • 1 gill sour cream • 1 egg yolk • a few drops of lemon juice (optional).

Cut up a plump, young chicken into pieces. Prepare stock from veal bones, carrots, parsnips, celeriac, black pepper and salt. Braise the chicken in butter together with finely chopped parsley and the very finely grated onion. Add a spoonful of stock every now and then to prevent burning. Take out the meat when tender and put aside. Sprinkle the butter which remained in the saucepan with flour, stir, and strain stock over it. Bring to the boil, add green peas, sliced mushrooms and asparagus cut into one-inch pieces and simmer till vegetables are tender. Meanwhile, pull the skin off the chicken, take the meat off the bones and cut into even pieces. Cut the carrots and celeriac into small cubes. Add this to the soup together with chicken meat and heat to boiling point. Pour it over egg yolk and sour cream mixed in soup tureen beforehand, stir, and serve. This soup should be as thick as a stew.

Ujházi Chicken Soup

Ingredients: 1 large chicken • 4 1/2 pints water • 1 lb. beef bones •
1 tbsp. salt • 6 whole black peppercorns • 1/2 tsp. paprika •
1 tbsp. tomato purée (or 1 large fresh tomato in summer) •
1/4 lb. carrots • 1/4 lb. parsnips • 2 oz. celeriac • 1 medium-sized onion •
1 clove of garlic • 5 oz. mushrooms • 1 tbsp. chopped parsley •
4 oz. green peas • 4 oz. vermicelli • liver dumplings •
1 egg per person.

Make stock of water, beef bones, pepper and salt. Strain carefully into a large saucepan. Put chicken into the stock together with carrots, parsnips and celeriac cut into finger-sized pieces, a whole onion, garlic, 2 or 3 whole mushrooms, tomato purée and paprika, cover, and simmer for about 2 hours. The slower you cook the soup, the clearer it will become. Put it aside when ready and allow to stand covered for about 10 minutes. Strain off the liquid very carefully into another saucepan. Now put the pieces of chicken onto a flat dish, cut the meat off the bones and cut it into even pieces. Heat the strained soup to simmering point, add the very thinly sliced mushrooms, green peas, allow to simmer 10 minutes, then add vermicelli, the vegetables previously cooked in the soup and sliced (do not add the garlic and onion). Make small dumplings with the scraped chicken-liver added, put these, too, in the soup. Simmer for another 10 minutes, break the eggs carefully one by one into the slowly simmering soup. Move the saucepan aside as soon as the whites are set but the yolks are still soft. Pour the soup carefully into a large soup tureen over the finely chopped parsley.

Cauliflower and Chicken Soup

Ingredients: 1/2 small chicken • 1 oz. carrots • 1 oz. parsnips • 1 oz. celeriac • 1 1/2 lb. cauliflower • 2 oz. butter • 1 tsp. chopped parsley • 1 oz. flour • 1 egg yolk • 1 gill sour cream • salt • 4 pints water.

Cook the chicken in water together with carrots, parsnips, celeriac and a generous pinch of salt, till tender. Break cauliflower into sprigs, melt butter, add cauliflower, chopped parsley and a ladleful of soup. Braise till tender then lift cover to let moisture evaporate. Sprinkle with flour, stir, and strain soup over it. Bring to the boil and after 10 minutes add chicken meat taken off the bones and cut into small pieces. Mix the sour cream and egg yolk in tureen, pour a ladleful of soup over it, stir well, then add the rest of the soup and serve.

Capon and Mushroom Soup

Ingredients: 1/2 fat capon • 2 oz. lard • 1 tbsp. flour • 1 level tbsp. salt • 1/3 tsp. ground black pepper • 4 pints veal bone stock • 1 tbsp. finely chopped parsley • 7 oz. mushrooms.

Cut the capon into small pieces. Heat 1 oz. lard in saucepan, add meat and fry it uncovered, stirring frequently with wooden spoon until all pieces are nicely browned. Now sprinkle with flour, black pepper, a generous pinch of salt and finely chopped parsley. Stir, reduce heat, then pour stock over it, bring to the boil and simmer till the meat can be easily taken off the bones. Strain soup into another saucepan. Cut mushrooms into thumb-sized pieces, fry in 1 oz. lard. Add to the soup when ready, together with the meat taken off the bones previously. After a final boil pull saucepan aside and add sour cream. Stir and serve.

Hubertus Soup

Ingredients: Legs and shoulders of 1 hare • 2 oz. carrots •
2 oz. parsnips • 1 oz. celeriac • 1 medium-sized onion •
8 whole black peppercorns • 2 bay leaves • 1/2 tsp. each of dried
juniper berries and coriander (optional) •
1 rounded tsp. mustard powder • 1 oz. lard • 1 oz. streaky bacon •
2 oz. flour • 4 1/2 pints water • 1 tbsp. salt •
1/4 pint good-quality red wine • 1 oz. capers • sippets.

Cut meat into regular pieces and braise in lard together with thinly sliced carrots, parsnips, celeriac and onion; add whole peppercorns, bay leaves, juniper and coriander, mustard powder, salt. Add a little cold water every now and then to prevent burning. When meat is really tender, lift out onto a plate and bone it. Mince one-half of the meat; cut the other half into small cubes. Mince the bacon and fry. Add some of the cooked vegetables, sprinkle with flour, stir and add 4 pints of cold water. Bring to the boil and allow to simmer for 1/2 hour. Strain into another saucepan, add wine, all the meat and the finely chopped capers, bring to boil and reduce heat. Serve with hot sippets dished separately.

Cream of Vegetable Soup

Ingredients: 4 pints veal bone stock • 1/4 lb. each of carrots •
parsnips • cauliflower • mushrooms • 2 oz. savoy cabbage •
2 oz. celeriac • 1 large onion • 2 tbsp. tomato purée • salt •
1/3 tsp. ground black pepper • 1 tbsp. finely chopped parsley •
3 oz. cooked rice • 1 egg yolk • sour cream • 3 oz. butter •
1 oz. flour.

Cut carrots, parsnips, savoy cabbage and celeriac into thin
strips, slice onion into rings, break cauliflower to springs and
cook in salted stock together with tomato purée. Cook slowly till vegetables are really tender, then strain, and put vegetables through a fine sieve. Make a yellow roux using 2 oz.
butter and 1 oz. flour. Add finely chopped parsley and
ground pepper and dilute with the stock. Add vegetable
purée. Bring to the boil, then reduce heat and simmer for 10
minutes. In the meantime mix in the soup tureen the egg
yolk and sour cream and add cooked rice. Pour hot soup
over it, stir, and serve.

Brown Vegetable Soup

Ingredients: 4 pints veal bone stock • 1 small onion • 2 oz. carrots •
2 oz. parsnips • 4 oz. mushrooms • 2 oz. savoy cabbage •
2 oz. French beans • 2 oz. green peas • 1 tbsp. salt • 2 oz. flour •
2 oz. lard • 1 tsp. sugar • 1 egg yolk • 1 gill sour cream •
golden drops.

Cut vegetables into small cubes and cook slowly in salted
stock till tender. Heat lard in saucepan, let it melt and brown
well. Add flour and, stirring continuously, pour the stock and
vegetables over it. Cover and cook slowly for 20 minutes.
Mix egg yolk and sour cream in the tureen and pour soup
over it. Stir well and serve with golden drops (see p. 59)

Spring Soup

Ingredients: 4 pints veal bone stock • 1 small onion • 2 oz. chopped
sorrel • 6 whole black peppercorns • 1/4 lb. tiny new potatoes •
1/4 lb. small young carrots • 1/4 lb. cauliflower • 1/4 lb. Brussels
sprouts • 2 oz. small mushrooms • 2 oz. butter • 2 oz. flour • 2 egg
yolks • 1 gill sour cream • 1 level tbsp. salt.

Melt butter in saucepan, add vegetables, black pepper and
1 tbsp. of stock. Cover and simmer till vegetables are half-
done. Sprinkle with flour, strain the salted stock over it. Boil,
then reduce heat and simmer for 1/2 hour. Mix the egg yolks
and sour cream well in the tureen, pour the hot soup over it,
stir and serve.

Minestrone

Ingredients: 2 lb. beef bones • 1 marrow-bone • 4 1/2 pints water •
1 tbsp. salt • 3 oz. carrots • 3 oz. parsnips • 1 oz. celeriac •
2 bay leaves • 2 green peppers • 2 medium-sized tomatoes •
3 oz. savoy cabbage • 1 small onion • 1 clove of garlic •
2 oz. mushrooms • 1 tbsp. finely chopped parsley • 1 sprig
finely chopped celery leaves • vermicelli or noodles.

Prepare the stock from bones, salt, green peppers, tomatoes,
bay leaves and onion. When ready, strain into another
saucepan and add the following ingredients: carrots,
parsnips and celeriac cut into cubes, mushrooms cut in
slices, savoy cabbage cut into strips, the finely chopped celery and parsley leaves. Lastly put in the marrow-bone.
Simmer till vegetables are tender, then put in sufficient
amount of vermicelli or noodles, boil soup 8 minutes longer.
Serve with grated Parmesan cheese sprinkled on top.

Potato Soup

Ingredients: 1 lb. potatoes • 4 pints beef and vegetable stock •
2 oz. lard • 2 oz. flour • 1 small onion • 1 tbsp. finely chopped parsley • 1/2 tsp. paprika • 1 level tbsp. salt • 1 gill sour cream.

Make a medium-brown roux of lard and flour. When it is
nicely browned, add finely chopped onion, parsley, stir and
add paprika. Dilute with the salted stock, add potatoes cut
into cubes, bring to the boil then reduce heat and cook till
potatoes are soft. Stir in the sour cream just before serving.

Cream of Potato Soup

Ingredients: 1/2 lb. smoked pork • 1 1/2 oz. butter • 1 oz. flour •
1 lb. potatoes • 1/2 pint milk • 3 1/2 pints water • 1 tsp. salt •
1 gill sour cream.

Simmer smoked pork in water till meat is tender. Lift out the
meat, put it aside, cut potatoes into cubes and add to the
stock. When they are cooked strain stock off into a bowl,
pass potatoes through sieve. Make a light yellow roux from
butter and flour. Keeping on low heat add the potato purée
and milk, stir, then add the stock. Bring to the boil and let it
simmer for about 20 minutes. Cut smoked pork into neat
cubes and add to the soup. Mix in the sour cream just before
serving.
I always put a pinch of marjoram in this soup; the subtle
blend of flavours improves it beyond expectation.

Cauliflower Soup

Ingredients: 1 lb. cleaned cauliflower • 4 pints bone stock •
1 tsp. sugar • 2 oz. butter • 2 oz. flour • 1 heaping tbsp. finely
chopped parsley • 2 egg yolks • 1 gill sour cream • 1 tbsp. salt •
butter dumplings.

Break cauliflower into flowerets and cook in the stock till
tender. Add the sugar when stock begins to boil. Make a light
roux with butter and flour, add parsley and strain the stock
over it. Bring to the boil and simmer for 1/2 hour. Add cauliflower. Mix egg yolks and sour cream in a soup tureen
together with 1 ladleful of soup, then pour the hot soup over
this mixture. Serve with butter dumplings (see p.58).

Savoy Cabbage Soup

Ingredients: 1 lb. savoy cabbage • 4 pints bone stock •
1/4 lb. potatoes • 1 tbsp. finely chopped parsley •
1/3 tsp. ground black pepper • 2 oz. lard • 2 oz. flour •
1 gill sour cream • 1 tbsp. salt.

Cut savoy cabbage into thin strips and the potatoes into
small cubes. Cook them in stock till tender. Prepare a light
brown roux from lard and flour, add parsley and black pepper, stir, and pour soup over it. Bring to the boil then reduce
heat and simmer for 15 minutes. Put sour cream into soup
tureen and, stirring constantly, add the hot soup. Serve with
sippets.

Cream of Savoy Cabbage Soup

Ingredients: 1 lb. savoy cabbage • 4 pints vegetable stock •
1 gill sour cream • 2 oz. flour • 2 oz. grated cheese • 2 oz. butter •
1 small onion • 1 level tbsp. salt.

Cook savoy cabbage in 1 pint of stock till very tender. Put through sieve, and add to the left-over salted stock. Make a nearly white roux, add grated onion, stir, put aside for five minutes, then add grated cheese, sour cream and 2 ladlefuls of soup. Stir thoroughly then put back on medium heat and add the remaining soup. Heat and serve with some grated cheese sprinkled on top.

Tomato Soup

Ingredients: 2 lbs. fresh tomatoes • 1 oz. flour • 1 oz. lard •
2 pints vegetable soup • 1 sprig of celery leaves • 1 small onion •
1 tsp. salt • 1 tbsp. sugar • 1 tsp. rice per person.

Break tomatoes into a saucepan, add whole onion, celery leaves, salt and sugar. Cook till tomatoes are soft, and put through sieve while hot. Prepare a golden-coloured roux with the lard and flour, pour salted vegetable stock over it, bring to the boil. Add tomato purée, the rice, bring to the boil then reduce heat and allow to simmer gently till rice is cooked. You can put 1/2 gill of sweet cream in the soup just before serving, but it is optional.

Cream of Celery Soup

Ingredients: 1 lb. veal bones • 1 large celeriac • 2 springs of celery leaves • 2 oz. butter • 2 oz. flour • 1 level tbsp. salt • 1/3 tsp. ground black pepper • 1 tbsp. finely chopped parsley • 1 egg yolk • 1 gill sour cream.

Cook the veal bones in salt water with celeriac and celery leaves. Prepare a light yellow roux from butter and flour, add chopped parsley and ground pepper. Strain stock over it. Pass cooked celeriac through a sieve, add it to the soup. Bring to the boil then simmer for 15 minutes. Mix egg yolk and sour cream in tureen, pour soup over it, stir. Serve with crackers.

Asparagus Soup

Ingredients: 3/4 lb. asparagus • 4 pints veal bone stock • 2 tsp. salt • 2 oz. butter • 2 oz. flour • 1/3 tsp. ground black pepper • 1 tbsp. finely chopped parsley • 1 egg yolk • 1 gill sour cream.

Scrape asparagus and cut into one-inch pieces. Pour boiling salt water over it, strain through colander. This will take away the bitter flavour. Now cook asparagus in the mildly salted stock till tender. Make a light yellow roux from butter and flour, add chopped parsley, ground black pepper and pour soup over it. Simmer for 15 minutes. Mix egg yolk and sour cream in the tureen, pour soup over it, stir, and serve.

Green Pea Soup

Ingredients: 1 1/2 lb. unshelled peas • 4 pints veal bone stock • 2 oz. flour • 2 oz. lard • 1 heaping tbsp. finely chopped parsley • 2 tsp. sugar • 1 level tbsp. salt.

Shell peas and cook empty pods in salted stock. Melt sugar in lard, add peas and chopped parsley. Sprinkle with flour, stir and strain stock over it.
Bring to the boil and reducing heat, simmer till peas are tender. Serve with crackers or sippets.

Cream of Green Pea Soup

Prepare exactly the same way as above, but purée the soup through sieve when peas are tender and, adding a 1 oz. piece of butter, simmer for 5 minutes before serving. Garnish with fried croutons.

Haricot Bean Soup

Ingredients: 1/2 lb. haricot beans • 4 pints vegetable and bacon rind stock • 3 bay leaves • 2 oz. lard • 2 oz. flour • 1 small onion • 1 tsp. salt • 1 gill sour cream • 1 tsp. paprika.

Soak beans overnight and cook in strained stock, adding salt and bay leaves. Prepare a brown roux from lard and flour, add finely chopped onion and paprika. Pour soup over it, stir, bring to the boil then reduce heat and simmer for 20 minutes. Add 1 gill sour cream to the soup just before serving.
An excellent cream soup can be made by passing soup through sieve when ready, adding a lump of butter, and reheating thoroughly. Serve with crackers.

French Bean Soup

Ingredients: 1 lb. tender French beans • 2 oz. streaky bacon • 2 oz. flour • 1 small onion • 2 tsp. finely chopped parsley • 1/2 tsp. paprika • 1 level tbsp. salt • 4 pints bone stock • 1 gill sour cream.

Cut bacon into small cubes and fry till brown and crisp. Strain the fat into a saucepan, add flour to make a golden-yellow roux. Add to it the very finely grated onion, chopped parsley and paprika. Stir, pour stock over it; bring to the boil. Add beans cut into inch-sized pieces. Simmer for 1/2 hour. Add sour cream just before serving.

Mushroom Soup

Ingredients: 1/3 lb. mushrooms • 2 oz. butter • 2 oz. flour • 1 small onion • 1 tbsp. finely chopped parsley • 1/3 tsp. ground black pepper • 2 tsp. salt • 4 pints veal bone stock • 1 gill sour cream • csipetke.

Prepare a light yellow roux from butter and flour, add coarsely chopped mushrooms, finely grated onion and ground pepper. Stir and add salted stock. Bring to the boil then reduce heat and simmer for 1/2 hour. Add sour cream just before serving. Serve with csipetke (see. p.58).

Cream of Mushroom Soup

Ingredients: 4 pints vegetable and veal bone stock • 2 oz. butter • 1 small onion • 1/2 lb. mushrooms • 1 heaping tbsp. finely chopped parsley • 1 level tbsp. salt • 1/3 tsp. ground black pepper • 2 oz. flour • 1 egg yolk • 1 gill sour cream.

Put uncooked mushrooms through mincer or — and this is the original method — chop them finely on wooden board together with parsley. Melt butter in saucepan, add the mushrooms, parsley, pinch of salt and pepper. Cover and simmer slowly till the moisture evaporates. Then sprinkle with flour, add 2 ladlefuls of stock, stir, bring to the boil, add rest of salted stock and simmer for 3/4 hour. Mix egg yolk and sour cream in tureen, pour hot soup over it. A small pinch of grated nutmeg improves the flavour.

Fish Soup with White Wine

Ingredients: 2 lb. fish • 2 pints water • 2 pints dry white wine • 1 large onion • 2 oz. parsnips • 3 bay leaves • 1 sprig of savory • 6 whole black peppercorns • 1 level tbsp. salt • 1 egg yolk • 1 gill sour cream • 1 tsp. flour.

For best results this soup should be prepared from fresh-water fish: carp, pike, sheat-fish and pike-perch. Turbot can be used as second choice.

Cut fish into even, finger-thick slices. Salt and put slices aside in a porcelain dish. Put the water in a saucepan together with the wine, thinly sliced onion and parsnips, savory, black peppercorns, bay leaves and the left-over salt. Bring to the boil and simmer for 1/2 hour. Put the fish into a saucepan, strain the stock over it and cook slowly for 20 minutes. Mix egg yolk, sour cream and flour in a small bowl, add 2 ladles of soup by degrees, then add this mixture to the soup. After a further 5 minutes' cooking, it is ready to serve. Serve with thin slices of bread and butter.

Fish Cream Soup

Ingredients: 2 lb. fish • 2 oz. carrots • 2 oz. parsnips • 1 large onion • 1 bay leaf • 5 whole black peppercorns • 1 tbsp. salt • 4 pints water • 1 tsp. white vinegar • 2 oz. flour • 2 oz. lard • 1 gill sour cream.

Boil the grated carrots, parsnips and onion adding the salt, bay leaf and black peppercorns. After 1/2 hour, add fish. Cook for 10 more minutes, then pass the whole soup through sieve. Prepare a light brown roux with lard and flour, pour soup over it, bring to the boil and simmer for 20 minutes. Flavour with vinegar and add sour cream just before serving.

Springtime Egg Soup

Ingredients: 4 pints veal bone and vegetable stock • 2 tbsp. French mustard • 6 hardboiled eggs • 2 oz. butter • 1 oz. flour • 1 tbsp. finely chopped chives • 1 gill sour cream.

Dice and put aside some of the vegetables from stock. Take out yolks of hard-boiled eggs, press through sieve. Cut whites into small cubes. Make a golden-brown roux from butter and flour, strain stock over it, bring to the boil, then reduce heat and allow to simmer. Mix egg yolk purée and mustard with a ladleful of stock, add to the soup together with chopped whites and diced vegetables. Mix the sour cream and chives in the tureen, pour the hot soup over it, and serve.

Caraway Seed Soup

Ingredients: 4 pints meat stock • 2 oz. lard • 2 oz. flour • 1 level tsp. caraway seed • 1–2 slices of lean bacon • 1 egg yolk • 1 gill sour cream • 1 level tbsp. salt.

Make a brown roux from lard and flour, add caraway seed, pour salted stock over it. Bring to the boil then add bacon. Simmer for 20 minutes. Mix sour cream and egg yolk in tureen, strain soup over it using a fine strainer. Serve with sippets.

Lebbencs Soup

Ingredients: 1/4 lb. pasta squares • 1/2 lb. potatoes • 1 oz. lard •
1 oz. flour • 1/2 tsp. paprika • 1 1/2 gill sour cream •
4 pints ham stock.

Whenever I cook ham, I keep the liquid for making this soup. Melt lard in saucepan, add pasta squares, stirring constantly, fry till squares are browned. Sprinkle with flour, and paprika, stir, then pour ham stock over it. Bring to the boil, add potatoes cut into small cubes, cook slowly for 20 minutes. Add sour cream just before serving. This soup needs no salt.

Morello Cherry Soup (Cold)

Ingredients: 1 1/2 lb. morello cherries • 3 pints water • 2 gills sour cream • 1/2 pint dry red wine • 1 egg yolk • 6 oz. sugar • the peel of half a lemon • 1 inch-sized piece of cinnamon • 2 tsp. flour • pinch of salt.

Stone the morello cherries, then put them to cook together with sugar, salt, lemon peel, and cinnamon. Allow to simmer. Meantime, mix in a bowl the flour, egg yolk and 1 gill of sour cream. Mix with a ladleful of soup, then add to the boiling soup stirring constantly. Finally, mix wine and other half of sour cream, and add this to the soup as well. After 10 minutes of simmering put soup aside and let it cool. Take lemon peel and cinnamon out before cooling. This soup is excellent when chilled. It can be made from gooseberries, blackberries, raspberries or red currants as well.

Wine Cream Soup

Ingredients: 2 pints light white wine • 1/2 pint water • 4 egg yolks •
3 oz. sugar • lemon peel.

For best results, use a heavy enamelled saucepan. Put yolks in the saucepan with sugar, beat well, gradually add the wine and water mixture. Add half a pinch of grated lemon peel. Put on medium heat and beat vigorously to prevent curdling till it begins to boil. Take off immediately and serve while hot.

GARNISHES FOR SOUPS

Vermicelli or Egg Squares

Ingredients: 1 egg • pinch of salt • about 4 tbsp. flour.

Knead ingredients very thoroughly together to make a stiff dough. Form into a round ball, then roll out on a floured board to the thickness of paper. Fold floured pasta into a roll, and keeping it on rolling pin, cut lengthwise and then crosswise into very thin noodles. Shake them apart to let flour fall off, then add to the slowly boiling soup and cook for about 6 minutes. It can be cut into small squares if preferred. Though dried vermicelli can be bought in delicatessen shops, the flavour and consistency of this pasta is definitely superior.

Butter Dumplings

Ingredients: 1 1/2 oz. butter • 2 oz. flour • 1 egg • pinch of salt • pinch of crushed mixed herbs.

Cream well the butter adding the egg, stir in the flour, salt and mixed herbs. Form small almond-shaped pieces with a teaspoon and drop them in the slowly boiling soup, one by one. Cover the saucepan and cook for about 10–15 minutes.

Csipetke (Thimble Dumplings)

Ingredients: 6 oz. flour • pinch of salt • 1 egg.

Sift flour into a bowl, add egg and salt. Knead ingredients into a stiff dough. Flatten the dough between your palms and pinch into small, beansized pieces, add to the soup and boil slowly for 10 minutes before serving.

Semolina Dumplings

Ingredients: 1 level tbsp. lard • 1 egg • pinch of salt • pinch of ground black pepper • 1 tbsp. finely chopped parsley • 2 1/2 oz. semolina.

Cream lard, add egg, salt, black pepper, parsley and finally the semolina. Mix well and let stand for 1/2 hour. Form almond-shaped pieces with a teaspoon and add dumplings to the slowly boiling soup one by one. Cover the saucepan and cook for about 15–20 minutes.

Trickled Pasta

Ingredients: 1 egg • pinch of salt • about 2 tbsp. flour • pinch of grated nutmeg.

Mix egg, flour, salt and grated nutmeg to a thin consistency. Put a colander over the boiling soup, pour mixture into it and stirring with a wooden spoon, let pasta trickle into the soup. Reduce heat and cook slowly for 6–7 minutes.

Golden Drops

Ingredients: 1 egg • 2 tbsp. flour • pinch of salt • 1 tbsp. milk • lard.

Beat together the flour, egg, salt and milk. Heat lard in a small pan, put a colander somewhat tilted over the pan, pour mixture into it and stirring constantly with a wooden spoon, let pasta trickle into the hot fat. Fry till golden brown, then lift out onto a warm plate.

Grated Pasta

Ingredients: 4 oz. flour • pinch of salt • 1 egg.

Knead a stiff pasta from ingredients. Grate the pasta on a coarse grater onto a plate. Dip the lump of pasta into flour every now and then to prevent sticking. Add to boiling soup and let cook for 6–8 minutes.

SAUCES

Mayonnaise Sauce

Ingredients: 2 egg yolks • pinch of salt • 1 gill olive oil • the juice of 1/2 lemon.

Beat egg yolks with whisk till light and frothy. Add the oil drop by drop, stirring vigorously all the time. When ready it should be stiff, the consistency of soft butter. Add salt and lemon juice last. An electric beater can be used, in which case it will take much less time.

Cooked Mayonnaise

Ingredients: 6 egg yolks • 5 gills sour cream • 1 gill olive oil • pinch of salt • juice of 1/4 lemon.

Mix well the egg yolks and sour cream in a saucepan. Put on medium heat, cook till it thickens, beating vigorously all the while. Take off, let cool. When the mixture is quite cold, add the oil by degrees, stirring constantly. Finally, stir in the salt and lemon juice. This mayonnaise can be kept for a considerable time without danger of spoiling.

Tartare Sauce

Take 1 cup of mayonnaise and add 1 tbsp. French mustard. Mix thoroughly.

Cold Game Sauce

Ingredients: 5 tbsp. red currant jelly • 2 tsp. French mustard • 8 morello cherries bottled in cognac or liqueur • 2 tsp. capers.

Chop morello cherries and capers, stir well with jelly and mustard. Add 2–3 spoonfuls of liqueur from the cherries.

Cold Anchovy Sauce

Ingredients: 6 anchovies • 3 hard-boiled eggs • 1/2 tsp. grated onion • 1 tbsp. finely chopped parsley • 2 tbsp. olive oil • 1 tsp. French mustard • 1/2 tsp. sugar • 2 gills sour cream.

Put the anchovies and hard-boiled eggs through a wire sieve. Mix with the rest of the ingredients except the sour cream. This you add by degrees as the last step, stirring the sauce constantly. Add a little lemon juice to taste.

Hot Anchovy Sauce

Ingredients: 1 oz. lard • 2 tbsp. flour • 4 anchovies • 3 ladles meat stock • 1 gill sour cream.

Chop anchovies very fine. Prepare a roux from lard and flour, add anchovies, stir and pour meat stock over it. Bring to the boil and simmer for 20 minutes. Add sour cream just before serving.

Hot Tomato Sauce

Ingredients: 1 oz. lard • 1 oz. flour • one 4-oz. tin of tomato purée • about 2 ladles vegetable stock • 1 tbsp. sugar • 1/2 green pepper • 1/2 tsp. salt.

Make a nicely browned roux from lard and flour, add tomato purée, bring to the boil and simmer for 20 minutes. Stir every now and then; add a little more stock if too thick. Take out green pepper before serving.

Mushroom Sauce

Ingredients: 1/2 lb. mushrooms • 1 oz. butter • 1 oz. flour •
1 tbsp. finely chopped parsley • pinch of ground black pepper •
1 gill sour cream • 1 egg yolk • pinch of grated nutmeg •
2 ladles of meat stock.

Chop mushroom coarsely. Make a light roux from butter and flour, add black pepper, parsley, salt, grated nutmeg and mushrooms. Stir and pour cold stock over it. Bring to the boil, then reduce heat and simmer for 20 minutes. Mix egg yolk and sour cream and add to the sauce. Take off the heat immediately when it begins to boil.

Horse-radish Sauce (Hot)

Ingredients: 2 oz. finely grated horse-radish • 2 gills sour cream •
pinch of salt • 1/2 tsp. sugar • 1/2 pint meat stock • 1 oz. flour.

Put 1 gill sour cream together with horse-radish in a saucepan and cook on low heat for 5 minutes. Mix flour and sour cream very thoroughly to avoid lumping, add to the horse-radish, and, stirring constantly, add the stock, salt and sugar. Bring to the boil. Add the remaining sour cream just before serving. This sauce is rather thin, so use 1/4 pint stock if you prefer it thicker.

Fresh Dill Sauce

Ingredients: 2 oz. finely chopped fresh dill • 1 1/2 oz. flour •
1 1/2 oz. lard • 1/2 pint meat stock • 1 gill sour cream • pinch of salt.

Make a light yellow roux from flour and lard, add chopped dill and salt, stir, and pour cold stock over it. Simmer for 20 minutes. Add sour cream, heat and serve.

Tarragon Sauce (Hot)

Prepare in the same way as dill sauce (see above), but add
1 oz. chopped tarragon leaves instead of dill, and flavour
with 1 tbsp. tarragon vinegar.

Sauce Béarnaise

Ingredients: 4 egg yolks • 3/4 pint milk • 3 oz. butter • 2 oz. flour •
1 large cup dry white wine • 1 small onion • 6 whole black peppercorns • 3 bay leaves • 1 tsp. tarragon leaves • the grated rind and
juice of 1 lemon and 1/2 orange • 1/2 tsp. salt • 1 gill sour cream •
1 1/2 oz. butter flavoured with 1 tsp. anchovy paste.

Mix egg yolks, flour, milk and 3 oz. butter very thoroughly,
heat in double saucepan till thickened, then pull aside and
add wine, grated onion, black pepper, bay leaves, the grated
rind and juice of 1 lemon, all the juice and half a grated rind
of an orange, salt and 1 gill of sour cream. Put saucepan
back on steam again and cook sauce, stirring constantly, till
it thickens. Then pass it through a sieve together with
anchovy butter, and gradually add the remaining milk. Pour
sauce back into the double saucepan, and keep warm over
hot, but not boiling water till needed.

Gooseberry Sauce

Ingredients: 3/4 lb. small, unripe gooseberries • 1/2 pint water • 1 gill
sour cream • 1 level tbsp. flour • 2 heaping tbsp. sugar • small pinch
of salt.

Clean gooseberries, cook slowly in 1/4 pint of water till soft.
Mix 1/2 gill sour cream with flour, add 1/4 pint water, stir
well. Pour on gooseberries, stir and bring to the boil, add
sugar and salt. The remaining sour cream should be added
just before serving.

Morello Cherry Sauce (Hot)

Ingredients: 1/2 lb. morello cherries • 2 oz. sugar • 1 gill sour cream • 1 cup water • 1 level tbsp. flour.

Stone ripe morello cherries and cut them in four. Cook slowly in their own juice till soft with the sugar, and 1 or 2 tbsp. water. Mix the flour, 1/2 gill sour cream, and the rest of water till smooth, add to cherries and boil slowly for 10 minutes. Add 1/2 gill sour cream just before serving.

Red Currant Sauce

Prepare in exactly the same way as Morello Cherry Sauce (see above), but using red currants, taking care not to crush the fruit while cooking.

Bechamel Sauce

Ingredients: 2 1/2 oz. butter • 2 oz. flour • 2 gill milk • 1 gill sour cream • 3 tbsp. grated cheese • 3 egg yolks • pinch of salt • pinch of ground white pepper.

Beat well together in a saucepan the egg yolks, sour cream, milk, flour, melted butter, cheese, salt and pepper. Stirring constantly, cook on medium heat till the sauce becomes thick and smooth.

FISH DISHES

Fisherman's Stew

Ingredients: 1/2 lb. each of carp • pike-perch • sterlet and sheat-fish
(whiting with cod, hake and plaice are a possible combination if
fresh-water fish are not available) • 1 oz. lard • 2 large onions •
1 level tbsp. paprika • 1 level tbsp. salt.

Clean fish, cut of heads and tails, and cut into thick slices.
Put slices on a plate, salt and put aside. Heat lard in
saucepan, add finely chopped onions, fry till golden. Put
saucepan aside, add paprika, stir, then put in the fish-heads
and tails. Pour 1 1/2 pints water on, bring to the boil, then
reduce heat and allow to simmer under lid for 3/4 hour. Now
strain liquid through a fine strainer into another saucepan,
arrange in it the salted fish-slices, taking care that the gravy
covers the fish. Cook slowly under lid for 1/2 hour, shaking
the saucepan every now and then. Do not stir. Serve in a
warmed soup tureen.

Fish Pörkölt

Ingredients: Several kinds of fish can be used for this. Fresh-water
fish like carp are preferable, but whiting with cod or hake may be
used. 2 lb. fish • 3 oz. lard • 2 large onions • 1 level tbsp. paprika •
1 level tsp. flour • 1 tsp. salt • 1 green pepper (optional).

Cut fish to thick slices, salt and put it aside. Heat lard, add
finely chopped onions, fry till golden, sprinkle with paprika
and flour, stir, then add 1/2 pint water. Simmer 1/2 hour,
then add sliced fish to gravy. Cover again and simmer for
20–25 minutes. Lift out slices of fish, arrange in a warmed

porcelain dish and pour the hot gravy over it. Decorate with thinly cut green pepper rings.

Fish in Paprika Gravy

Prepare it in exactly the same way as fish pörkölt, except that no water is added. Instead mix 2 gills of sour cream with the gravy about five minutes before serving.

Sheat-fish Steaks of Szeged

Ingredients: 1 lb. thick sheat-fish slices (if not available, use cod) •
5 oz. streaky bacon • 1 large onion • 1 level tbsp. paprika •
2 tbsp. tomato purée • 1 1/2 gills sour cream.

Cut bacon into small pieces and fry in a large saucepan till crisp. Lift out fried bacon, put aside. Fry the finely chopped onion in the bacon fat in the saucepan to golden-yellow, pull aside, stir in the paprika, then arrange the fish steaks in it. Add tomato purée and sour cream, cover, and simmer for 20–25 minutes. Serve fish with the gravy poured over it, and garnish with boiled potatoes and crisp bacon.

Tihany Pike-perch

Ingredients: 1 large pike-perch (about 3 lbs.) • 3 gills sour cream •
6 eggs • 3 oz. butter • 1 tsp. finely chopped tarragon leaves •
1 tsp. finely chopped capers • 1 small onion • 1 sp. anchovy paste •
pinch of grated lemon-peel • 2 tbsp. finely chopped chives •
2 tbsp. finely chopped parsley • 1 tbsp. vinegar • 1/2 tsp. salt.

Cover fish with water in a large saucepan, add salt and vinegar, then cook fish slowly, for about 15 minutes. Taking it out, lift the meat off the back carefully, taking care not to break the two fillets. Now mix well in a brain the following ingredients: sour cream, the yolks of 6 eggs, melted butter, tarragon, capers, grated onion, anchovy paste, grated lemon-peel, chives and parsley. Pour half of this mixture into the bottom of an oval fireproof dish, and arrange the fish-fillets on it. Beat egg whites stiffly, fold it in the rest of sauce and pour the mixture over the fish. Bake in a medium-hot oven for about 1/2 hour. Serve with buttered new potatoes.

Pike-perch with Asparagus

Ingredients: 3 lb. pike-perch • 1 lb. fresh asparagus • 1 tsp. salt • 3 oz. butter • 2 gills sour cream • 2 level tbsp. flour • 3 egg yolks.

Cut each asparagus in half, tie both halves in separate bunches, cook in gently boiling salt water. Put the fish in a suitable saucepan, strain asparagus stock over and cook fish in the gently simmering stock for 20 minutes. Lift the two fillets off the bones. Melt 1 1/2 oz. butter in a fireproof dish, and arrange the fish-fillets in it. Keep warm while preparing the following sauce: beat together 4 egg yolks, the sour cream and melted butter, add 1/2 pint of the fish-and asparagus stock. Arrange asparagus around the fish, pour sauce on top. Bake in a hot oven for 20 minutes. Garnish with buttered potatoes.

Jacksalmon in Wine Sauce

Ingredients: 3 (about 1 lb.) jacksalmons • 3 oz. butter • 1 small onion • 1/2 pint red wine • 3 tbsp. tomato purée • 1/2 tsp. salt.

Remove fillets, cook the bones, tails, heads in 1/2 pint salt water, for 1/2 our. Heat butter in a saucepan, add the finely chopped onion and fry till golden. Add wine, tomato purée and the strained stock from the fish-bones, bring to the boil, then simmer for 10 minutes. Now add the rolled-up fillets of fish and cook slowly for 20 minutes. Serve with boiled rice.

Stuffed Carp Normandy

Ingredients: 1 (about 2 lb.) carp • 1/3 lb. halibut or hake •
1 pint vegetable stock • 1/4 pint milk • 5 oz. butter • 2 egg yolks •
2 tbsp. flour • 1 tsp. anchovy paste • 1 tbsp. finely chopped parsley •
pinch of ground black pepper • 1/4 pint white wine • 1 tsp. salt.

Gut carp and, cutting the bone through at the neck and pulling it away from the fish, take out backbone, rub fish with salt and let it stand for 15 minutes. Cook halibut in vegetable stock, strain, bone and skin it, then mash the fish with a fork. Beat well together the milk, flour, 2 oz. butter and 2 egg yolks. Cook this sauce on low heat, stirring all the while, till it thickens. Mix in the mashed halibut, chopped parsley, pepper, a pinch of salt, and anchovy paste. Fill the fish with this stuffing, sew up the opening, then arrange in a fireproof dish. Pour 3 oz. melted butter and the wine over it and basting frequently, bake in a medium oven for 3/4 hour.

Stuffed Füred Carp

Ingredients: 1 (2 1/2 lb.) carp • 1 bread-roll soaked in milk •
3 1/2 oz. mushrooms • 1 tbsp. finely chopped parsley •
1 tsp. grated onion • 1 pinch of grated lemon peel • 2 eggs •
1 tsp. anchovy paste • pinch of ground black pepper • 4 oz. butter •
1 1/2 gills sour cream.

Gut, then rub the carp with salt. Mix in a saucepan the soaked and well-squeezed roll, the chopped roe from the carp, chopped mushrooms, parsley, grated onions and 2 oz. butter. Cook mixture on low heat for 20 minutes, put aside and add grated lemon peel, pepper, 2 eggs and anchovy paste. Stuff the fish with this, and secure with toothpicks. Melt the rest of butter and heat together with sour cream and a pinch of salt. Place carp in an oval fireproof dish, pour sour cream and butter mixture over it, and bake in a medium-hot oven for 1/2 hour. Serve with mixed salad.

Carp Piquant

Ingredients: 6 slices carp (1 inch) • 1/2 tsp. salt • 1 level tsp. grated onion • 1 tsp. finely chopped parsley • the juice of 1/2 lemon • 2 oz. flour • fat to fry.

Rub the slices of fish with salt. Mix the onion, parsley and lemon juice; spread this mixture over the fish and let it stand for 20 minutes. Dip slices into flour, tapping them with your palm and shaking off surplus, and fry in hot fat. Serve tartare sauce separately, mixed with a tsp. of chopped chives.

Casseroled Pike with Sauerkraut

Ingredients: 1 (about 3 lb.) pike • 2 lb. sauerkraut • 3 oz. lard • 1 heaped tbsp. granulated sugar • 1 ladleful of stock • 1 oz. streaky bacon • 2 gills sour cream.

Gut pike and rub with salt. Put aside for 1 hour. Heat lard, add sugar. When chocolate-brown, add sauerkraut well pressed out. Simmer for 1/2 hour, stirring every now and then to prevent burning. Take a large oval fireproof dish, pour a ladleful of stock in the bottom, then arrange on it evenly half of the cooked sauerkraut. Lay the pike on this, then cover with the remaining sauerkraut, sprinkle with chopped and fried bacon, and pour over the sour cream. Cook in a medium-hot oven for 3/4 hour. Serve in the casserole.

Pike-perch in White Sauce

Ingredients: 1 (about 7 oz.) fish for each person • 4 oz. butter •
2 heaped tbsp. flour • 1/2 pint vegetable stock • 1 large cooked
celeriac • 1 tbsp. salt • 1 1/2 gills sour cream • 1 pinch of ground
white pepper.

Gut fish, put them in an oblong baking tin and pour boiling
salt water over them. Leave to stand for 10 minutes. Heat
butter, add flour, stir till frothy but still white, dilute with cold
stock. Stirring constantly, bring sauce to the boil, add pepper, a little salt and the celeriac pressed through sieve. Lastly
add sour cream, then put saucepan aside. Butter a suitable
fireproof dish, arrange the fish in it, then pour sauce over it.
Bake in a medium-hot oven for 25 minutes. Serve with
boiled, buttered or mashed potatoes.

Baked Sheat-fish with Tomatoes

Ingredients: 6 slices of fish • 4 oz. butter • 1 lb. tomatoes •
6 oz. cooked rice • 1 tsp. salt • 1/3 tsp. ground black pepper.

Salt fish, let stand for 20 minutes. Dip firm, even-sized tomatoes in hot water, pull off skin. Arrange fish-slices in an oval
fireproof dish on a bed of cooked rice, put tomatoes around
and sprinkle with pepper. Pour melted butter over it. Bake in
a hot oven for 20–25 minutes basting frequently with the
gravy. Serve grated cheese separately.

Pike-perch with Mayonnaise

Ingredients: 3 (about 1 lb.) pike-perch • 2 gills sour cream •
2 egg yolks • pinch of salt • 1 heaped tsp. sugar • 1 tbsp. vinegar •
1 tbsp. water.

Cook fish in salt water. Lift out carefully and allow to cool. Mix in a double saucepan egg yolks, sour cream, pinch of salt, 1 heaped tsp. sugar, vinegar and water. Cook this sauce over steam, stirring constantly, till it thickens. Take off heat and stir till it cools. Arrange fish on an oval porcelain dish, and pour sauce over it. Decorate with parsley leaves and lemon butterflies.

Carp Slices in Walnut Sauce

Ingredients: 6 slices of carp • 1 celeriac • 1 carrot • 1 parsnip • 3 lumps of sugar • 4 oz. coarsely ground walnuts • 3 level tbsp. flour • pinch of ground black pepper • 1 tsp. salt • 2 oz. lard.

Grate celeriac, carrot and parsnip on a fine grater. Bring to the boil pints of water in a wide saucepan, add 1/2 tsp. salt, and grated vegetables. Cook for 20 minutes. Heat lard in another saucepan, melt the sugar in it, add ground walnuts, flour and ground pepper, dilute with the strained vegetable stock and, stirring constantly, allow to simmer till sauce thickens a little. If very thick, add a little water. Arrange the fish-slices on the grated, cooked vegetables left in the large saucepan, pour walnut-sauce over and cook slowly for about 20–25 minutes shaking the saucepan now and then. Do not stir, because the fish breaks easily. Serve fish with the sauce poured over.

Baked Carp with Walnut Stuffing

Ingredients: 1 (3 lb.) carp • 1 bread-roll soaked in milk • 7 oz. coarsely ground walnuts • 1 level tsp. salt • 1 good pinch of marjoram • 2 eggs • 2 oz. butter.

Gut and salt fish, then leave to stand for 20 minutes. Mix in a basin the lightly squeezed roll, egg yolks, ground walnuts, a little salt and marjoram. Lastly add whipped egg whites. Stuff the carp with the mixture, pin the slit together with toothpicks. Spread the butter on the fish and bake for 1/2 hour in a medium-hot oven. Serve hot.

Jellied Carp

Prepare Fisherman's Stew (see p. 65). Lift out meat, bone, then arrange in individual dishes. Boil remaining gravy for 1/2 hour. Put aside, add 2 sheets of gelatine, stir till gelatine dissolves. Strain gravy over the fish, pouring equal amount on each portion. Serve chilled with lettuce salad.

Herring Salad

Ingredients: 3 large pickled herrings • 1/2 lb. boiled potatoes •
4 oz. cooked carrots • 1/2 lb. apples • 4 egg yolks • 1 cupful olive
oil • pinch of salt • 1 level tsp. sugar • 1 tbsp. French mustard •
1 gill cream • juice of
1/2 lemon.

Skin and bone herrings, and cut meat to strips. Beat egg yolks till frothy, add oil drop by drop, stirring continually. Then add to this mayonnaise the following ingredients: salt, sugar, cream, mustard, lemon juice, and the potatoes, apples and carrots cut into small cubes. Lastly add herrings cut to strips. Mix well and chill for about 6–8 hours. Pile up on a glass dish just before serving, sprinkle with a little chopped chives. Serve with lettuce salad.

Jacksalmon with Anchovies

Ingredients: 1 large (2 lb.) jacksalmon • 1/2 pint milk • the juice of
1/2 lemon • 4 oz. butter • 1 gill sour cream • anchovies.

Scale and gut fish. Soak in the milk to which a little water and a pinch of salt have been added. Cut three anchovies to matchstick-thin strips. Remove fish from milk and dry with a cloth. Push anchovy-strips with a larding-pin in the two sides of the fish, in an even row. Brush jacksalmon with the juice of 1/2 lemon, then arrange neatly in an oval fireproof dish. Pour half of the melted butter over it, and bake in a medium-hot oven for 20–25 minutes. A few minutes before serving mix melted butter and sour cream, pour it over the fish, put it back in the oven for 3 minutes. Serve hot with mixed salad.

Home-made Caviar

Ingredients: 6 oz. smoked cod's roe • 1 heaped tsp. grated onion • 6 tsp. olive oil • juice of 1 lemon.

Peel, then scrape roe off the inner membranes. Mix well with the ingredients, put in a glass jar or deep dish, allow to stand in a cool place for 24 hours before use. Serve with buttered toast.

Fried Soft Roe with Tartare Sauce

Ingredients: 1 (1/2 lb.) soft roe • 2 tbsp. flour • 1 tsp. salt • fat to fry.

Put roe in a deep dish, pour boiling salt water over. After 5 minutes strain and turn the roe in the salted flour. Using a deep-fryer, fry in medium-hot fat, lift out onto absorbent paper. Serve on a heated plate, with tartare sauce in a separate dish.

MEAT DISHES

BEEF

Alföld Braised Beef

Ingredients: 2 lb. braising steak • 1 large or 2 medium-size onions •
1 tsp. salt • 1 heaped tsp. paprika • 3 oz. streaky bacon • 2 oz. lard •
1 1/2 gills sour cream • 1 green pepper.

Cut meat into 6 slices. Cut bacon to short strips and, using a
larding pin, lard the slices in even rows. Heat the lard in a
large frying-pan and fry larded steaks for 3 minutes each
side, then put them aside. Lowering the heat, fry in the fat
remaining in pan, the finely chopped onions to a nice golden colour, stir in paprika, put back the meat, add salt and 2
tbsp. water. Cover and simmer, adding a spoonful water
once or twice to prevent burning. When meat is tender, pour
on the sour cream, bring to the boil. Serve in a hot dish, decorate with green pepper sliced in thin rings. Garnish with
boiled potatoes.

Tailor's Steak

Ingredients: 2 lb. braising steak • 1 tsp. salt • 1 oz. bacon •
1 tbsp. finely chopped parsley • 2 tbsp. breadcrumbs •
pinch of grated lemon peel • 2 eggs • pinch of ground black
pepper •
2 gills sour cream.

Cut meat into two large even slices, trim edges, and salt. Put
through mincer the cut-off bits of meat together with the

bacon. Add to the minced meat the chopped parsley, bread-crumbs, lemon peel, eggs, pepper and 1/2 tsp. salt. Mix well, then spread on one slice of the meat. Cover with the other slice, then sew edges together all round. Put in a baking-tin in which you heated some fat beforehand and, basting frequently, roast in a medium oven for about 1 hour. Strain off fat and pour sour cream in the tin, stir well and bring to the boil on the stove. Cut the meat into thick slices — do not forget to take out the thread — lay slices on a hot dish and pour some of the gravy over, serving the rest separately in a sauce-boat. Garnish with steamed cabbage and boiled potatoes.

Braised Steak

Ingredients: 2 lb. braising beef • 1 oz. lard • 1/2 tsp. salt • 1 level tbsp. finely chopped onion • pinch of ground black pepper.

Heat lard in a skillet, put in the meat and fry for no longer than 3 minutes on both sides. Lift out meat, add to the fat the finely chopped onions, and fry till pale yellow. Put the meat back, add salt, pepper and 1/2 cup of stock or water, cover and simmer slowly till meat is tender. Garnish with steamed Brussels sprouts, cabbage, or rice.

Stuffed Steak

Ingredients: 2 lb. stewing steak • 2 bread-rolls soaked in milk • 1 tbsp. French mustard • 4 oz. mushrooms • 1 large onion • 1 gill sour cream • pinch of ground black pepper • 1/2 tsp. salt • 1/2 pint vegetable or meat stock • 3 oz. lard.

Tell the butcher to cut the meat in four slices, without cutting right through; the slices should be kept together by a hinge of uncut meat. Divide this in two before preparation, so that you get two pairs of thick slices. Trim, shape, then flatten with a meat-beater, sprinkle with salt and spread with mustard. Mince the bits of meat cut off while trimming. Heat 1 oz. lard in a saucepan, add 1 tsp. finely chopped onion, fry till pale yellow, then add the coarsely chopped mushrooms. Add salt and pepper, cover and allow to simmer till water evaporates. Knead together the minced meat, cooked mushrooms and squeezed-out rolls. Spread this mixture over the two large flattened steaks, roll them up and tie with thread. Heat 2 oz. lard in a saucepan, add the remaining chopped onion, the two rolls of meat and 1/2 pint of stock. Cover and allow to simmer till meat is tender. Remove cotton, cut the meat into slices one-inch thick, arrange them on a flat dish, and pour the gravy over it. Serve with macaroni or noodles.

Braised Beef with Savoy Cabbage

Ingredients: 2 lb. joint of beef • 4 oz. streaky bacon • 1/3 tsp. salt • pinch of ground black pepper • 1 carrot • 1 parsnip • 1 large onion • about 1 lb. heart of a savoy cabbage • 1 gill sour cream • pinch of mixed herbs • 1 celeriac • 1 oz. lard.

Leave the joint whole. Grate carrots celeriac, onion and parsnip. Cut bacon in rather thick strips and lard the meat deeply all over with the help of a larding-pin, then place the joint into a roasting-pan. Sprinkle with the grated vegetables, cover with savoy cabbage cut to strips. Pour melted fat over it and 1 or 2 ladlefuls of water. Cook in a medium oven, basting frequently. When joint is tender, lift out, then pour sour cream over the vegetables remaining in the pan. Cut the meat in 6 slices, arrange on a dish and pour the vegetables and gravy over it. Serve with boiled potatoes.

Rolled Steak with Carrots

Ingredients: 2 lb. braising steak cut in 6 slices • 1/2 lb. carrots •
1 large onion • 1 egg • 1/2 tsp. salt • pinch of ground black pepper •
good pinch of marjoram • 3 oz. fat bacon • 1 gill sour cream.

Flatten the slices of meat with beater. Cook carrots and
onion, strain, then press them through sieve. Add 1/4 tsp.
salt, black pepper, marjoram and the egg, and beat well
together. Spread this mixture on the meat, roll and tie slices.
Grill sliced bacon, pour the rendered fat into a saucepan,
heat, then add meat-rolls. Fry all around, salt, then pour
some of the vegetable stock over it, cover and allow to simmer till meat is tender. Add sour cream, bring to the boil,
then serve in own gravy. Arrange the crisp fried bacon over
the meat. Garnish with boiled potatoes.

Layer Roulade of Transylvania

Ingredients: 6 oz. slice of beef • 6 oz. slice of pork • 6 oz. slice of
veal • 6 oz. calf's liver • 3 oz. streaky bacon • 1/2 tsp. salt • pinch
of ground black pepper • a good pinch of marjoram • about 1/2 pint
of meat stock • 3 oz. lard • 2 gills sour cream.

Flatten the large slices of meat with beater, sprinkle them
with a little salt. Chop bacon very finely, put liver through
mincer, add to the bacon, together with a little salt, the black
pepper and marjoram. Beat mixture well, then spread thickly
on the 3 slices of meat. Place the slice of pork over the beef,
then the veal. Roll meat layers carefully together, tie securely with cotton. Heat lard in a saucepan, fry the meat-roll
quickly and evenly in it, then add a little of the stock, cover,
and allow to simmer till meat is tender. Remove meat onto a
warm dish, add a spoonful of paprika and the sour cream to

the gravy, bring to the boil and serve in a sauce-boat. Garnish with boiled rice.

Fried Steaks with Tomatoes

Ingredients: 2 lb. thick fillet steak • 3 oz. lard • 6 large firm tomatoes • potato chips.

Heat lard in a large frying-pan, put in the thick, round fillets. Fry meat quickly, turning slices several times with a slicer. In the meantime cut tomatoes in two and fry them in a separate frying-pan. Pile the fried tomatoes in the middle of a heated-up round flat dish, arrange fillets around it. Serve immediately.

Hungarian Fillet of Beef

Ingredients: 2 lb. piece of fillet steak • 2 oz. lard • 3 oz. streaky bacon • 2 large onions • 1 tbsp. paprika • 1 tbsp. tomato purée • 1 tbsp. white wine vinegar • 1 ladleful water • 2 gills sour cream • salt.

Cut bacon to strips and lard the meat deeply with the help of a larding-pin. Melt fat in a saucepan, put in the meat and fry quickly to a golden-brown colour on all sides. Take meat out on a hot plate and fry in the fat remaining in saucepan the finely chopped onions till golden-yellow, add paprika, tomato purée, 1 tbsp. wine vinegar and a ladleful of water. Bring to the boil, then put meat back, cover and simmer till meat is tender. Then cut to thick slices and arrange on a hot oval dish. Pour sour cream on the gravy left in the saucepan, bring to the boil, then pour some over the sliced meat, serving the rest in a sauce-boat. Garnish with galushka (see p. 154) or boiled noodles.

Fillet of Beef in Sour Cream

Ingredients: 2 lb. piece of fillet steak • 4 oz. streaky bacon •
2 gills sour cream • 1/4 pint water • pinch of salt • pinch of ground
black pepper.

Apart from the bacon, you do not need any fat. Use a thick, heavy saucepan. Lard meat with the help of larding-pin, using up all the given quantity. Pour 1 glass of water in the saucepan, rub the meat with pepper and put in the saucepan. Cover and simmer slowly, adding a spoonful of sour cream every now and then. When meat is tender, lift off lid for 5 minutes and let the surplus moisture evaporate. This meat dish be served hot with potato purée and green peas, or cold with mixed salad.

French Fillet of Beef

Ingredients: 2 lb. fillet steak • 6 oz. goose-liver • 3 oz. mushrooms •
1 pork-lace • 2 oz. lard • 3 oz. bacon • 3 tbsp. tomato purée •
1 medium-sized onion • 1 1/2 gills cream • pinch of salt •
pinch of ground black pepper.

Make deep, even slits in the meat, push slices of goose-liver into the openings. Arrange a layer of thinly sliced mushrooms on the spread-out lace, rub the meat with salt and pepper and wrap it in the lace. Tie securely. Put meat in a roasting-pan and pour the following sauce on: mix the very finely chopped or minced bacon with 1/4 pint water, add lard and tomato purée, heat mixture and pour over the meat. Put whole onion in the pan as well. Basting frequently, roast till meat is nearly tender, then add sour cream and leave in the oven 15 minutes longer. Serve sliced, on a hot dish, with gravy separately. Garnish with boiled rice and potato chips.

Braised Mignon Fillets

Ingredients: 2 lb. fillet steak • 2 oz. lard • 1 tbsp. grated onions • 3 oz. thinly sliced streaky bacon • 2 gills of wine • 1 tbsp. finely chopped parsley • a pinch of ground white pepper • salt.

Trim, and cut meat into thick round slices. Mix grated onion, chopped parsley and pepper, spread this mixture on the top of the slices. Lay a piece of bacon on each, secure with toothpicks. Place meat in a saucepan, and pour the heated lard and half the wine over it. Braise slowly under lid, adding a little wine every now and then to prevent burning. Serve with mushrooms, rice, and tomato salad.

Savoury Fillet of Beef

Ingredients: 2 lb. fillet steak (thick end) • 2 tbsp. French mustard • 3 oz. lard • 1 tsp. flour • 1 gill cream • pinch of salt • pinch of ground white pepper.

Brush the joint with mustard, and, placing it in a small roasting pan, pour the hot lard over it. Bake in a hot oven, basting frequently. When done, lift meat out of pan, put aside. Sprinkle flour on gravy in pan, stir, add cream and a spoonful of water, salt and white pepper, boil well together. Serve meat on a hot dish, with gravy separately. Garnish with vegetables according to season.

Tokány of Marosszék

Ingredients: 1 lb. end of fillet • 1 lb. shoulder of pork • 3 oz. lard • 3 large onions • 1/2 tsp. salt • 1 tsp. paprika • 1/2 pint dry white wine • 2 gills sour cream.

Cut meat into small squares, chop onions finely. Heat the lard, add onions, together with the meat. Salt, add the paprika, cover and allow to simmer. Add wine gradually. When meat is tender, add the sour cream and boil for about 5 minutes. Serve in a deep dish together with its gravy. Garnish with boiled potatoes.

Transylvanian Tokány

Ingredients: 2 lb. round of beef • 3 oz. lard • 1/2 tsp. salt •
3 medium-sized onions.

Cut meat into 2-inch squares, heat lard in a saucepan, add meat and salt. Cover and allow to simmer for 1/2 hour. Cut the onions into rings, add to the meat together with a ladleful of water. Simmer till onions are tender. Serve in a deep dish, garnish with galushka (see p. 154).

Fillet with Mushroom and Tomato Sauce

Ingredients: 2 lb. fillet of beef • 1 large onion • 3 oz. lard • 1/2 pint
tomato juice • 4 oz. mushrooms • 1/2 tsp. salt • 2 gills sour cream •
1 tsp. sugar.

Cut meat into thick slices, sprinkle with salt and put aside. Chop onions finely. Heat lard in a saucepan, add onions and mushrooms, fry till onions are golden-yellow. Add the meat, pour tomato juice over it. Cover and allow to simmer till meat is tender, adding a spoonful of tomato juice every now and then to prevent burning. When meat is ready, add the sugar and 2 gills of sour cream. Serve in a deep dish together with its gravy. Garnish with boiled rice.

Braised Steak with Béarnaise Sauce

Ingredients: 2 lb. fillet of beef • 2 oz. lard • 1/2 tsp. salt • 1 cup white wine • 2 tbsp. wine vinegar • 4 bay leaves • grated rind of 1/2 lemon • 2–3 springs of tarragon • 1 level tbsp. finely chopped parsley • 1 small onion • 10 whole black peppercorns • about 3 tbsp. flour • 2 egg yolks • 4 oz. butter • 1 tbsp. sugar.

Cut meat into thick slices, salt, then put aside for 15 minutes. Heat lard in saucepan, add meat, fry quickly on both sides, then add a little water, cover with lid and allow to simmer till meat is tender. Mix in a saucepan the wine, vinegar, bay leaves, grated lemon rind, tarragon, chopped parsley, thinly sliced onion, whole black pepper and a little salt. Allow to simmer for 1/2 hour, then strain. Heat the butter in another saucepan, add flour, cook stirring constantly till frothy and pale yellow, and dilute with half of the spiced wine. Cook slowly, stirring constantly, till sauce is very thick and smooth. To the other half of spiced wine add 2 egg yolks, sour cream, and 1 oz. of melted butter. Beating constantly, add this mixture to the sauce, then pour sauce over the tender meat-slices. Cook slowly for 10 more minutes, then serve on a flat dish, with some of the sauce poured over, and the rest in a sauce-boat.

Boiled Beef with Mixed Garnish

Ingredients: 2 lb. smoked brisket of beef • 1/2 lb. tomatoes • 3 tbsp. boiled rice • 1/2 lb. green peas • potato chips • 1/2 lb. cauliflower • 1 gill cream • 1 large celeriac • 3 oz. butter • pinch of salt and black pepper • sprig of mint.

Put meat in a saucepan, pour cold water over it, bring to the boil, then pour off the water. Pour cold water over the meat again, bring to the boil, then allow to simmer slowly. Add a large celeriac after 1 hour of cooking. Prepare garnish meantime. Cut off the tops of tomatoes, scrape out seeds and fill loosely with boiled rice. Put a dab of butter over each and bake in the oven for 20 minutes. Cook green peas with a pinch of salt and a sprig of mint. Cook cauliflower, strain well, pour some melted butter over, sprinkle with chopped parsley. Fry chips. Take out cooked celeriac, mash well with fork, and adding the cream and a pinch of black pepper, beat well. Now lift the cooked meat onto a heated dish, pour a ladleful of the stock over it. Arrange the vegetables around it, except the chips which should be served in a separate dish. Serve celeriac sauce in a small glass bowl.

Boiled Beef in Mushroom Sauce

Ingredients: 2–3 lb. brisket of beef • 2 oz. lard • 1 medium-sized onion • 1/2 tsp. paprika • 1 tsp. salt • 5 oz. mushrooms.

Boil beef slowly in salt water till nearly tender, then cut into thick slices. Heat lard in a saucepan, add thinly sliced onion, paprika and a pinch of salt. Dilute with 1/2 pint of stock, place in the meat, cover with sliced mushrooms and cook rather briskly for 20 minutes until the gravy is reduced. Serve with boiled rice, boiled potatoes and lettuce salad. Make some gravy from part of the stock and serve separately.

Hungarian Sirloin Steak

Ingredients: 2 lb. sirloin steak (3 large slices) • 2 large onions • 3 oz. lard • 1 level tbsp. paprika • 1 level tsp. salt • 4 green peppers • 4 large tomatoes • 4 oz. rice • 1/2 lb. mushrooms.

Heat lard in a large saucepan, add finely chopped onions, fry till golden, then add the meat. Sprinkle with paprika and salt, add a ladleful of stock or water, cover, and allow to simmer slowly till water evaporates. Slice green peppers and tomatoes into thick rings, cut mushrooms in four. Spread them over the meat, and rice on top. Add more water or stock, cover and simmer again gently till rice is tender. Lay the steaks on a warm round dish, and arrange the rice and vegetables all around it.

Stuffed Sirloin Steaks

Ingredients: 2 lb. sirloin steaks • 2 stale bread-rolls • 4 oz. mushrooms • 1 level tbsp. finely chopped parsley • 1 tsp. grated onion • 3 oz. lard • 2 eggs • 1 level tsp. salt • pinch of blackpepper • 1 tsp. French mustard.

Bone meat, cut into even, medium-thick slices, trim off edges, flatten slices with meat-beater, then sprinkle with a little salt and pepper. Spread mustard on the steaks and put them aside. Soak bread-rolls in milk, then squeeze and put them in a bowl. Add coarsely chopped mushrooms, parsley, pepper, pinch of salt, grated onion, 1 tsp. cold lard, 2 eggs, flavour mixture with salt and pepper and knead together thoroughly. Spread this stuffing thickly on the steaks, roll them up and tie each with thread. Heat the remaining lard in a saucepan, put in the rolled steaks and fry quickly on both sides. Add a little stock, cover, and allow to simmer slowly, adding a little stock every now and then to prevent burning, till meat is tender. Cook the last 5 minutes without lid. Serve with boiled rice and mixed salad.

VEAL

Veal Pörkölt

Ingredients: 2 lb. boned knuckle of veal • 2 large onions •
4 oz. lard • 1 tbsp. paprika • 1 green pepper • 1 tomato • 1 tsp. salt.

Cut meat into 2-inch cubes. Chop onions finely. Heat the
lard in a saucepan, add chopped onions, fry till golden. Add
paprika, meat and salt. Cover and allow to simmer slowly,
adding a little water every now and then. After 1/2 hour add
tomato and green pepper cut in four. When meat is tender,
remove pepper and tomato skins from the gravy. Serve
pörkölt in a deep round dish, garnished with golden drops
(see p. 59).

Veal Paprikash

Prepare in exactly the same way as pörkölt but add 2 gills of
sour cream to the gravy 10 minutes before serving.

Gamekeeper's Veal Stew

Ingredients: 2 lb. leg of veal • 1/2 lb. mushrooms • 1 heaped tbsp.
finely chopped parsley • 1 large onion • 1 tsp. salt • 1/3 tsp. ground
white pepper • 1 heaped tbsp. flour • 3 gills sour cream.

Cut meat into inch-sized cubes. Heat lard in a saucepan, add
meat, thickly sliced mushrooms, parsley, grated onion, salt
and pepper. Cover and allow to simmer till meat is tender.
By then the gravy should be quite short. Sprinkle with 1 level
tbsp. flour, stir, then add sour cream. Boil for 5 minutes with
sour cream, then serve in a deep dish, garnished with boiled
rice.

Wiener Schnitzel

Ingredients: 2 lb. leg of veal, cut to even, thin slices • 1/2 tsp. salt • 3 oz. flour • 2 eggs • 3 oz. toasted breadcrumbs • lard for frying.

Flatten slices of meat with meat-beater, salt, then put aside for 1/2 hour. Dip in flour, then in beaten eggs, lastly in toasted breadcrumbs. Pat slices between your palms. Heat lard in a frying pan, add slices one by one, turning them over when one side is nicely browned. Lift onto absorbent paper, keep hot. Serve with potato chips and lettuce salad or with potato salad.

Breaded Veal

Ingredients: 2 lb. leg of veal • 1 level tsp. salt • 4 oz. toasted breadcrumbs • fat to fry.

Cut meat into slices not thicker than your little finger, nick edges and flatten them well with meat-beater. Sprinkle with salt, then put aside on a plate for 1/2 hour. Spread the sieved fine breadcrumbs on a board, then take the moist meat-slices turning them over on the board and patting with your palm to make breadcrumbs stick. Fry in hot fat, lifting the basket out of the deep-fryer once or twice. When meat is nicely browned, put the slices on absorbent paper for a minute or two. This veal is excellent with vegetables prepared in gravy in the Hungarian way, but either beetroot or potato salad can be a good accompaniment to this dish.

Goodwife's Veal Steak

Ingredients: 1 1/2 lb. leg of veal • 1/2 lb. sliced ham • 1 egg yolk •
3 oz. grated cheese • flour • 2 eggs • toasted breadcrumbs and lard
for frying.

Flatten slices with the help of a meat-beater. Mix egg yolk
and grated cheese well together adding a spoonful of milk if
the mixture is too dry. Spread it on the steaks, then cover
with slices of ham, trimmed to same size. Press well together
with your palm, dip first in flour, then in beaten egg, and
toasted breadcrumbs, fry in hot lard. Serve immediately.

Baked Veal with Bechamel

Ingredients: 1 1/2 lb. leg of veal cut in 3 large even slices • 3 large
slices of ham • 1 oz. lard • 3 eggs.
For bechamel sauce: 2 egg yolks • 1 gill sour cream • 3 heaped tsp.
flour • 2 oz. butter • 3 tbsp. grated cheese.

Flatten slices of meat with meat-beater. Heat lard in a frying
pan and fry slices of veal separately on both sides until golden-brown. Beat up one egg, and brush steaks thickly with it,
then press a slice of ham on each slice of meat. Butter generously the bottom of a fireproof dish, and arrange the flat
meat-slices on it. Prepare the bechamel. Beat well together in
a saucepan the 2 egg yolks, sour cream, flour, 1 1/2 oz. melted butter and the grated cheese. Stirring constantly cook on
medium heat till sauce becomes thick and smooth. Spread
thickly and evenly on the top of ham slices covering the
veal, put the dish in a hot oven and bake for 10–12 minutes.
The top of the bechamel should be nicely browned by then.
Serve hot with potato chips and green peas or with mixed
salad.

Roast Veal in Lace

Ingredients: 2 lb. fillet of veal • 3 oz. mushrooms • 3 oz. lean bacon •
3 oz. calf's liver • pork-lace • 1 tsp. salt • 3 oz. lard • 1 gill sour
cream.

Salt meat, then make deep, narrow slits all over with a sharp,
narrow knife. Push into the openings the liver cut into thick
strips, the slices of bacon rolled up tightly and some of the
smaller mushrooms. Put the remaining mushrooms on the
top and roll the stuffed meat in the pork-lace, and tie securely. Put in a roasting-pan and pour hot lard over it. Bake in a
medium-hot oven for 1 hour. Add sour cream to the gravy
after 1/2 hour, baste meat frequently. Serve with buttered
cauliflower and small potatoes baked in the pan together
with the meat.

Braised Veal Julienne

Ingredients: 1 lb. fillet of veal • 3 oz. lard • 6 oz. vegetable
macédoine • 1 small onion • 1 bunch of parsley • 2 oz.
mushrooms •
2 oz. bacon • 1/2 pint white wine • 1 level tsp. salt • pinch of ground
black pepper • 1 gill sour cream.

Salt meat. Line the bottom of a saucepan with thin slices of
bacon, add thinly sliced mushrooms, the whole onion, and
the bunch of parsley. Put the meat in the saucepan, pour
1/4 pint wine under it. Cover and allow to simmer slowly.
Remove onion and parsley when wine evaporates, drain
macédoine and add to the meat, first lifting out the slices of
bacon and putting them on the top of the meat. Add another
1/4 pint wine, cover and allow to simmer again. When meat
is tender, cook for 5 more minutes without lid to let the
moisture evaporate, stir and turn the meat to prevent

burning. Add sour cream and stirring, bring to the boil. Cut
into slices and serve with the sauce poured over it.

Fricassee of Veal

Ingredients: 1 1/2 lb. boned knuckle of veal • 4 oz. carrots •
4 oz. parsnips • 4 oz. mushrooms • 1 tbsp. finely chopped parsley •
finely chopped tarragon leaves • a good pinch of ground black
pepper •
2 oz. butter • 2 heaped tbsp. flour • 1/2 lemon • 1 gill sour cream •
1 tsp. salt.

Cut meat into 2-inch cubes. Cut carrots, parsnips and mushrooms to thick slices. Bring 1 pint of water to the boil in a
saucepan. Add meat, vegetables, mushrooms and salt, cover
and allow to simmer till meat and vegetables are tender.
Heat the butter in a saucepan, add flour. Stir till pale golden,
then add the finely chopped parsley, pepper and tarragon.
Dilute with a ladleful of cold water, stir thoroughly, then
pour this mixture into the meat and vegetable stew. Bring to
the boil, stirring every now and then, reduce heat and allow
to simmer for 20 minutes. Add the lemon juice and sour
cream about 5 minutes before serving. Serve in a deep dish.
Add some boiled rice as garnish.

Veal Ragout

Ingredients: 2 lb. knuckle of veal • 4 oz. carrots • 4 oz. parsnips •
4 oz. celeriac • 1 small onion • 1 small clove of garlic • 1 tsp. salt •
1 cup milk • 2 egg yolks • 2 tbsp. flour • 2 oz. butter • pinch of
grated lemon peel • 1 gill sour cream.

Let the butcher cut the knuckle to 3 pieces, then it is easier to
deal with. Cook the meat and vegetables in a saucepan,
using just enough water to cover the contents. Add salt and

bring to the boil. Reduce heat and allow to simmer till meat comes easily off the bone. Strain the stock into a smaller saucepan, cut meat and vegetables into small cubes, put aside. Mix in a basin the milk, egg yolks, flour, and melted butter, then beat well. Add mixture to the stock, which should not be more than about 1/2 pint. Bring to the boil, stirring constantly till sauce is thick and smooth. Add the chopped meat and vegetables, heat up again. In a deep dish mix the sour cream with a pinch of finely grated lemon peel, pour ragout over it, and after a final stirring, serve.

Veal in Savoury Sauce

Ingredients: 2 lb. leg of veal • 3 oz. thick streaky bacon rashers • 1 oz. lard • 1/2 pint white wine • 1/2 tsp. finely chopped tarragon leaves • 2 oz. capers • 1 tbsp. anchovy paste • 1 large potato • 1 1/2 gills sour cream • pinch of grated lemon peel.

Cut the thick rashers of bacon into strips and, with the help of a larding-pin, lard the meat in even rows all over. Place in a deep saucepan, then heat lard and pour over the meat. Brown meat, turning it in the hot fat to colour all sides, then add the wine, chopped tarragon, chopped capers, the anchovy paste, and a coarsely grated large raw potato. Cover and allow to simmer till meat is tender. If the gravy is too much reduced and the meat still needs cooking, add 2–3 spoonfuls of sour cream. Lift the meat onto a dish when ready, pour 1 1/2 gills sour cream into the gravy, bring to the boil and boil briskly for 4–5 minutes. Garnish the meat with asparagus, mashed potatoes or mushroom-rice. Serve the gravy separately.

Roast Loin of Veal with Tarragon

Ingredients: 3 lb. loin of veal • 4 oz. butter • 1 tbsp. anchovy paste •
1 tsp. finely chopped tarragon leaves • 1 gill sour cream • 1 level
tbsp. flour.

Knead well together 2 oz. butter and anchovy paste. Chill
thoroughly. With a sharp, narrow knife cut deep, narrow slits
in the joint and push pieces of hard anchovy butter in the
openings. Now rub the joint thoroughly with the finely
chopped tarragon, put in a small roasting-pan, pour 2 oz. of
hot melted butter over the meat, and cook in a medium
oven, basting once or twice with the sour cream. Lifting the
meat out onto dish, sprinkle gravy with flour, stir, then dilute
with water or stock and boil for 5 minutes. Serve gravy separately. Add boiled macaroni as garnish.

Stuffed Roast Veal

Ingredients: About 3 lb. leg of veal • 5 oz. calf's liver • 5 oz. ham •
5 oz. mushrooms • 1 small onion • 3 stale bread-rolls soaked in milk
and well squeezed • a good pinch of pepper • 1/3 tsp. marjoram •
1 tbsp. anchovy paste • 3 oz. lard • 1/4 pint red wine • 2 eggs.

This is enough for 8 people. Choose a flat, boned piece of
meat, preferably fillet. Let the butcher make a long slit
lengthwise so as to obtain a wide hole running through the
length of the joint. Heat 1 oz. lard in a saucepan, then add
onion and mushrooms, both finely chopped. Cover and
allow to simmer till moisture has evaporated, then add the
scraped liver, and lastly the finely chopped ham. After stirring for 5 minutes, put aside, add well-squeezed rolls, pepper, marjoram, anchovy paste, and the 2 eggs. Knead the
stuffing well together and stuff the meat tightly. You need
someone to hold up the meat and keep the slit open during

the procedure. Sew the opening with thread, put the joint in a roasting-pan and, adding the lard, roast in a fairly hot oven. Baste with the wine, using up all of it while roasting the joint. Serve with green peas and potato purée.

PORK

Kisalföld Pork Gulyás

Ingredients: 1 lb. shoulder of pork • 1 large onion • 1 tsp. salt • 1 tbsp. paprika • 1/4 clove of garlic • 1/2 lb. green peppers • 1/2 lb. fresh tomatoes • 1/4 lb. green beans • 1/4 lb. green peas • 1/4 lb. rice • 4 oz. lard.

Bone and cut meat into 2-inch cubes. Heat lard in a large saucepan, add finely chopped onion, fry till golden. Add a tiny piece of crushed garlic, the paprika and the meat, stir, add salt and a spoonful of water, cover and allow to simmer for 1/2 hour. Cut tomatoes and green peppers in four, slice beans, shell peas. Add vegetables to the stew, sprinkle rice on top, add 1/4 pint water, cover and simmer on low heat till gravy is quite short and rice soft. Do not stir, only shake the saucepan once or twice. Serve in a deep dish.

Wooden Platter

Ingredients: 6 thick loin chops • 6 small slices of fillet steak • 1 large onion • 1/2 tsp. ground black pepper • 1 tsp. salt • 1/2 oz. lard • a bunch of parsley.
The garnish: potato chips, steamed rice, braised cabbage, pickled gherkins sliced, cooked beetroot, green pepper rings.

This is a mixed grill of beef and pork. Cover each slice of meat with some crushed parsley, thinly sliced onion and black pepper. Lay them on each other in a deep dish and put aside for 1/2 hour. Heat the grill, melt lard in a small saucepan. Brush off the parsley, pepper and onion-rings, and brush the meat with melted lard; grill on both sides until brown. Pile up potato chips on the middle of a wooden platter, arrange grilled meat around in a ring. There should still be 4–5 inch space left around the meat. Put the rest of the garnish there in small heaps. Serve hot.

Sour Tokány

Ingredients: 1/2 lb. shoulder or best end of pork • 1/2 lb. pig's kidney • 1/2 lb. pig's or calf's liver • 2 large onions • 1 tsp. salt • 1/3 tsp. ground black pepper • the juice of 1 lemon • 1 1/2 gills sour cream • 3 oz. lard.

Bone meat, trim kidneys, wipe the liver. Cut each into finger-thick strips, then put aside in separate plates. Heat lard in a saucepan, add finely chopped onions, fry to a golden-brown colour, add meat only, stir, then add salt and pepper. Cover and simmer for 1/2 hour, adding a spoonful of water to prevent burning. Now add the kidneys, cook under lid for 20 minutes. Squeeze lemon over it, stir, then add sour cream and the liver, bring to the boil and boil briskly for 5–6 minutes. Serve with steamed rice.

Stuffed Cabbage

Ingredients: For the stuffing: 1 1/2 lb. shoulder or best end of pork • 2 oz. streaky bacon • 1 egg • 2 oz. cooked rice • 1 oz. lard • 1 small onion • pinch of salt • pinch of ground black pepper. For the stew: 1 lb. sauerkraut • 6 large sour or fresh cabbage leaves • 2 oz. lard • 2 tbsp. flour • 1 tsp. paprika • 1 gill sour cream.

Cut cabbage leaves in two, trimming of the thick vein in the middle. Mince the meat together with the bacon. Heat lard in small saucepan, add finely chopped onion and fry till golden-yellow. Pour it over the minced meat, then add cooked rice, 1 egg, salt and pepper. Knead mixture well together, spoon even heaps onto the cabbage leaves. Roll them up, push the edges of leaves in at both ends. Put the sauerkraut into a large saucepan, add 1/2 pint water, bring to the boil. Arrange the stuffed cabbage leaves on top, cover and simmer slowly for 1 hour. Remove stuffed cabbage leaves from top into a deep dish but keep them hot under cover. Heat 2 oz. lard in a small saucepan, add flour and fry till golden-brown, then add this roux into the sauerkraut. Stir well, bring to the boil, add sour cream and boil briskly for 5 minutes. Spoon sauerkraut and gravy over stuffed cabbage leaves and serve hot. In Hungary garnish is not served with stuffed cabbage, but I found that suet dumplings flavoured with mixed herbs are a good accompaniment.

Old-fashioned Stuffed Cabbage

Ingredients: 1 large piece of bacon-skin • 4 lb. pork belly •
1/2 lb. streaky bacon • 4 oz. cooked rice • 1 small onion •
pinch of salt • pinch of ground black pepper • 1 tsp. paprika •
1 oz. lard •
2 lbs. sauerkraut • 12 large sour or fresh cabbage leaves •
1 1/2 gills cream • 2 tbsp. flour • 1 fried garlic sausage and fried pork chop per person • 2 eggs.

Line a large iron saucepan with a large piece of bacon-skin. Put a 2-inch layer of sauerkraut in the bottom. Cover with a flat piece of lean belly, then add another layer of cabbage. Mince 2 lb. fat pork, mix with cooked rice, finely chopped onion fried in 1 oz. lard, pinch of salt, pinch of ground black pepper, 1 tsp. paprika and 2 eggs. Put sufficient amount of stuffing on the cabbage leaves, wrap them up and push in edges. Arrange them in the pan on the top of the cabbage layer, pour 1 pint of meat stock over them. Cover and cook slowly for 2 hours. Put the stuffed cabbages in one side of the pot, mix the double cream and flour, stir carefully into the gravy. Arrange stuffed cabbage in a layer again, cover the pot and boil briskly for 5 minutes. Put the pot to cool. Heat up next day 1 hour before you want to serve. Serve heaped up on a large platter; decorate with fried garlic sausages and fried pork chops.

Stuffed Vine Leaves

Ingredients: 1 lb. lean pork • 5 oz. streaky bacon • 4 oz. cooked rice • 1 egg • pinch of salt • pinch of ground black pepper • 30–40 tender vine leaves • 1 gill sour cream • 1 level tbsp. flour.

Mince pork and bacon, add the cooked rice, egg, pinch of salt, pinch of black pepper. Knead mixture well, then put a spoonful on 12 vine leaves. Wrap them up, push in edges and tie each with cotton. Cut the remaining vine leaves into wide strips, put in the bottom of a saucepan. Arrange stuffed leaves over this, then pour boiling water to cover. Cook slowly under lid for 3/4 hour. Mix sour cream and 1 tsp. flour, add to the vine stew and boil for 5 more minutes. Arrange stuffed vine leaves on a dish, strain some of the gravy over, serve the rest separately in a sauceboat.

Pork and Savoy Pie

Ingredients: 1 1/2 lb. cooked savoy cabbage • 1 lb. minced pork • 1/2 tsp. caraway seeds • 2 oz. lard • 2 oz. streaky bacon • 1/2 tsp. salt • pinch of ground black pepper • 4 oz. cooked rice • pinch of mixed herbs • 2 gills sour cream.

This is a good way to use up left-over roast or boiled meat. Lard thickly an oblong fireproof dish, put in a layer of cooked and well pressed-out savoy cabbage, then a thick layer of minced meat. Add mixed herbs to the cooked rice, arrange it over the minced meat, and pour 1 gill sour cream evenly over it. Cover with the remainder of savoy cabbage, and pour the rest of sour cream over it. Cover with thin slices of bacon and bake in a medium-hot oven for about 40 minutes. Serve in the fireproof dish. The gravy should be served separately.

Breaded Pork Chops

Ingredients: 2 lb. chops • 1 large onion • a bunch of parsley • 10 coarsely broken black peppercorns • 1 level tsp. salt • 2 eggs • flour • toasted breadcrumbs • fat to fry.

The chops should not be thicker than your little finger. Flatten them with meat-beater, nick fatty edges to prevent curling. Put a layer of thinly sliced onion on a plate. Crush the peppercorns, sprinkle a few over the onionrings, crush the sprigs of parsley between your palms, place 1 or 2 on the onions. Put some of the chops on this savoury mixture, repeat the layer again, till the last chops are covered with the mixture. Cover the plate and put aside for at least 1 hour. Beat eggs, put flour and breadcrumbs on separate plates. Brush the flavourings off the chops, sprinkle with salt, then dip into flour, then the beaten eggs and lastly the toasted breadcrumbs. Pat the chops between your palms to make breadcrumbs stick. Heat cooking-fat in a shallow frying-pan, and fry chops on medium heat, turning them over when one side is golden-brown. Put on absorbent paper, and keep hot. Arrange on a hot dish when ready. Serve with potato chips and mixed salad.

Roast Pork of Ráckeve

Ingredients: 2 lb. loin of pork • 3 oz. streaky bacon • 1 medium-
sized onion • 3 tomatoes • 1 green pepper • 4 oz. mushrooms •
2 oz. lard • 1 tsp. salt.

Slice meat into finger-thick slices without cutting it off the
bone. This way the joint will remain whole yet there will be
plenty of room between the slices for stuffing. Slice the
onion, green pepper, tomatoes and mushrooms thinly, and
mix them together. Place a slice of streaky bacon into each
slit and 1 tbsp. of the vegetable mixture; when every slit is
filled, tie joint securely with twine. Place in a roasting-tin,
sprinkle with salt, and pour hot lard over. Basting frequently,
cook in a medium oven for about 1 hour. Leave the joint to
stand for 10 minutes, then using a long, sharp knife, carve
the meat off the bone, holding the cutlets together with fork.
Place on an oval dish, remove twine, arrange cutlets neatly,
keeping the vegetables between the slices. Serve with
steamed vegetables and gravy.

Harvester's Pot Roast

Ingredients: 2 lb. spare rib • 5 oz. streaky bacon • 2 large onions •
1 tbsp. paprika • 2 tomatoes • 1 green pepper • 2 oz. butter •
about 1 lb. potatoes.

Bone meat, then cut into finger-thick slices. Line a deep,
thick saucepan with slices of bacon. Heat butter in a small
saucepan, add sliced onions and, stirring fry for one minute
or two, then stir in the paprika. Do not brown the onions. Put
aside and put a thin layer of the fried onions over the bacon
in the large saucepan, arrange a layer of meat-slices over
this. Now comes a layer of onions, then meat again, till you

run out of meat. Add a layer of sliced tomatoes and green peppers. Peel potatoes, cut in four and fill the remaining space. Pour over 1/2 pint water, cover with a tight-fitting lid. Leave on medium heat for 15 minutes, after which cook on low heat for 2 hours. Serve in a deep dish together with the potatoes and the gravy. This ancient dish is still popular in harvest-time, but is a strong favourite with tourists, too. The heavy iron pot is bedded in embers and hot ashes, the lid is secured with stones.

Pork Tenderloin in Lace

Ingredients: 2 lb. tenderloin of pork • 6 oz. mushrooms •
1/2 tsp. salt • 1 level tbsp. finely chopped parsley • pinch of ground black pepper • a piece of pork lace • 2 oz. lard •
2 gills sour cream.

Heat lard in a small saucepan, add chopped mushrooms, salt, pepper and chopped parsley, cover and simmer till moisture evaporates. Flatten the pork lace and spread mushroom-mixture on evenly. Wrap the trimmed tenderloin in the lace carefully, then tie with cotton. Roast in a medium-hot oven for 1 hour basting frequently with sour cream. Let the meat stand 6–8 minutes before carving. Slice with a sharp knife to avoid tearing the lace. Brown the gravy and serve in a sauceboat.

Roast Pork with Caraway Seeds

Ingredients: 2 lb. leg of pork • 1/2 tsp. caraway seeds • 1/2 tsp. salt •
lard or dripping.

Crush caraway seeds, mix with salt. Rub meat with the mixture thoroughly, then place in a roasting pan. Leave meat to stand for 1 hour. Then pour hot lard or dripping over it and roast in a medium oven for 1 hour. If you roast potatoes with the joint, it will need 1/4 hour longer cooking. Serve with vegetables and gravy.

Meat Loaf

Ingredients: 1 1/2 lb. shoulder of pork • 2 oz. bacon • 1/2 tsp. salt •
pinch of ground black pepper • pinch of marjoram • 1 egg •
1 small onion • 2 oz. lard.

Bone meat, cut into strips and put through fine mincer together with the bacon. Add salt, pepper, marjoram, egg. Grate the onion, fry in a very little lard to a golden colour, and add to the minced meat. Knead mixture thoroughly, and shape into a loaf. Grease a roasting-tin thickly with half the lard, put in the meat-loaf, dab the remaining lard on top. Cook in a medium-hot oven for 45 minutes. Serve hot with vegetables, or cold with mixed salad.

Roast Suckling Pig

Ingredients: 1 six-week-old piglet • 4 oz. lard • 1 oz. fat bacon •
1 apple • a good pinch of marjoram • 1 tsp. salt.

To my mind it was not without reason that Charles Lamb found this dish worthy of an immortal essay. Suckling pig is still a traditional roast in Hungary at New Year's Eve, and it is the pride of the housewife to serve it with the dark-gold transparent crackling crisp, yet melting in the mouth. I have several recipes — some of them with a very distinctive local emphasis — collected from different counties. This one is from the Bakony region, that wooded part of the country which, with its gentle hills and rich valleys, is one of the most picturesque parts of Hungary.

Wipe the pig thoroughly, inside and out. Rub with salt all over, and then rub the inside with marjoram. Place in a roasting tin, press the end of the spine well down, to make the legs lie flat in the tin. The front part should be propped up on the knuckles. Place an apple in the mouth, wrap ears and tail in greased paper. Let stand for 1 hour. Pour boiling hot lard over it evenly. Pour 1/4 pint water in the pan and roast the pig in a medium oven for 2 hours. Baste frequently till all water evaporates, then spear a lump of fat bacon on the end of a skewer and, dipping it in the fat underneath, use it to brush the pig all over three or four times while roasting. Lift the pig onto a board when ready and cut the head off immediately. This will let the steam escape and the crackling will remain crisp. Carve in the kitchen with the help of a chopper and a sharp knife, cutting off the legs and shoulders first, then cut the body across with the help of the chopper into 5 even-sized pieces. Cut the head in two lengthwise. Heat a large oval dish and, fitting the pieces together on it in the original shape, put the dish in the oven till the gravy is prepared. Make a thin gravy with the drippings and juices in the pan, and serve separately. Roast pig does not call for elaborate garnish; a little apple sauce and some boiled potatoes served with Maître d'Hôtel butter is all it needs.

Budafok Stuffed Roast Pig

Ingredients: 1 suckling pig • 4 oz. lard • 5 oz. mushrooms • 1 tsp. grated onion • 1 tbsp. finely chopped parsley • 2 stale bread-rolls soaked in milk • 3 eggs • 1 heaped tsp. salt • 1/4 tsp. ground black pepper.

Heat 1 oz. lard in a saucepan, add coarsely chopped mushrooms, 1 tsp. grated onions and chopped parsley. Chop the liver, heart and lungs of the pig (do not use the kidneys), and add to the mushrooms, together with 1/2 tsp. salt and the pepper. Cover, and simmer for 15 minutes. Squeeze the rolls, add the eggs and the mushroom mixture, mix well. Now turn the pig on its back and fill cavity with the stuffing, then sew the opening with thread. Proceed further according to the roast suckling pig recipe above, except that stuffed pig needs to cook 1/2 hour longer in the oven. Scoop out stuffing before carving and put in even heaps all around the roast pig.

LAMB AND MUTTON

Mutton Pörkölt (Paprika Stew)

Ingredients: 2 1/2 lb. shoulder of mutton • 2 large onions • 3 green peppers • 2 medium-sized tomatoes • 3 oz. lard • 1 tbsp. paprika • 1 tsp. salt.

Bone, then cut the meat into 2-inch cubes. Heat lard in a saucepan, add finely chopped onions, fry till onions are pale-golden. Pulling the saucepan aside, add the meat and the paprika, stir one minute or two, then add the sliced green pepper, tomatoes and the salt. Cover and allow to simmer under lid, adding a spoonful water every now and then to prevent burning. It should be ready in about 1 hour, unless the meat is exceptionally tough. Serve on a hot dish, garnished with boiled rice.

Larded Leg of Mutton

Ingredients: 2 1/2 lb. piece of leg • 2 oz. streaky bacon • 1 small onion • 1 bay leaf • 3 oz. lard or dripping.

Do not use a large tin, unless you want to roast potatoes with it. Cut the thick rashers of bacon into strips and lard the joint in even rows with the help of a larding pin. Lard deeply, do not leave the ends of the bacon sticking out. Place the joint in the roasting tin, add dripping, the onion cut in two, the bay leaf and 1 tbsp. water. Roast in a medium-hot oven, basting frequently for 1 hour; do not add any more water. Serve with vegetables and gravy.

Hungarian Boiled Mutton with Cabbage

Ingredients: 2 lb. shoulder of mutton • 1 1/2 lb. cabbage • 1 green pepper • 1/4 tsp. caraway seeds • 1 tbsp. salt • 1 1/2 oz. lard • 1 oz. flour • 1 level tsp. paprika • 1 gill sour cream.

Cook meat together with salt, green paprika and caraway seeds in just enough water to cover. Allow to simmer slowly till meat is tender. Quarter the small, firm cabbage-heads, cook in briskly boiling salt water, then strain off the water. Heat lard in a frying-pan, add flour, and, stirring constantly, fry till flour is nicely browned, then pull aside and stir in the paprika.

Dilute this roux with 3 ladlefuls of stock strained off the meat, stir and pour over the cabbage. Allow to simmer for 10 minutes. Cut boiled meat into finger-thick slices, arrange them in a dish, put the cabbage around the meat and pour the gravy over it. Serve with boiled potatoes. Spoon the sour cream over the dish just before serving.

Stewed Mutton in Casserole

Ingredients: 2 lb. shoulder of mutton • 2 oz. lard • 2 large onions • 2 oz. celeriac • 2 oz. parsnips • 2 oz. carrots • 1 small savoy cabbage • large bunch of parsley • 2 bay leaves • 8 whole black peppercorns • 1/3 tsp. marjoram • 1 clove of garlic • 1 lb. potatoes.

Cut meat into 2-inch cubes. Peel onions, celeriac, parsnips and carrots, cut them in four, slice savoy cabbage to wide strips. Tie the parsley, bay leaves, peppercorns, marjoram and garlic in a piece of muslin or gauze. Peel and quarter potatoes. First, using the lard, fry the meat very quickly in a frying-pan to a nice red colour, stirring with a wooden spoon. The process shouldn't take more than 5–6 minutes. Lift meat into a deep, large casserole. Arrange vegetables over it, add the bag of herbs, sprinkle with salt. Add enough water to cover well, cook in a moderate oven under lid for 1 hour, then add potatoes. Cook for another hour, remove herbs, then serve in the casserole.

Roast Lamb of County Fejér

Ingredients: 1 leg of lamb • 1/2 lb. carrots • 1 small celeriac • 1/2 lb. parsnips • 1/4 lb. mushrooms • 1/2 lb. cauliflower or Brussels sprouts • 1 tsp. salt • 1/4 pint tomato juice • 1 gill sour cream • 2 oz. lard or dripping • 4 oz. tinned peas.

This is enough for 10 people. Place the joint in a roasting tin, heat fat and pour over. Cut root vegetables to 2-inch pieces, break cauliflower into sprigs, cut mushrooms in two. Arrange vegetables around the joint. Roast in a medium oven, basting the meat frequently. After 1/2 hour pour the tomato juice over the vegetables; do not omit to stir every now and then. When ready (about 2 hours), place joint on a large dish, keep hot. Lift out vegetables onto a separate dish, heat up green peas, mix with the vegetables. Pour off surplus fat from tin, add sour cream to the drippings and, stirring with a wooden spoon, bring to the boil. Add a little more stock or water if you find gravy too thick, and serve separately.

Stuffed Roast Lamb

Ingredients: 2 lb. breast of lamb • 1/2 lb. lights and liver of lamb •
4 oz. bacon • 1 breadroll soaked in milk • 2 hard-boiled eggs •
5 oz. chopped mushrooms • 1 small, finely chopped onion • 1 egg •
1 tbsp. finely chopped parsley • pinch of ground black pepper •
pinch of grated nutmeg • salt.

Bone the meat. With the help of a wooden spoon part the upper layer of meat from the lower, thus producing a cavity. Rub meat with salt and let stand for 1/2 hour. Put through the mincer the liver and lights together with the bacon and the squeezed-out roll; add the chopped mushrooms, the coarsely chopped hard-boiled eggs, chopped parsley, onions, 1 raw egg, 1/2 tsp. salt, pinch of black pepper and grated nutmeg. Knead well together, then stuff the meat with this mixture. Sew the opening with thread. Place stuffed meat in a roasting-tin, pour hot fat over, and roast in a medium oven basting frequently, for about 1 1/2 hours. Serve with green peas and spring potatoes. Serve the gravy and mint sauce separately.

GAME

Game Pickle

Ingredients: 2 pints water • 1/2 pint red claret or burgundy • juice of
1 lemon • 3 bay leaves • 1 tbsp. salt • 1 tsp. granulated sugar •
8 whole black peppercorns • 1 carrot • 1 parsnip •
1/2 tsp. juniper berries (latter only for wild boar).

Many dishes of game require, or are improved by, the marination in game pickle of the meat for three or more days, to bring out the delicate flavour of wild game.

Cook the thinly sliced vegetables in 2 pints water, adding the bay leaves, peppercorns and salt. When vegetables are tender, add the wine, lemon juice, sugar and, in the case of wild boar, juniper berries. Put the meat into a deep earthenware or porcelain dish, and pour the hot pickle over it. The meat should be covered by the liquid. Keep in a cool place. Strain the liquid off once a day and boil up, then pour back again over the meat. After 3–6 days the meat can be either boiled or roasted.

Börzsöny Stuffed Pheasant

Ingredients: A brace of pheasants • 2 oz. streaky bacon • 1 tsp. salt •
a pinch of marjoram • 2 medium-sized apples • 4 oz. mushrooms •
1 gill sour cream • 1/4 pint wine.

Pluck, draw and truss pheasants, rub them all over with salt, rub insides with marjoram as well. Peel, then cut the apples in two, hollow out carefully, leaving only an inch-thick shell. Stuff finely chopped mushrooms tightly in the apples, then, placing the halves together again, put a stuffed apple inside each bird, then tie thin slices of bacon on the breast and legs.

Spread 1 oz. lard on the bottom of a roasting-tin, put in the birds and cover with greaseproof paper. Roast in a medium oven. After 20 minutes remove greaseproof paper, pour 1/4 cup wine under the pheasants and, basting frequently, roast them for 30 more minutes. Lift out the birds, but keep them hot. Add sour cream mixed with 1/4 cup wine to the gravy, boil well together, stirring constantly. Serve with steamed rice, fried potato straws and redcurrant jelly.

Roast Pheasant with Chestnut Stuffing

Ingredients: A brace of pheasants • 1/2 lb. peeled chestnuts •
1 bread-roll soaked in milk • 1 egg • 1 oz. cold lard • 1 oz. melted
lard • pinch of marjoram • 2 tbsp. red wine • 2 tbsp. sour cream •
salt • 2 oz. bacon.

Pluck, draw and truss birds, rub all over with salt, rub insides with marjoram. Cut chestnuts deeply across and put in a hot oven for 10 minutes: you will find that the skins can be easily peeled off. Chop chestnuts coarsely, mix with the finely chopped livers and gizzards, add the well squeezed-out roll, a good pinch of salt, 1 egg, 1 oz. cold lard and 2 tbsp. wine. Knead well together and stuff birds with this mixture. Lift the skin away from the breast and slip slices of fat bacon under. Cover with thickly greased paper and roast in a medium-hot oven for 20 minutes. Then take off the paper, brush the birds generously with sour cream and roast 30 minutes longer, basting frequently. Remove and keep hot while preparing gravy with a little thickening. If you carve the birds in the kitchen, arrange the stuffing on the two ends of the dish. Serve with steamed rice and redcurrant jelly.

Braised Partridges

Ingredients: 6 partridges • 3 oz. bacon • 3 oz. butter • 1/2 pint red wine • 1 heaped tsp. flour • 1/2 gill cream • 1 tsp. salt.

Pluck and drew partridges. Cut off breast and legs. Rub pieces with a little salt and put aside. Chop carcasses to small pieces with a chopper. Heat butter in a saucepan, add the chopped meat and bones, salt, and, stirring frequently, fry over a brisk heat, taking care not to burn. When golden-brown (in about 10–15 minutes), add 1/4 pint wine, cover, reduce heat and allow to simmer slowly. Chop bacon finely, put in another saucepan together with the breast and legs, add 1/4 pint wine, cover and cook till meat is tender, adding a spoonful of water every now and then to prevent burning. When ready, lift out meat and keep hot. Sprinkle the flour in the fat in the saucepan, stir, then add a 1/4 pint water and the wine stock strained off the bones. Bring to the boil and add the cream. Serve partridges with a little of the sauce poured over them. Add the rest of the sauce separately. Serve with lentil purée.

Partridges in Piquant Sauce

Ingredients: 4 partridges • 1/2 lb. button mushrooms • 1 level tbsp. finely chopped parsley • 5 oz. streaky bacon • 1 large onion • 1 carrot • 1 parsnip • 1 tsp. granulated sugar • 1 heaped tbsp. finely chopped capers • 1/4 cup red wine • the juice of 1/2 lemon.

Pluck, draw and truss partridges. Stuff them with the raw button mushrooms. Line the bottom of a large saucepan with slices of bacon, cover this with a layer of sliced carrots, parsnips and onion, add 1/4 pint water or stock and arrange partridges on top. Cover and allow to simmer till all moisture evaporates and the birds are tender. Lift them out onto a flat dish, and keep hot. Add sugar to the vegetable mixture remaining in the saucepan, brown contents to a deep golden colour; stir constantly to prevent burning. Sprinkle a tsp. flour on when sufficiently browned, stir, then add the wine mixed with 1/2 cup water, the finely chopped capers and lemon juice. Bring to the boil, then allow to simmer for 10 minutes. Scoop out the mushrooms and arrange them around the dish. Strain the sauce, pour a little over the birds, serve the rest in a sauceboat. Serve with watercress salad and fried potato straws.

Mock Fillet of Hare

Ingredients: 2 lb. round of beef • 5 oz. bacon • 1 bread-roll soaked in milk • 1 oz. finely chopped capers • 3 eggs • 2 oz. finely chopped mushrooms • 1 gill sour cream • 1 heaped tbsp. flour • a small piece of lemon peel • the juice of 1/2 lemon • 1 heaped tsp. granulated sugar.

Marinate the beef according to the game pickle recipe (see p. 105); omit juniper berries. Keep in the liquid for 3 days. Wipe meat before use, cut into strips, put through fine mincer together with bacon, the well squeezed-out roll and the capers. Then add the 3 eggs and the finely chopped mushrooms, knead the mixture well together. Take an oblong narrow baking tin, brush inside with melted lard, then put in the meat rolled to a loaf-shape. Brush top with lard, then bake in a fairly hot oven for 3/4 hour. Meantime heat 1 oz. lard in saucepan, add sugar, stir till sugar turns to a nut-brown colour. Add flour, stir again, then reduce heat and pour 1/2 pint of the pickling liquid over it. Add lemon peel, lemon juice, bay leaf and the sour cream. Bring to the boil, then allow to simmer for 10–15 minutes. Turn mock hare onto an oblong dish, strain some of the sauce over it, serve the rest in a sauceboat. Garnish with potato dumplings or potato chips.

Eger Roast Hare

Ingredients: 1 hare (marinated in game pickle) • 1/2 pint red claret
or burgundy • 3 oz. bacon • 2 oz. lard • 5 oz. mushrooms •
2 gills sour cream.

The hare should be marinated for 3 days before use. Wipe
the meat, cut off forepart just behind the shoulders, use only
the saddle and hind legs. Trim off surplus skinny bits and
ends of ribs. Cut bacon into strips and lard the back in two
even rows. Place hare in a roasting tin, and pour boiling hot
lard over it. Roast in a hot oven for about 15 minutes, then
reduce heat a little, pour the wine over it and add the mushrooms. Basting frequently, roast for about 1 1/2 hours. Take
out the meat and mushrooms when ready, keep hot. Strain
surplus fat off the pan, then pour sour cream on the sediment. Boil, stirring meanwhile, for 5–6 minutes. Pour some
of the gravy over the meat, serve the rest separately. Serve
with potato straws and redcurrant jelly.

Cold Hare Mould

Ingredients: 1 hare (marinated in game pickle) • 2 oz. lard • 2 bread-
rolls soaked in milk • 4 oz. streaky bacon • a good pinch of mixed
herbs • 1 tbsp. French mustard • 2 eggs • 1 tbsp. sour cream •
1 medium-sized onion • 1 level tsp. paprika.

The hare should be in the pickling liquid for at least 3 days
before use. Joint the hare, cut carcass into 3 pieces. Take a
large saucepan and heat the lard in it. Add very finely
chopped onions and fry to a golden colour. Sprinkle with
paprika, then add the meat, a pinch of salt, and, stirring
every now and then, cook slowly adding a little of the pickling liquor to replace the evaporated gravy. The meat should
be tender enough in 1 hour to lift it off the bones easily.

Remove meat from bones and put through fine mincer, together with the well squeezed-out rolls and the bacon. Add mixed herbs, mustard, a spoonful of sour cream and 2 eggs. Knead the mixture well together, then put into a greased pudding shape, leaving space enough for mixture to rise a couple of inches during cooking. Close shape tightly, put into boiling water and cook for about 1 hour. Cool, then turn out. Serve cold, with potato, beetroot or mixed salad.

Wild Boar in Mustard Sauce

Ingredients: 3 lb. piece of leg • 2 tbsp. French mustard • 1 carrot • 1 parsnip • 1/2 celeriac • 1 medium-sized onion • 4 bay leaves • 2 sprigs of tarragon • 1 tbsp. salt • 8 whole black peppercorns.

Bone the joint and spread the mustard on the meat evenly. Leave to stand for 1 hour. After this put the meat into slowly boiling salt water and cook for 1 hour. Slice the vegetables, tie tarragon, peppercorns and bay leaves in a piece of muslin, add them to the slowly boiling meat. Continue cooking till meat is tender, then lift out, strain stock off into a basin, put vegetables through sieve. Then put the vegetable purée back into the saucepan together with 1 tbsp. cranberry sauce and 2 tbsp. sour cream. Stir, then dilute with 1 cup off the stock. Slice the meat, arrange neatly on a hot dish, pour some of the gravy over it, serve the rest of the gravy separately. Garnish with potato chips.

If boar is not available, a tough joint of pork is improved beyond recognition if prepared this way.

Braised Fillets of Venison

Ingredients: 2 lb. fillet of venison • 6 oz. butter • 1/4 pint wine vinegar • 1 heaped tsp. salt • 1/4 pint red wine • 1 1/2 gills sour cream • 1 lb. cauliflower • steamed rice for garnish.

Cut the ripe fillet into finger-thick slices. Heat 3 oz. butter in a saucepan and fry fillets in it quickly on both sides to a golden-brown colour. Lift out the slices, increase heat under saucepan and brown the butter left in it (beurre noir). Pull saucepan aside, put the meat-slices in it again, add the remaining butter, the vinegar mixed with 1/4 pint water and the salt, cover and allow to simmer till meat is nearly tender, adding a little water every now and then to prevent burning. Now add cauliflower broken into sprigs, 1/4 pint wine and the sour cream, cover and allow to simmer till cauliflower is tender. When ready, arrange cauliflower around a hot dish, put the slices of meat in the middle and pour the sauce over it. Serve with steamed rice.

Saddle of Venison with Caper Sauce

Ingredients: 1 (4 lb. piece) of saddle of venison marinated in game pickle • 3 oz. bacon • 2 oz. lard • 1 heaped tbsp. finely chopped capers • 1 gill of sour cream.

The meat should be pickled for at least four or five days. Do not grudge the extra work which pickling entails; it is worth the trouble several times over. Put the wiped meat in roasting tin, cut the bacon into strips and lard the meat in even rows. Heat the lard thoroughly, then pour over the meat. Add a ladleful of pickling juice under it and roast in a moderately hot oven, basting frequently. When nearly ready, add the finely chopped capers and 1 gill of sour cream. After further 20 minutes cooking lift out the joint, keep on a hot dish. Add a ladleful of the pickling juice to the gravy in the tin and, stirring, boil for 5 minutes. Pour into a sauce-boat. Serve with potato chips and redcurrant jelly.

Braised Stag Steaks

Ingredients: 6 finger-thick slices of the haunch • 1 medium-sized onion • 1 bunch of parsley • 2 bay leaves • 6 whole black pepper-corns • 1 thin piece of lemon peel • 1 tbsp. salt • 3 oz. lard • 1 gill sour cream.

Take a deep earthenware or porcelain dish. Put a layer of thinly sliced onions and a few springs of parsley in the bottom. Put on a layer of meat, repeat the procedure covering the top with onions and parsley again. Boil 1/2 pint water together with salt, lemon peel, pepper and bay leaves. Pour the boiling liquid over the meat, taking care to cover the meat completely. Stand in a cool place for 24 hours. Next day heat the lard in a saucepan, and first shaking off the sliced onions and parsley, place the steaks in. Fry quickly on both sides, then add a little of the pickling juice, cover and allow to simmer, adding a little of the juice every now and then to prevent burning. When steaks are tender, lift out onto a hot dish, add sour cream to the gravy remaining in the saucepan, bring to the boil and pour a little over the steaks. Serve the rest of the sauce separately. Garnish with potato chips.

POULTRY

Roast Chicken (Parboiled)

Ingredients: 1 large chicken • 3 oz. lard • pinch of salt • pinch of marjoram.

This is a good way to make an old fowl palatable. Put the plucked, drawn and trussed chicken in boiling salt water, reduce heat and allow to simmer very slowly for about 1 hour. Lift it out of the stock, rub inside with a little salt and a good pinch of marjoram, place on a sieve to drain for 1/2 hour. Then place the bird in a roasting tin, pour hot lard over and roast in a fairly hot oven for 20–30 minutes, basting once or twice. Prepare a thinnish gravy with the drippings and some gravy thickening, serve with bread sauce, tomato and green pepper salad and potatoes with Maître d'Hôtel butter.

Stuffed Capon of Eger

Ingredients: 1 large fat capon, or a good-sized chicken • 3 oz. calf's liver • 1 oz. bacon • 1 bread-roll soaked in milk • a pinch of ground black pepper • a good pinch of marjoram • 2 eggs • 5 oz. mushrooms • 1 heaped tsp. finely chopped parsley • 1 tsp. salt • 1/2 pint red wine • 1 gill sour cream.

The unique Medoc, grown on the hills around the town of Eger, gave the inspiration for this really festive dish. The red wine of Eger, known as Bull's Blood, is far too good to use for cooking in general, yet in this case I am willing to stretch the point; the happy blending of flavours fully justifies the extravagance.

Pluck, draw and truss a capon or a large roasting chicken. Rub with salt and put aside for 1 hour. Trim the liver and gizzard, put through fine mincer, together with the calf's liver and the well squeezed-out roll. Chop bacon very finely, add to the mixture, together with pepper, marjoram and 2 eggs. Mix well, then chill this stuffing for 1/2 hour. Chop mushrooms coarsely, and mix with chopped parsley. Add very little salt, keeping in mind that the chicken is already salted. Now lift the skin on the breast carefully, the handle of a wooden spoon will help you to reach all around the breast as well. Push the stuffing under the skin, pressing evenly all round. Stuff tightly the inside of the bird with the mushroom and parsley mixture. Put capon in a roasting-tin, pour the hot lard over it with half the wine. Roast in a medium hot oven, basting frequently, and pouring a spoonful of wine over it every now and then. If it browns too quickly, cover with greaseproof paper. The capon will be ready in 1 1/2 hours, then lift out onto a hot dish. Pour off surplus fat, and boil up sediment with 1 gill sour cream and the remaining wine. Serve with at least 3 kinds of vegetables, according to season.

Chicken Casserole à la Hungária

Ingredients: 1 large boiled chicken • yolks of 4 eggs • 1/2 tsp. salt • 1/2 pint chicken stock • 4 1/2 oz. butter • 4 level tbsp. flour • 5 tbsp. grated cheese • 5 oz. mushrooms • 1 heaped tbsp. chopped chives • 1 tbsp. chopped capers.

Skin the boiled chicken, then remove meat from the bones; put aside. Heat 3 1/2 oz. butter, add flour, stir till frothy but still white, add cold stock of the chicken. Keep on stirring and cook on low heat till sauce is very thick. Pull aside, add a pinch of salt, the egg yolks one by one, then the grated cheese, chives and capers. Heat 1/2 oz. butter in a frying pan, add coarsely chopped mushrooms, fry till water evaporates, and add it to the sauce. Stir well. Put half of this mixture in the bottom of a deep casserole, arrange the boneless pieces of chicken over it, then cover with the other half of the sauce. Cook in a medium oven for 30 minutes. Serve with spring carrots, green peas and French beans.

Chicken in Lemon Sauce

Ingredients: 1 chicken • 1 tsp. salt • a large bunch of parsley • juice of 1 lemon • 1 tbsp. flour • 3 oz. butter • 3/4 cup milk • 2 oz. bacon • 1 oz. lard • a pinch of nutmeg.

Pluck and draw chicken, then cut to neat pieces. Line the bottom of a casserole with slices of bacon, arrange the pieces of chicken over it. Add parsley tied in a tight bunch, salt 1/4 cup water and the juice of 1/2 lemon. Cover and cook in a medium-hot oven till chicken is tender. Heat butter in a saucepan, add a heaped tbsp. flour, stir and cook till frothy but still white, add 3/4 cup milk and stir till sauce is thick and smooth. Pull aside, add grated nutmeg, sour cream, and lastly stir in the juice of 1/2 lemon. Remove parsley and pour sauce over the chicken. Cook uncovered in a brisk oven for 15–20 minutes. Serve in the casserole with vegetables in season.

Chicken Paprikash

Ingredients: 1 large chicken • 2 large onions • 3 oz. lard • 1 tbsp. paprika • 1 green pepper • 1 tomato • 1 tsp. salt • 2 gills sour cream • 1 level tsp. flour.

Pluck, draw, then cut chicken into neat pieces. Heat the lard in a saucepan, add finely chopped onions, fry till golden yellow. Pull aside, add paprika, salt and the chicken. Stir. Cover and allow to simmer slowly, adding a little water every now and then. After 1/2 hour add tomato and green pepper cut in four. When meat is tender, remove the pepper and tomato skins from the gravy, sprinkle the chicken with a level tsp. flour, stir, then add sour cream. Cook slowly 10 minutes longer. Serve in a deep round dish, garnish with golden drops (see p. 59).

Chicken in Piquant Sauce

Ingredients: 1 large chicken • 3 oz. bacon • 3 tbsp. tomato purée •
1 oz. finely chopped capers • 1 tsp. French mustard •
1/4 pint vegetable stock • 1/4 pint wine • 1 gill sour cream •
1 tsp. anchovy sauce.

Pluck, draw, then cut chicken into neat pieces. Line the bottom of a deep casserole with thinly sliced bacon, arrange the pieces of chicken on it; add tomato purée, capers and mustard, cover with slices of bacon. Lastly pour on the vegetable stock. Cover and cook in a fairly hot oven under lid. When meat is tender, lift the lid to allow the bacon to brown. Mix the wine, sour cream and anchovy sauce together and pour over the chicken. Leave casserole in the hot oven 10 minutes longer. Serve chicken in the casserole. Garnish with rice and mushroom.

Chicken Ragout

Ingredients: 1 chicken • 2 oz. carrots • 2 oz. parsnips •
2 oz. celeriac • 1 small onion • 1 clove of garlic • 1 heaped tsp. salt •
bunch of parsley • a pinch of grated nutmeg • 2 oz. flour •
3 oz. butter • 1/2 lemon.

Joint, then cook the chicken, together with the vegetables, salt, parsley, onion and garlic in 1 1/2 pints water. Lift out pieces of chicken when tender, skin and bone them, and cut the meat into small, neat pieces. Strain the stock, put aside to cool. Heat butter in a saucepan, add flour and fry, stirring constantly till just golden. Dilute with 3/4 pint of the cold stock and, stirring constantly, bring to the boil. Add meat and grated nutmeg; simmer 5 minutes longer, then serve in a deep dish. Garnish with green peas and new potatoes, or rice and mushroom. Serve lemon, cut into thin rings, separately.

French Fried Chicken

Ingredients: 2 young chickens • 1/2 tsp. salt • 2 oz. flour • 3 eggs.

You need quite young birds for this. Pluck, draw, then cut each chicken in four, pull of the skin, then sprinkle with salt and allow to stand for 1/2 hour. Separate egg yolks and whites, beat whites till stiff. Dip the pieces of chicken first in flour, then egg yolks, and lastly in the stiffly whipped egg whites. Fry in hot deep fat, lifting the basket once or twice for a moment, to let surplus steam escape. Put the cooked pieces on absorbent paper to drain off fat. Serve immediately with sour cream.

Chicken Pilaf

Ingredients: 1 large chicken • 2 oz. carrots • 1 oz. parsnip •
1 oz. celeriac • 1/2 lb. rice • 1 small onion • 1 level tsp. salt •
1 heaped tbsp. finely chopped parsley • 1/2 lb. green peas •
1/2 lb. mushrooms • pinch of ground black pepper • 3 oz. lard.

Joint a large boiling chicken and cook in 2 pints salt water, together with carrots, parsnip and celeriac. Heat lard in a saucepan, add the rice and, stirring constantly, fry till the grains become opaque. Then add grated onion, finely chopped parsley, pepper and sliced mushrooms, stir, then add green peas. Dilute with stock strained off the chicken; add just enough to cover with two fingerbreadths. Bring to the boil, then reduce heat immediately, cover with lid and cook on a very low heat without stirring. Skin and bone the pieces of chicken, cut meat to neat, small pieces. Add it to the cooked rice; mix carefully with a wooden spoon to prevent rice becoming mushy. Serve heaped up in a round dish.

Camp Chicken

Ingredients: 2 small chickens • 2 oz. bacon • a pinch of salt •
3 medium-sized tomatoes • 1 green pepper • 3 eggs.

This is an excellent dish to serve at a garden picnic, or camping week-end. Cut the bacon into small cubes. Place a heavy frying pan on embers or over a barbecue grid, and fry bacon to a pale golden colour. Cut the small tender chicken in four, place in the frying pan skin-side down. Sprinkle with a very little salt, cover pan tightly and let the chicken cook for about 20 minutes. Shake the covered pan every now and then, but do not lift the lid while it is cooking. When ready, put the chicken between two tin plates, keep hot at the side of the fire. Core, then chop green pepper coarsely, fry in the fat in the pan, add quartered tomatoes after three or four minutes. Sprinkle with a pinch of salt, fry briskly. Lastly add well-beaten eggs, stir once or twice. Serve the chicken on individual plates, add a spoonful of the savoury scrambled eggs on each plate. Potato salad on a lettuce bed is a satisfying accompaniment.

Duck with Sauerkraut

Ingredients: 1 nice, fat duck • 1 1/2 lb. sauerkraut • 1/4 pint red
wine • 1 gill sour cream • 1 tsp. salt • 1–3 oz. lard.

Use the legs, breast and liver only. Cut legs in two at the joint, bone the breast carefully, keeping the meat whole. The amount of lard used depends on the fatness of the bird. Rub meat with a little salt, let stand for 1/2 hour. Heat lard in a saucepan and fry the pieces quickly on both sides to a golden-brown colour. Put a layer of sauerkraut in the bottom of a deep casserole, arrange the meat on it, add the raw liver cut to strips, cover with the rest of sauerkraut. Heat lard in the saucepan, add wine and sour cream, spoon this mixture in the sauerkraut. Cover and cook in a fairly hot oven for about 1–1 1/2 hours. Serve with potato dumplings or boiled potatoes.

Savoury Roast Duck

Ingredients: 1 young duck • 2 oz. lard • 1 tsp. anchovy paste • grated rind of 1/2 lemon • 1 tbsp. finely chopped capers • 1 egg • 1 tbsp. fine breadcrumbs.

Pluck and draw a plump duck, cut off feet, head and neck and the end joint of the wings. Cook these in 1/2 pint water, then put aside. Rub the outside of the bird with salt. Mix anchovy paste, grated lemon rind, capers and 1 heaped tbsp. breadcrumbs with the egg. Spread this mixture in the inside, place the trimmed liver in the cavity, then truss. Place the duck breastside down in a deep casserole, add 1/4 pint wine and 1/4 pint stock. Cover and cook in a medium oven for 1 hour, then turn the bird over and cook, without lid, 1/2 hour longer. Cover with greaseproof paper if it browns too quickly. Prepare a brown gravy with the remaining wine and stock. Remove liver before serving, slice and place it beside the duck. Serve with roast potatoes and French beans.

Minced Goose Breast

Ingredients: Breast of 2 geese • 4 oz. cooked ham • 1 bread-roll soaked in milk • pinch of marjoram • 1 tsp. salt • pinch of ground black pepper • 1/2 tsp. grated onion • 2 oz. lard or goose fat • 2 eggs.

Pull the fat skin of the breasts carefully, put aside. Remove meat from the breastbone, cut to strips, then put through fine mincer together with the well squeezed-out roll. Heat 1 tsp. lard, add grated onions, stir till onions are golden-yellow, pour on the minced meat. Add salt, marjoram, pepper and eggs. Knead mixture well together, then put it back on the breastbones to resemble the original shape. Cover with the skins. Fasten the skins to the bone with a few stitches of cotton. Melt the fat in a roasting-tin, place in the two breasts, cover them with a piece of well-greased paper, and roast in a medium oven, basting frequently. When ready, place meat on a warmed dish, pour off surplus fat and, sprinkling a little flour in the pan, stir and add a little water or stock. Do not make the gravy very thick. Serve with vegetables according to season and potato purée.

Stuffed Roast Goose

Ingredients: For 8–10 people: 1 plump goose • 4 hard-boiled eggs • 6 oz. mushrooms • 1 tsp. finely chopped chives • 1/2 gill sour cream • 2 1/2 tsp. salt • a good pinch of ground black pepper • a good pinch of marjoram • 2 eggs • 2 tbsp. burgundy • 2 oz. lard.

Rub the goose all over with 2 tsp. salt and leave to stand for 2 hours. Meantime prepare the stuffing; put in a deep bowl the following ingredients: 4 hard-boiled eggs coarsely chopped, the mushrooms chopped finely, sour cream, chives, the liver of the goose cut to small cubes, salt, pepper, marjoram, 2 raw eggs and 2 tbsp. wine. Knead the mixture well together and stuff the goose with it. The whole of the stuffing should go in, then pin the skin together with a couple of toothpicks. Spread the lard on a piece of greaseproof paper, cover the bird with it, pour about 1/4 cup water in the roasting tin and then put in the goose. Roast in a medium-hot oven, basting frequently, for at least 2 hours. Remove greaseproof paper after an hour. Roast goose does not need elaborate garnish: the gravy, stuffing and a mixed salad should be sufficient.

Stuffed Goose's Neck

Ingredients: Skins taken off the necks of 3 geese • 1/2 goose-liver and heart • some leftover goose meat • 2 large boiled potatoes • 1 tsp. salt • a good pinch of ground black pepper • 6 oz. mushrooms • 2 oz. lard or goose-fat • 1 tbsp. finely chopped parsley • a pinch of marjoram • 2 eggs.

Pull the skin off the neck and sew the opening of one end with cotton. Salt and put aside for 1/2 hour; meantime prepare the stuffing. Put through fine mincer the meat, hearts and potatoes. Fry the finely chopped onions in a very little fat, add thinly sliced mushrooms, pinch of salt and the parsley, cover and cook for 10 minutes, then add it to the minced meat together with pepper, marjoram and two eggs. Mix well, then stuff the mixture tightly into the skins. Sew the open end, then put the sausage-shaped stuffed skins in an oblong casserole. Pour a spoonful or two of water under them, dot with lard. Cover and cook in a fairly hot oven under lid for 1/2 hour, and cook for another 1/2 hour without lid, basting once or twice. When ready, the skins should be crisp and nicely browned. Remove cotton before dishing, then cut necks to slices with a sharp knife. Serve with braised red cabbage, boiled potatoes and gravy.

Stuffed Roast Turkey

Ingredients: For 12 people: 1 medium-sized turkey • 2 oz. bacon • 2 bread-rolls soaked in milk • 4 oz. goose-liver • 1 tsp. grated onion • 1 tbsp. finely chopped parsley • 6 oz. mushrooms • pinch of ground black pepper • 1 tbsp. salt • pinch of marjoram • 2 eggs • 4 oz. lard • 1 lb. chestnuts • 1/4 cup wine.

Rub the turkey with salt, loosen the skin over the breast, and crop with the help of a wooden spoon. Leave to stand for 1 hour. Cut chestnuts deeply across, put in the hot oven for 15 minutes, then peel and cut in half. Put aside. Cook gizzard, etc. with the exception of the liver in 1/2 pint slightly salted water, allow to simmer. Now prepare the stuffing. Heat a spoonful of lard in a small saucepan, add grated onions and fry till onions are yellow. Add sliced mushrooms and finely chopped parsley, cover and allow to simmer for 10 minutes. Meantime put through the mincer the raw liver of the turkey, 2 oz. bacon, and the well-squeezed rolls. Add cooked mushrooms to it, together with the goose-liver cut into tiny cubes, the yolks of 2 eggs, and lastly, the stiffly whipped egg whites. Mix well, then stuff the mixture under the skin of the crop and breast. Fill the inside of the bird with the chestnuts. Now put the turkey into a large roasting tin, heat the remaining 3 oz. lard and pour over the bird. Cover drumsticks and the top of the breast with greaseproof paper, then roast the turkey in a medium-hot oven. Pour 1/4 cup wine under it while cooking, baste frequently. After 2–2 1/2 hours the turkey should be ready. Remove from the tin, keep hot. Prepare gravy, using the stock made with the giblets. Serve with vegetables according to season.

Roast Turkey with Mushrooms

Ingredients: 1 young turkey • 3 oz. fat bacon • 3 oz. lard • 1/4 pint stock • 1/2 lb. mushrooms • 2 gills sour cream • 1 heaped tsp. salt.

Rub the turkey all over with salt, and leave to stand for 1/2 hour. Loosen the skin on the breast and legs — you can do this easily with the handle of a wooden spoon — then push the slices of bacon under the skin, smoothing it out to make the slices lay flat. Chop mushrooms coarsely, stuff the inside of the bird with it. Place the turkey in a roasting pan, heat lard and pour over the bird. Add 1/4 pint stock, then roast in a medium-hot oven, basting frequently. After 1 hour brush the turkey thickly all over with sour cream; repeat this after 15 minutes. 1 1/2 hour's cooking should be enough for a really young bird. Taking it out of the tin, pour off the surplus fat, add the remaining sour cream to the drippings and stirring, bring to the boil. Serve with mixed salad and roast potatoes.

ONE-COURSE MEALS AND LUNCHEON DISHES

For additional ideas see also "Hot Entreés" (p. 21–38).

Vegetarian Stuffed Cabbage

Ingredients: 1 1/2 lb. sauerkraut • 6 cabbage leaves •
1/2 lb. mushrooms • 1 small onion • 1 tsp. finely chopped parsley •
1 oz. lard • 1 tsp. paprika • 7 oz. rice • 1/4 pint tomato juice •
1/2 tsp. salt • 1 tsp. flour.

Strain sauerkraut, then arrange in a layer in the bottom of a thick saucepan. Place the cabbage leaves in a colander and scald. Chop separately the mushrooms, onion and parsley. Heat lard in a saucepan, add finely chopped onion and, stirring every now and then, fry till pale yellow. Add finely chopped parsley and mushrooms, sprinkle paprika over it, add salt, then cover and allow to simmer till moisture evaporates. Put aside and stir in the uncooked rice, place even heaps of this mixture on each cabbage leaf, roll up, tuck in the ends of the leaves, and tie with cotton. Arrange the stuffed leaves over the sauerkraut. Dilute a small tin of tomato purée with 1/4 pint water and pour over it. Cover and leave to simmer for about 1 hour. Thicken with a tbsp. of roux, boil up again, then serve.

Whole Stuffed Cabbage

Ingredients: 1 firm head off cabbage (about 2 lb.) • 2 oz. fat • 2 small onions • 1 lb. minced pork • 1 bread-roll soaked in milk • 1 egg • bacon • 1 tbsp. sour cream • 2 oz. cooked rice.

Choose a nice hard cabbage, remove outer leaves and cut off surplus stalk. Place the cabbage in a colander and pour boiling hot water over it. Now open the outer 8–10 leaves and, with a sharp knife, cut out the inner part, leaving a shell of leaves, held together with the remaining stalk. Chop the cut-out part. Melt 1 oz. lard in a saucepan, add chopped cabbage, 1 finely chopped onion, pinch of ground black pepper and salt, cover and simmer for 10–15 minutes. Put saucepan aside and pour contents into a bowl. Add minced pork, the wellsqueezed roll, 1 egg, 1 tbsp. sour cream and rice. Stir well, then put the mixture into the scooped-out cabbage, pressing the leaves on to get the original shape. Line the bottom of a deep casserole with thinly sliced bacon, place the stuffed cabbage on it, put 2–3 slices of bacon and a few thin slices of onion on top. Pour 1 cup stock or water under the cabbage, cover, and cook in a medium oven for about 1 hour, then brush top of cabbage thickly with sour cream and cook 10 minutes longer without lid. Serve in the casserole. Easier to prepare than it looks at first sight, and it is tasty and economical.

Transylvanian Mince

Ingredients: 1 1/2 lb. cold roast or boiled beef • 2 bread-rolls soaked in milk • 1 level tbsp. mustard • 2 oz. butter • 1/2 gill sour cream • 2 tbsp. tomato purée • 1 oz. grated cheese.

Put meat through mincer together with the well squeezed-out rolls. Flavour with salt and mustard. Butter thickly the bottom of a shallow fireproof dish and heap minced meat in the middle. Melt, but do not heat the remaining butter, add tomato purée and sour cream. Spread this mixture over the meat, sprinkle with grated cheese and bake in a medium oven for about 1/2 hour. Serve with salad or vegetables.

Baked Pork Chops

Ingredients: 6 pork chops • 1 1/2 lb. potatoes • 1 medium-sized onion • 1 1/2 gills sour cream • 1/2 tsp. paprika • 1 tsp. salt • 1 oz. lard.

Peel potatoes and cut into thin slices. Slice onion thinly. Grease thickly the bottom of a roasting tin, arrange on it a layer of sliced potatoes and thinly sliced onions. Sprinkle with paprika and salt, then place pork chops on top. Put a dab of lard on each chop. Bake in a hot oven for about 1/2 hour, then pour the sour cream over and put the tin back in the oven for another 20 minutes. Serve with mixed salad.

Haricot Bean Stew

Ingredients: 10 oz. haricot beans • 7 oz. pearl barley • 2 oz. carrots • 2 oz. parsnips • 1 medium-sized onion • 1 green pepper • 1 tomato • 2 oz. lard • 1 tsp. ground paprika • 1 heaped tbsp. flour • 10 oz. smoked sausages • salt.

Soak beans overnight. Put on to cook in 2 pints water, together with pearl barley, carrots, parsnips, the whole onion, green pepper and tomato. Cover and allow to simmer for 1 hour. Heat lard in a frying pan, add flour, stir till nicely browned, then dilute with a ladleful of cold water. Stir, add to the stew, bring to the boil. Put sliced smoked sausage in the bottom of a deep casserole and pour the stew over. Cook in a medium oven for another hour, then serve in the casserole.

Goose Giblets with Rice

Ingredients: One set of goose giblets • 3 oz. carrots • 2 oz. parsnips • 1 small onion • 6 whole black peppercorns • 1 tbsp. salt • 1/2 lb. rice • 1/2 lb. shelled green peas • 7 oz. mushrooms • 2 oz. lard or goose-fat • 2 oz. grated Parmesan cheese.

Cook giblets in 2 pints water, adding cubed carrots, parsnips, whole onion, peppercorns and 1/2 tbsp. salt. When meat is tender, strain off the stock into a bowl, leave the giblets in the saucepan, cover, and put aside. Heat fat in a saucepan, add sliced mushrooms, stir, then add rice, chopped parsley, green peas, and salt. Pour just enough of the stock on the rice to cover a finger-breadth. Cover and allow to simmer very slowly indeed, till rice is tender. Now stir the cooked giblets into the rice carefully, turn the mixture into a casserole, cover and heat well through in a hot oven. Serve in the casserole with grated cheese in a separate dish.

Risotto Mould

Ingredients: 1 1/2 lb. potatoes • 1/2 cup milk • 1 1/2 oz. butter • 1 tsp. flour • 1 lb. cooked rice • 5 oz. liver • 5 oz. ham • 5 oz. mushrooms • 3 oz. grated cheese • salt • pinch of ground black pepper.

Peel and cook potatoes, press them through sieve, then add 1 oz. butter, salt and pepper to taste, 1 tsp. flour and 1/4 pint milk. Beat well together to a smooth stiff purée. Line a deep, oblong casserole with a thick layer of the purée, pressing well to the sides and bottom. Put a layer of rice, on top then arrange on the rice the chopped liver, ham and mushrooms. Mix the remaining rice with grated cheese, cover the meat with it. Cover top with the remaining potato purée. Press down lightly, then bake in a hot oven for about 1/2–3/4 hour. Put aside for 5–6 minutes after removing from the oven, then loosen sides carefully with a blunt knife and turn risotto out onto a flat dish. Serve with tomato sauce.

Paprika Veal Casserole

Ingredients: 1 lb. shoulder of veal • 1 large onion • 2 1/2 oz. lard • 1 level tbsp. paprika • 1 level tbsp. salt • 2 lb. potatoes • 1/4 pint milk.

Cut meat into 2-inch cubes. Heat lard in a saucepan, add finely chopped onions and fry till golden. Add paprika, 1/2 tbsp. salt, and the meat, stir, cover and allow to simmer for 1 hour. Add a spoonful or two of water while cooking, but the gravy should be kept quite short. Peel and cook potatoes, press through sieve, add remaining salt and the milk and, stirring constantly, cook till purée thickens. Place half of the purée in the bottom of a deep round casserole, arrange the paprika-meat over it, then cover with the other half of the purée. Bake in a medium-hot oven till top browns nicely. Serve with mixed salad.

Minced Pork Casserole

Ingredients: 1 lb. minced pork • 1 pig's kidney and brains • 1/2 lb. liver • 1 small onion • 1 level tbsp. paprika • 1 level tbsp. salt • 3 oz. lard.

Cook peeled potatoes in salt water, mash thoroughly when cooked and put aside. Heat 2 oz. lard in a saucepan, add finely chopped onions and, stirring, fry till onions are pale yellow. Add paprika, minced meat and salt, cover and allow to simmer for 1/2 hour. Line a deep casserole with half of the mashed potatoes, pour the cooked meat mixture into it, then cover with the rest of mashed potatoes. Brush top thickly with melted lard and bake in a fairly hot oven till top is nicely browned. Serve garnished with braised red cabbage.

Pork Chops and Spinach Casserole

Ingredients: 6 pork chops • 3/4 lb. spinach • 1 oz. lard • 1 large cup bechamel sauce • 2 egg whites • 1 oz. grated cheese • 1 tsp. salt • pinch of ground black pepper.

Heat lard in a saucepan and fry pork chops in it to a golden-brown. Now reduce heat and placing all the chops back into the saucepan, add a ladleful of stock, cover with lid and leave to simmer for 3/4 hour. Throw cleaned spinach into boiling salt water and cook for 10 minutes. Drain well, then arrange in the bottom of a casserole. Place cooked chops on top, adding the gravy as well. Cover first with bechamel sauce, then with the stiffly whipped egg whites; sprinkle grated cheese over. Bake in a fairly moderate oven for about 1/2 hour, by this time the top should be nicely browned. Serve in the casserole.

Mushroom and Potato Stew

Ingredients: 1/2 lb. fresh or 3 1/2 oz. dried mushrooms • 1 medium-sized onion • 2 oz. lard • 1 tsp. paprika • 1 tsp. finely chopped parsley • 1 level tbsp. tomato purée • 1 1/2 lb. potatoes • 1 1/2 gills sour cream • 1 level tbsp. flour • 1/2 tbsp. salt.

If you are using dried mushrooms, soak them first in warm water for about 2 hours. Boil potatoes in their skins, peel, then put aside. Heat lard in a saucepan, add finely chopped onions. Stirring, fry onions till just pale yellow, then add chopped parsley, paprika, sliced mushrooms and salt. Let it simmer for 10 minutes and then add sliced boiled potatoes. Mix flour with sour cream and stir into the stew. Boil slowly for 5 minutes and it is ready to serve.

Savoury Mushroom Roll

Ingredients: 1 1/2 lb. potatoes • 3 oz. butter • 1/4 cup milk • 1 level tbsp. flour • 1 tsp. salt • 7 oz mushrooms • a pinch of mixed herbs • 1 egg.

Peel and cook potatoes, then press through sieve. Add flour, 1 oz. butter, 1/2 tsp. salt, and just enough milk to bind mixture. Heat 1 1/2 oz. butter in a saucepan, add the finely chopped mushrooms, 1/2 tsp. salt and a pinch of mixed herbs. Cover and allow to simmer till water evaporates. Place the potato purée onto a floured pastry-board and roll out lightly to finger-thickness. Spread the mushroom mixture on evenly, roll up into a tight roly-poly and place into a greased baking-pan. Brush top with beaten egg and bake in a hot oven for about 15–20 minutes. Serve with vegetables and gravy.

Potato Letcho

Ingredients: 1 1/2 lb. potatoes • 1/2 lb. green peppers • 1/2 lb. tomatoes • 1 large onion • 1 level tbsp. paprika • 1 tsp. salt • 2 oz. lard.

Peel, then cut potatoes into 1-inch cubes. Heat lard in a saucepan, add finely chopped onions and fry till onions are pale yellow. Add potatoes, paprika and salt, stir and pour 1/2 cup of water on it. Cover and allow to simmer for 20 minutes. Core and slice green peppers, slice tomatoes, and add them to the potatoes. Stir well, then cover the saucepan again and cook slowly for about 15–20 minutes. Serve in a heated casserole.

Green Pepper with Rive Stuffing

Ingredients: 6 large green peppers • 6 oz. uncooked rice • 1 level tbsp. finely chopped parsley • 2 oz. carrots • 2 oz. parsnips • 2 oz. celeriac (celery root) • 2 oz. shelled green peas • 2 oz. lard • 1 level tbsp. salt.
Sauce: 1 lb. fresh tomatoes • 2 oz. lard • 1 tbsp. flour • pinch of salt • 1 tbsp. granulated sugar.

Prepare the sauce first. Cut tomatoes in half and cook in a saucepan. When soft, put through sieve. Heat 1 oz. lard, add flour and stir till brown, then pour the tomato juice over it. Keep on stirring till sauce begins to boil, then add salt and sugar and put aside. Now chop carrots, parsnips and celeriac into tiny cubes, shell peas. Heat 2 oz. lard in a saucepan, add the rice and stir till the grains turn white and opaque. Add chopped vegetables, shelled peas, parsley, and salt, stir, then add enough water to cover the rice with a fingerbreadth. Cover and allow to simmer for 20 minutes. Core the green peppers and stuff them with the rice-mixture, then place in an oblong fireproof dish and pour the tomato sauce over it. Cover and cook in a medium oven for about 3/4–1 hour. Serve in the casserole, with boiled potatoes.

Stuffed Green Pepper

Ingredients: 1 lb. minced pork • 10 green peppers • 3 lb. fresh toma-toes • 14 oz. lard • 2 1/2 oz. onions • 2 1/2 oz. flour • 2 oz. sugar • salt • pinch of ground black pepper • pinch of marjoram • 1 1/2 eggs • 4 oz. rice • 1 clove garlic • small bunch parsley • tomato sauce.

Wash and core peppers. Parboil the rice, strain, and put aside to cool. Place the minced meat in a bowl, add the rice, 1 oz. of the chopped onions fried in 1 oz. of the lard, the finely chopped parsley, one whole egg and one yolk, salt and pepper and sprinkle with marjoram. Fry the rest of the onions lightly with the crushed garlic, add to the stuffing and knead well together. Stuff the peppers with the meat and cook slowly in the tomato sauce, until ready. If the peppers are too hot, pour boiling water over them, and then rinse in cold water before stuffing. Serve with boiled potatoes.

Stuffed Potatoes

Ingredients: 1/2 lb. left-over meat • 6 large boiled potatoes • 1 1/2 gills sour cream • 1 tsp. paprika • 1/2 tsp. salt • 1 small onion • 2 oz. lard • 6 eggs • 1 oz. butter.

Peel, then scoop out the insides of boiled potatoes opening them at the side, not on the top. Mince the meat, mix with salt, paprika and a pinch of ground black pepper. Fry the finely chopped onion in 1 oz. lard and add to the minced meat. Put a spoonful of the mixture into each potato. Place the stuffed potatoes into a well-greased fireproof dish, break one egg into each. Spoon sour cream over and add a dab of butter on top of each. Bake in a hot over for 20 minutes then serve with salad.

Stuffed Baked Potatoes

Ingredients: 6 large potatoes • 1 1/2 gills sour cream • pinch of paprika • 1/2 tsp. salt • 1/2 tbsp. finely chopped chives • 4 oz. scraped liver • 2 oz. lard.

Peel 6 large potatoes and bake in the oven, turning over once or twice to let both sides brown nicely. Take out when ready, cut a shilling-sized hole in the middle of each and scoop out insides. Place the scraped raw liver. Mix well and stuff the hollowed-out potatoes with it. Arrange stuffed potatoes in shallow fireproof dish, and pour melted lard and sour cream over it. Bake in a hot oven for about 20–30 minutes. Serve hot.

Potato and Cottage-cheese Casserole

Ingredients: 1 1/2 lb. potatoes • 1/2 lb. cottage cheese • 1 tsp. salt • 2 oz. lard • 1 1/2 gills sour cream.

Cook potatoes in their jackets, peel, then slice them. Grease thickly a deep fireproof dish and put a layer of sliced potatoes in the bottom. Cover with a layer of cottage cheese and repeat procedure till the casserole is full; the top layer should be potatoes. Mix melted lard and sour cream, add salt and pour over the top. Cover and cook in a hot oven for about 1/2 hour. Serve with salad.

Green Peppers and Potato Casserole

Ingredients: 1 lb. boiled potatoes • 3 hard-boiled eggs • 3 oz. butter • 1 1/2 gills sour cream • 1/2 lb. tomatoes • 1/2 lb. green peppers • 1 level tbsp. salt.

Peel and slice boiled potatoes and hard-boiled eggs. Slice tomatoes, core and slice green peppers. Mix melted butter and sour cream, add salt. Grease well a deep fireproof dish and put sliced potatoes, peppers, hard-boiled eggs and tomatoes in it, in alternative layers. Pour the sour cream mixture over, cover and bake in a hot oven for about 30–40 minutes. Serve in the casserole.

Mushroom and Potato Casserole

Ingredients: 1 lb. boiled potatoes • 1/2 lb. mushrooms • 3 oz. lard •
1 tsp. salt • pinch of ground black pepper • 1 1/2 gills sour cream •
1 level tbsp. finely chopped parsley.

Select even-sized mushrooms, cut off stalks. Heat lard in a
saucepan, add mushrooms, salt and black pepper, cover and
allow to simmer for 10 minutes. Grease an oblong fireproof
dish, and line the bottom with a fork, arrange them on the
potatoes, cover with a layer of sliced potatoes. Add the sour
cream to the mushroom-gravy left in the saucepan, heat up,
but do not boil, then spoon over the top of the potato layer.
Bake in a hot oven for 1/2 hour. Sprinkle top with finely
chopped parsley just before serving.

Savoy Casserole

Ingredients: 1 lb. nice firm savoy cabbage • 1/2 lb. boiled potatoes •
4 hard-boiled eggs • 3 oz. butter • 1 1/2 gills sour cream • 1 egg
yolk • 1 tsp. salt.

Peel and slice boiled potatoes and hard-boiled eggs. Parboil
savoy cabbage in salt water, then place on a sieve to drain.
Butter thickly a deep fireproof dish, put half of the sliced
potatoes and eggs into it. Cut the savoy to finger-thick slices,
place into the casserole, top with the remaining half of sliced
potatoes. Melt butter and mix with the sour cream, add egg
yolk and pepper. Pour this mixture into the casserole, cover
and cook in a hot oven for about 1/2 hour.
Serve hot.

Vegetable Risotto

Ingredients: 1/2 lb. green peas • 1 kohlrabi • 1/4 lb. carrots •
1/4 lb. parsnips • 1/4 lb. mushrooms • 1/2 lb. rice • 4 oz. butter •
2 oz. grated cheese • 1/2 gill sour cream • 1 tsp. salt •
1/2 cup tomato juice.

Shell peas, clean vegetables and cut them into small cubes.
Cook peas and vegetables in salt water till tender, then drain.
Mix in a basin 3 oz. melted butter, grated cheese, sour cream,
tomato juice and 1/2 tsp. salt, add cooked rice and cooked
vegetables. Stir well, then pour the mixture into a thickly
buttered casserole. Cover and cook in a hot oven for 1/2
hour.

Stuffed Savoy in Casserole

Ingredients: 2 medium-sized firm savoy cabbages •
10 oz. pig's or calf's liver • 1 egg • 3 tbsp. fine breadcrumbs •
1 1/2 gills sour cream • 2 oz. butter • 1 oz. lard • 1 tsp. salt.

Parboil savoys in salt water after removing outer leaves.
Place in a colander to drain. Cut liver to palm-sized pieces.
Heat lard in a saucepan, add liver and fry quickly, stirring
every now and then. Put aside to cool after 5–6 minutes of
cooking. Put liver through mincer, then add to it the egg,
breadcrumbs and 2 tbsp. sour cream. Mix well. Pull cabbage-
leaves apart carefully so as not break them off the stalk,
place the liver-stuffing between the leaves, then smooth
leaves back. Place stuffed savoys in a thickly buttered fireproof dish, rather closely to each other. Mix sour cream and
melted butter, add a pinch of salt, then pour the mixture
over the savoys. Bake in a medium oven for about 3/4 hour.
Baste with their own gravy once or twice while cooking.
Serve hot.

Vegetable Marrow and Rice Casserole

Ingredients: 2 lb. vegetable marrow • 4 oz. cooked rice •
3 oz. butter • 1 gill sour cream • 2 oz. grated cheese • 1 tsp. salt.

Peel and clean vegetable marrow, then cut into 2-inch wide slices. Parboil sliced marrow for 10 minutes, then drain. Butter an oval casserole. Melt the remaining butter and mix with the sour cream. Put alternative layers of marrow and cooked rice into the casserole, sprinkle each layer with melted butter, grated cheese and sour cream. Top with grated cheese and bake in a hot oven for about 1/2 hour.

Stuffed Vegetable Marrow

Ingredients: 1 medium-sized marrow • 4 oz. rice • 1 small onion •
3 oz. lard • 2 tbsp tomato purée • 2 oz. grated cheese • 1 egg •
1/2 gill sour cream • 1/2 tsp. paprika-pepper • 1/2 tsp. salt

Peel marrow, then cut across the middle and scrape out seeds. Heat 1 1/2 oz. lard in a saucepan, add finely chopped onion and stirring constantly, fry till onion turns pale yellow. Now add the tomato purée, paprika-pepper, 1 tsp. salt and rice. Stir well, pour enough cold water over to cover the rice with a finger-breadth and allow to simmer under lid for 20 minutes. Pull aside, stir in the grated cheese and 1 egg. Stuff the two halves of marrow with the mixture, fit cut ends together, tie and place marrow in a roasting tin. Pour a mixture of hot melted lard and sour cream over and bake in a medium oven for about 3/4 — 1 hour, basting occasionally. Add a little gravy-thickening in the last quarter of an hour. Lift stuffed marrow carefully onto a dish, remove cotton and pour over the sauce.

Stuffed Morels

Ingredients: 1 1/2 lb. morel mushrooms • 2 oz. lard • 3/4 lb. boneless veal • 1 level tbsp. finely chopped parsley • 1 stale bread-roll soaked in milk • 2 egg yolks • pinch of ground black pepper • 1 heaped tsp. salt • 1 gill sour cream.

Trim morels, remove stalks and put the heads aside. Chop the stalks coarsely, cut veal into 1-inch pieces. Heat 1 1/2 oz. lard in a saucepan, add the chopped stalks and meat, sprinkle with parsley and salt, cover and fry briskly for 20 minutes. Put aside to cool, then put through mincer, together with the well-squeezed-out roll. Add the egg yolks and stir throughly. Grease the bottom of an oblong fireproof dish. Fill morel heads with the stuffing and arrange them in the dish. Spoon sour cream over the morels and sprinkle with chopped parsley. Bake in a medium oven for about 1/2 hour.

Stuffed Tomatoes

Ingredients: 1 lb. left-over meat • 4 oz. cooked rice • 1 tsp. finely chopped parsley • 1 lb. even-sized fresh tomatoes • 1 tsp. salt • pinch of ground black pepper • 1 1/2 gills sour cream • 1 tsp. flour • 1 tsp. sugar • 1 oz. grated cheese • 2 oz. lard.

Cut off the stalk ends of tomatoes and scrape the insides into a bowl. Put meat through mincer, add cooked rice, chopped parsley, salt and pepper, stuff tomatoes with the mixture. Heat lard in a saucepan, add to it the carped-out tomato-pulp, together with 1 tsp. sugar. Stirring every now and then, cook pulp for 10–15 minutes, then press through sieve. Arrange the stuffed tomatoes in a greased fireproof dish. Mix sour cream, flour and tomato purée throughly, pour over the stuffed tomatoes, then cook in a medium hot oven for about 3/4 hour. Sprinkle a little grated cheese on top just before serving.

Stuffed Carrots in Casserole

Ingredients: 1 1/2 lb. carrots • 3 oz. cooked rice • 4 oz. mushrooms • 4 oz. butter • 2 gills sour cream • 1 tsp. salt.

Choose very thick, short carrots. Scrape, then cut carrots in half length-wise, cook in salt water for 20 minutes. Drain, then scrape out insides, leaving half-inch-thick shells. Heat 2 oz. butter in a saucepan, add finely chopped mushrooms, salt and allow to simmer till moisture evaporates. Add the rice and stir well together. Butter thickly the bottom of an oblong fireproof dish. Place a heaped tablespoonful of the stuffing into each half-carrot, and arrange them in the dish. Melt the remaining butter and mix with the sour cream. Pour this mixture over the stuffed carrots, cover and cook in a hot oven for 1/2 hour. Serve with mashed potatoes.

Green Pepper and Egg Casserole

Ingredients: 6 green peppers • 6 eggs • 2 oz. grated cheese • 2 oz. butter • 1 1/2 gills sour cream • 1 large tbsp. tomato purée • 1 tsp. salt.

Choose a deep round casserole. Cut off the stalk ends of the peppers, take out core and seeds. Butter casserole thickly, then fit peppers with open side upwards, tightly in the casserole. Put a dab of butter in the bottom of the peppers, then break one egg into each one and sprinkle thickly with grated cheese. Mix sour cream and tomato purée, spoon this mixture carefully over the peppers. Cook in a medium oven for 1/2 hour.

Special Egg and Ham Soufflé

Ingredients: 6 eggs • 1/2 lb. minced ham • 1 pint milk •
3 1/2 oz. cheese • 1 gill sour cream • 4 oz. flour • 3 oz. butter •
pinch of salt.

Beat well together egg yolks, sour cream, flour, add a pinch of salt and fold into the mixture the stiffly whipped egg whites. Boil the milk in a wide saucepan and, dipping a tablespoon first into the boiling milk, cut egg-sized dumplings from the mixture, placing each separately into the boiling milk. Strain off the milk as soon as the dumplings have risen to the top. Place a layer of the dumplings into a buttered casserole. Spread a thick layer of minced ham over it, add a spoonful melted butter, cover with the remaining dumplings. Sprinkle thickly with cheese, dot with small pieces of butter. Bake in a medium oven for 1/2 hour, then serve.

Summer Macaroni

Ingredients: 1/2 lb. macaroni • 1/2 lb. tomatoes • 1/2 lb. green
peppers • 2 oz. lard • 2 gills sour cream • 1 level tbsp. salt •
2 oz. grated cheese.

Boil macaroni in salt water, then drain, rinse. Choose small, even-sized tomatoes and peel them, first dipping in hot water. Core and slice pepper. Cut tomatoes in half. Grease thickly an oblong fireproof dish and put in the macaroni, tomatoes and sliced peppers in alternative layers. Sprinkle each layer generously with sour cream and melted lard. Top with a layer of grated cheese and cook in a medium oven for 3/4–1 hour.

Cottage-cheese Rissoles

Ingredients: 1 lb. cottage cheese • 3 eggs • 3 tbsp. flour • 1 level tsp. salt • toasted breadcrumbs • fat to fry.

Crumble cottage-cheese, add salt, 2 egg yolks, 2 heaped tbsp. flour and stiffly whipped egg whites. Shape round flat rissoles from the mixture, dip each in flour, then in beaten egg, and lastly, into toasted breadcrumbs. Fry rissoles in hot fat till both sides are nicely browned and serve immediately.

VEGETABLES AND GARNISHES

VEGETABLES

I mention here, at the beginning, that in Hungarian cooking nearly all the vegetables are prepared and served in a flavoured sauce, using roux or plain flour for thickening. These methods are practically unknown abroad. Here are the basic recipes for both types. The amounts are for 2 lb. of vegetables.

With Roux

Ingredients: 2 oz. lard • 1 1/2 oz. flour.

Heat lard in a saucepan, add flour and stirring constantly, fry to a goldenbrown colour. Pulling saucepan aside, add the flavourings according to the given recipe. Add a small ladleful of cold water or stock, stir, then pour the mixture over the vegetable. Bring to the boil, then allow to simmer for 10 minutes.

Without fat: 1 gill sour cream, 1/4 pint milk or stock, 1 tbsp. flour. Put the flour in a small dish and add liquid gradually, stirring constantly. The mixture must be smooth, without the tiniest lump. Pour it on the boiling vegetable, stir well. Reduce heat after adding the thickening and stir the food once or twice; just like other sauces it catches easily.

Potatoes in Sour Sauce

Ingredients: 2 lb. cooked potatoes • 2 oz. lard • 1 1/2 oz. flour •
1/2 tsp. pepper • 2 bay leaves • 1 tbsp. wine vinegar • 1 tsp. salt.

Prepare a medium-brown roux with lard and flour, pull saucepan aside, add paprika and 1/2 pint cold water or stock. Add vinegar, salt and bay leaves. Stirring constantly bring to the boil, add the sliced, cooked potatoes and allow to simmer for 10 minutes. Stir in the sour cream just before serving.

Potatoes in Tomato Sauce

Ingredients: 2 lb. cooked potatoes • 2 oz. lard • 1 1/2 oz. flour •
1 1/2 cup tomato juice • 1 tsp. granulated sugar • 1/2 tsp. salt •
1 rasher of streaky bacon.

Prepare a brown roux with lard and flour, dilute with the tomato juice, then add salt, sugar, and rasher of bacon. Bring to the boil, stirring constantly, then add sliced, cooked potatoes. Allow to simmer for 10 minutes before serving.

Braised Kohlrabi

Ingredients: 1 lb. young kohlrabis • 2 oz. lard • 1/2 tsp. salt •
1 tsp. granulated sugar • 1 tbsp. finely chopped parsley • 1/4 pint
stock or water • a pinch of ground black pepper.

Peel, then cut tender kohlrabis to cubes, together with some of the tender middle leaves. Heat lard in a saucepan, add sugar, stir till sugar is a golden brown colour. Pull aside, add 1/4 pint cold stock or water, the kohlrabis, parsley, salt and the pepper. Cover and allow to simmer till kohlrabis are tender. Stir once or twice while cooking. Serve as a garnish to roast meat.

Cauliflower au Gratin

Ingredients: 1 1/2 lb. cauliflower • 2 egg yolks • 2 gills sour cream • pinch of salt • 1/2 tsp. granulated sugar • 1 oz. grated cheese.

Cook cauliflower in salt water, drain, then put in a casserole. Mix 2 gills sour cream, 2 egg yolks, pinch of salt and sugar; pour this sauce over the cauliflower, sprinkle with grated cheese. Cook in a medium-hot oven for about 20–25 minutes. Serve in the casserole.

Cauliflower in Breadcrumbs

Ingredients: 1 1/2 lb. cauliflower • 2 oz. butter • 3 oz. breadcrumbs • 1 tsp. salt.

Cook cauliflower in salt water, drain. Heat butter in a saucepan, add breadcrumbs together with a pinch of salt, and, stirring constantly, fry till breadcrumbs are nicely browned. Spoon it over the cooked cauliflower, shaking the saucepan to coat the springs evenly with the breadcrumbs. Serve hot.

Brussels Sprouts

Ingredients: 1 1/2 lb. small Brussels sprouts • 1 tsp. salt • 2 oz. butter • 1 1/2 gills sour cream • 1 tbsp. breadcrumbs.

Cook Brussels sprouts in salt water, then drain. Put in a fireproof dish, mix melted butter and sour cream, spoon the mixture over the sprouts. Sprinkle with breadcrumbs and brown in a hot oven for 10–15 minutes.

Carrots in Parsley Sauce

Ingredients: 1 lb. carrots • 1 heaped tbsp. finely chopped parsley •
2 oz. lard • 1 1/2 oz. flour • 1 tsp. salt • 1 tsp. granulated sugar •
pinch of ground white pepper • 1 tbsp. cream.

Cut carrots into cubes. Heat lard in a saucepan, add sugar,
stir till sugar melts, then add carrots, chopped parsley, salt
and pepper. Add 1/4 pint cold water, cover and leave to simmer till carrots are tender. Sprinkle with flour and stir.
Adding 1 1/2 cup water or stock, bring to the boil and allow
to simmer for 10 minutes. Add a spoonful of cream just
before serving.

Asparagus in Butter Sauce

Ingredients: 1 1/2 lb. asparagus • 1 tsp. salt • 1 gill sour cream •
1/2 tsp. sugar • 1 heaped tbsp. flour • 2 oz. butter.

Trim asparagus, cut each piece in three. Scald, then cook in
salt water, to which 1/2 tsp. sugar has been added. Use just
enough water to cover. When cooked, mix the flour with
1 gill sour cream, add to the asparagus, then allow to simmer
for 10 minutes. Pull aside, stir in the cold butter and the
remaining sour cream, and serve immediately.

Asparagus in Parsley Sauce

Ingredients: 1 1/2 lb. asparagus • 1 tsp. salt • 1/2 tsp. sugar •
3 oz. butter • 2 oz. flour • 1 gill sour cream • 1 heaped tbsp. finely
chopped parsley.

Trim asparagus, then cut each piece in three. Blanch, then
cook in just enough salt water to cover, adding 1/2 tsp. sugar.
Heat butter in a saucepan, add flour, stir till frothy but still

quite white, then add finely chopped parsley. Pull aside, dilute with 1/4 pint milk, stir, then add sauce to the asparagus. Bring to the boil, then allow to simmer for 10 minutes. Add sour cream just before serving.

Creamed Spinach

Ingredients: 1 1/2 lb. spinach • 1 pint milk • 1 bread-roll • 3 oz. lard • 2 oz. flour • pinch of ground black pepper • 1 tsp. salt.

Cook the spinach in salt water, then pour into a colander and drain. Soak the bread-roll in the milk. Put spinach through fine mincer, together with roll. Pour the milk in which the roll was soaked over this purée, then put aside. Heat lard in a saucepan, add flour and, stirring, cook till light yellow, then add the pepper. Put the diluted purée over the roux and stirring constantly bring to the boil. Allow to simmer for 10 minutes before serving.

Spinach Rissoles

Ingredients: 1 lb. spinach • 1 bread-roll soaked in milk • 1 tsp. salt • pinch of grated nutmeg • 2 eggs • toasted breadcrumbs

Cook the spinach in salt water, pour into a colander when cooked and drain well. Put through the mincer together with the well squeezed-out roll. Add a pinch of salt, grated nutmeg, 1 tsp. flour, 1 egg. Mix well, shape small rissoles, dip in flour, beaten egg and toasted breadcrumbs. Pat with your palms to make breadcrumbs stick. Fry quickly in deep fat, lifting the basket out once or twice to let steam escape. Serve with mushroom sauce or with cheese sauce.

Spinach au Gratin

Ingredients: 2 lb. spinach • 1 heaped tbsp. salt • 3 1/2 oz. butter •
2 oz. flour • 1/2 pint milk • 3 oz. grated cheese • pinch of ground
white pepper • a pinch of paprika.

Cook spinach in salt water, pour on a sieve to drain. Prepare
cheese sauce: heat 3 oz. butter in a saucepan, add flour, stir
till frothy but still white. Add milk, pepper and grated cheese,
and, stirring constantly, cook till sauce thickens. Butter a fireproof dish and put in half of the coarsely chopped spinach.
Spoon on it an even layer of cheese sauce and repeat the
procedure. Sprinkle top with a pinch of paprika and bake in
a fairly hot oven without cover for about 20 minutes. Serve
in the casserole.

Celeriac Fritters

Ingredients: 1 1/2 lb. celeriac • batter made with about 3/4 cup wine
(or wine and water) • the stiffly whipped whites of 2 eggs • salt.

Wash celeriac and cook in salt water till tender. Cool, then
peel and cut into thick slices. Sprinkle with salad oil, put
aside. Prepare thick pancake batter with the wine and some
water, fold in the stiffly whipped egg whites last. Dip the
slices of celeriac in the batter with the help of a fork, and fry
in deep hot fat. Drain on absorbent paper and serve hot.

Stuffed Celeriac

Ingredients: 1 1/2 lb. even celeriac • 4 oz. mushrooms •
3 oz. grated cheese • 2 oz. butter • 1/2 gill sour cream • salt.

Cook the peeled celeriac in salt water till nearly done. Lift
out and scoop out insides carefully. Chop mushrooms finely

together with the scooped-out bits of celeriac, mix with the grated cheese. Stuff the celeriac with this mixture, place in a fireproof dish. Put 1 tsp. sour cream and a knob of butter on the top of each. Bake in a medium oven for 1/2 hour, then serve.

Haricot Beans in Onion Sauce

Ingredients: 1 lb. haricot beans •
1 pint smoked–meat or vegetable stock • 2 bay leaves •
2 oz. flour • 1 small onion • 1/2 tsp. paprika • 1/2 gill sour cream.

Soak beans overnight in 1 pint water to which a pinch of bicarbonate of soda has been added. Strain, then wash the beans and put on to cook on enough water or stock to cover 3–4 inches. Add bay leaves, bring to the boil, then allow to simmer slowly till beans are tender. Prepare a medium-brown roux with the lard and flour, pull aside, add finely chopped onions and paprika. Dilute with 1/4 pint cold water or stock, stir well, and pour over the beans. Bring to the boil, then allow to simmer for 10 minutes. Add sour cream, boil up again, then serve as a garnish to boiled bacon or smoked meat of any kind.

Haricot Beans in Paprika Sauce

Ingredients: 1/2 lb. cooked haricot beans • 1 1/2 oz. lard •
1 medium-sized onion • 1 tsp. paprika • 1/4 pint stock •
1 green pepper • 1/2 clove of garlic • 1 fresh tomato.

Heat lard in a saucepan, add finely chopped onions, fry till onions are golden. Pull the saucepan aside, add the thoroughly crushed garlic, green pepper and tomato cut in two, paprika, stock and the beans. Cover and allow to simmer till gravy is absorbed. Serve on toast or on fried bread with fried bacon.

French Beans in Brown Sauce

Ingredients: 2 lb. green beans • 2 oz. lard • 1 1/2 oz. flour • 1 small onion • 1/3 tsp. paprika • 1 gill sour cream • 1 tsp. salt.

Top and tail, then cut beans into 2-inch pieces. Cook in enough salt water to cover. Prepare a golden-brown roux with the lard and flour, pull aside, add grated onions and paprika, dilute with the cooled water strained off the cooked beans. Stir, then pour sauce over the beans and allow to simmer for 10 minutes. Add sour cream 5 minutes before serving.

French Beans in Tomato Sauce

Ingredients: 2 lb. green beans • 2 oz. lard • 1 1/2 oz. flour • 1 tsp. salt • 1 heaped tsp. granulated sugar • 1 rasher of bacon • 3 tbsp. thick tomato purée • 1 tbsp. cream.

Slice the beans and put on to cook, together with salt, in just enough water to cover. Prepare a medium-brown roux with the lard and flour, dilute with 1/4 pint cold water, pour over the beans. Stir, then add tomato purée, sugar, and slice of bacon. Simmer for 10 minutes, then serve.

French Beans in Casserole

Ingredients: 1 lb. green beans • 1/2 lb. tomatoes • 1 tbsp. salt • 1 1/2 gills sour cream • 1 1/2 oz. butter • the yolk of 1 egg.

Top and tail beans, cook in boiling salt water. Strain off the water when cooked and arrange half in a buttered fireproof dish. Put a layer of sliced tomatoes on it, sprinkle with a little salt, add beans again, cover with sliced tomatoes. Melt butter, and mix with the egg yolk and sour cream. Pour over the top layer of tomatoes. Put casserole in a fairly hot oven and cook for 20–25 minutes. If preferred, a little grated cheese can be sprinkled on top. Serve in the casserole.

Green Peas in Parsley Sauce

Ingredients: 2 lb. green peas • 1 heaped tbsp. finely chopped parsley • 2 oz. butter • 1 heaped tsp. granulated sugar • 2 oz. flour • 1 tsp. salt.

Shell peas, then pick out the tender shells and those with undeveloped peas, put them on to cook in 1 pint mildly salted water, after 1/2 hours cooking put aside to cool. Heat the butter, add sugar, stir till it melts but do not brown, then add green peas and parsley. Add some of the stock off the shells, a pinch of salt, then cover and allow to simmer slowly till peas are tender and the stock evaporates. Sprinkle with flour, stir, then add the remaining stock, bring to the boil, and allow to simmer for 10 minutes. Serve in a deep dish or casserole.

Braised Green Peas

Ingredients: 1 1/2 lb. shelled peas • 2 tsp. granulated sugar • 1 heaped tbsp. finely chopped parsley • 1 oz. lard • 1 large ladleful of cold chicken stock or water • pinch of salt.

Heat lard, add sugar. Brown to a golden colour, pull saucepan aside and pour in the stock or water. Add peas, salt and parsley, cover and allow to simmer till peas are tender. The gravy under it should be quite short by them. Serve as garnish to mixed grill or fried liver and bacon.

Vegetable Marrow in Dill Sauce

Ingredients: 2 lb. tender vegetable marrow • 1 heaped tbsp. salt • 2 oz. lard • 1 1/2 oz. flour • 1/2 tsp. paprika • 1 heaped tbsp. finely chopped fresh or dried dill • 1 level tsp. sugar • 1 gill sour cream.

Peel young vegetable marrow, cut in two, scrape out inside. Cut marrow into thin strips and, putting it in a dish, sprinkle with 1 tbsp. salt. Leave to stand for 1/2 hour, then drain off liquid, pressing the marrow well between your hands to remove surplus juice. Prepare light-yellow roux in a saucepan from the lard and flour, pull aside and add chopped dill and paprika. Put in the squeezed-out marrow, add 1/4 pint cold water and the sugar, stir, cover and allow to simmer for about 1/2 hour, stirring every now and then. After this time add the sour cream, cook for 5 more minutes and serve.

French Vegetables

Ingredients: 3 oz. each of asparagus • green peas • carrots • cauliflower • savoy cabbage • 2 oz. of spinach • 1 oz. sorrel • 1 heaped tbsp. finely chopped parsley • 4 oz. butter • 1 1/2 gills sour cream • 1 tbsp. tomato purée • about 1 tbsp. salt • 1 level tsp. granulated sugar.

Cook vegetables except spinach and sorrel, separately in salt water. Cook the chopped spinach and sorrel in very little butter. Strain and mix vegetables when ready, with the exception of spinach and sorrel mixture. Melt butter in a saucepan, pull aside, then add sour cream, parsley, spinach and sorrel, a tbsp. tomato purée, pinch of salt, sugar. Put on low heat and stir till sauce thickens. Pour over the mixed vegetables. Serve hot.

Braised Cabbage

Ingredients: 2 lb. red cabbage • 1 oz. granulated sugar •
1 level tbsp. salt • 1/4 cup vinegar • pinch of ground back pepper •
3 oz. lard.

Remove all outer leaves, then slice cabbage to very thin strips. Mix well with salt and leave to stand for 1/2 hour. Then squeeze out the liquid by pressing handfuls of cabbage between your palms, pour off the liquid. Heat lard in a saucepan, add sugar, stir till sugar turns to a pale yellow colour. Pull aside, add the squeezed-out cabbage, pepper, and the vinegar mixed with 1/4 cup water. If you like the taste, add a piece of bacon-rind as well. Cover and allow to simmer slowly till all moisture evaporates. Stir once or twice, to prevent burning. Serve with roast pork, boiled bacon or smoked meat.

GARNISHES

Potato Casserole

Ingredients: 2 lb. cooked potatoes • 1 medium-sized onion •
2 oz. lard • 2 tbsp. sour cream • 1 tsp. salt.

Slice cold boiled potatoes, put in a basin. Heat lard, add finely chopped onions and fry till golden-yellow. Pour over the potatoes, add 2 tbsp. sour cream, salt, mix well together. Grease a casserole, put the potatoes in, press down top with your palm. Brush top thickly with sour cream. Bake in a hot oven for 1/2 hour. Take casserole out of the oven, cover with lid; in 4–5 minutes you can turn out onto a flat dish; it will retain its shape.

Potato Purée

Ingredients: 2 lb. potatoes • 3 oz. butter • about 1/4 cup milk •
pinch of ground white pepper • 1 tsp. salt.

Choose mealy kind of potatoes. Peel, then cut into cubes, cook in salt water till potatoes are tender. Strain water well. Shaking the drained potatoes over heat for a minute or two will remove surplus moisture. Add cold butter cut to pieces and mash thoroughly; add pepper and milk, beat till creamy. Serve immediately.

Potatoes in Horse-radish Sauce

Ingredients: 1 lb. potatoes • the juice of 1/2 lemon •
2 tbsp. grated horse-radish • 1 1/2 oz. butter • 1 tbsp. flour •
1 1/2 gills of sour cream • pinch of sugar •
1/2 tsp. salt.

Boil potatoes in their skins, peel, then cut to cubes. Sprinkle with salt and put aside. Heat butter in a saucepan, add flour, fry till frothy but still white, add sour cream, sugar and grated horse-radish and, stirring constantly, allow to simmer for 5–6 minutes. Pour it on the potatoes, add lemon juice, mix well. Serve hot with boiled beef.

Potatoes in Paprika Sauce

Ingredients: 1 1/2 lb. potatoes • 3 oz. lard • 1 large onion •
1 rasher bacon • 1 tsp. salt • 1 tsp. paprika • 1 green pepper •
1 fresh tomato.

Peel potatoes, cut them in four. Heat lard, add finely chopped onion, fry till golden. Pull aside and add paprika, sliced green pepper, tomato, potatoes, salt and a slice of bacon. Stir. Bring to the boil, then reduce heat and add just enough water to cover. Cook on low heat under lid, till potatoes are ready. Serve in a deep dish; sprinkle the top with a spoonful of sour cream.

Boiled Potato-and–cheese Dumplings

Ingredients: 1 lb. cooked mashed potatoes • 3 eggs •
3 oz. grated cheese • 4 oz. butter.

Cream the butter, with 3 whole eggs, add mashed potatoes, and 2 heaped tbsp. grated cheese. Mix well, then shape into dumplings. Cook in fast boiling salt water. When ready, strain, then turn in grated cheese. Serve hot, piled up on a flat plate.

Fried Potato-and–cheese Dumplings

Ingredients: 3–4 lb. cooked mashed potatoes • 1 oz. butter • 3 eggs •
5 oz. grated cheese.

Beat well together the egg yolks, softened butter and grated cheese. Knead together with mashed potatoes. Lastly mix in the stiffly beaten egg whites. Form dumplings between your floured palms, fry in hot deep fat till golden-brown. Drain in absorbent paper. Serve hot as garnish to game.

Potato Croquettes

Ingredients: 1 1/2 lb. mashed potatoes • 2 eggs • 2 tbsp. semolina •
1 tsp. salt • pinch of grated nutmeg • 1 oz. toasted breadcrumbs.

Mix mashed potatoes, semolina, salt, grated nutmeg and eggs. Knead well together, then shape mixture into croquettes. Roll in toasted breadcrumbs and fry in hot deep fat. Serve immediately.

Rice with Mushroom

Ingredients: 1/2 lb. rice • 3 oz. lard • 1/4 lb. mushrooms • 1 heaped tsp. salt • 1 heaped tbsp. finely chopped parsley • a good pinch of ground black pepper • about 1 pint of stock or water.

Heat 1 oz. lard in a saucepan, add coarsely chopped mushrooms, a pinch of salt and the parsley. Cover and allow to simmer till water evaporates. Put aside. Heat the remaining 2 oz. lard in a larger saucepan, add rice and stir till it becomes opaque but still white. Pull aside, add mushrooms, salt and pepper, pour cold water or stock on. The liquid should just, cover the rice. Cover and bring to the boil, then reduce heat and allow to simmer very slowly indeed, till rice is soft (about 30 minutes). Stir once, just before serving, very carefully, to avoid breaking the rice (each grain must be separate). Serve hot.

Savoury Rice

Ingredients: 1 cup rice • 2 oz. butter • 2 oz. grated carrots •
2 oz. grated celeriac • 1 green pepper • 1/2 lb. tomatoes •
3 oz. grated cheese • 1 heaped tsp. salt.

Heat butter in a saucepan, then add rice. Stir till rice is just beginning to turn light-yellow, add the cored green pepper cut in two, grated vegetables, salt sand 2 cups water. Cover and allow to simmer slowly under lid for 1/2 hour. Cut tomatoes in half and fry in lard, or dripping. Remove the green pepper. Heap up rice on a round plate. Put the fried toma-toes over it, then sprinkle with grated cheese. Serve hot.

Galushka (Midget Dumplings)

Ingredients: 10 oz. flour • 1/2 oz. lard • 3/4 cup water •
1 heaped tbsp. semolina • 2 oz. butter • 1 level tsp. salt.

Cream the lard, add the flour, semolina, salt and the water. Mix ingredients together with the help of a wooden spoon to a medium-soft consistency. Form small dumplings with a teaspoon dipped into hot water, drop the dumplings into slowly boiling salt water. Melt butter in a saucepan. Using a perforated ladle, lift out dumplings as soon as they have risen to the top; place them in the melted butter. Shake the saucepan once or twice to prevent sticking. Serve as a garnish with any kind of meat prepared in paprika sauce.

Midget Dumplings in Cheese Sauce

Ingredients: 2 eggs • 1 cup milk • pinch of salt •
flour to make a soft dough • 1 oz. butter • cheese sauce.

Beat well together the milk and egg, add salt and enough flour to bring to a soft, runny consistency. Form small dumplings with the help of a teaspoon, drop them in slowly boiling salt water. Melt butter in a saucepan. Using a perfo-rated ladle, lift out dumplings as soon as they have risen, place in the melted butter. Shake the saucepan once or twice to prevent sticking. Put dumplings in a fireproof dish, pour cheese sauce over and brown top in hot oven. Serve in the casserole.

Boiled Cheese Dumplings

Ingredients: 5–6 bread-rolls • 1/2 pint vegetable stock • 3 oz. butter •
pinch of salt • 4 eggs • 3 oz. grated cheese.

Cut rolls into cubes, and, putting in a saucepan, spoon the
stock over. Add 1 1/2 oz. butter and a pinch of salt, cook on
medium heat, stirring constantly, for about 10–15 minutes.
Put aside to cool. When cold add 2 whole eggs and 2 eggs
yolks, stir well, then add the stiffly whipped whites of 2 eggs
and the grated cheese. Shape into dumplings and cook in
slowly boiling salt water. Serve in a deep dish. Pour 1 1/2 oz.
Hot butter over dumplings just before serving.

Hungarian Macaroni

Ingredients: 1/2 lb. macaroni • 3 oz. lard • 1 small onion •
1 tsp. each of finely chopped parsley • fresh dill • marjoram •
tarragon and savory • 1 tbsp. flour • 1 tsp. salt • 2 gills sour cream •
1 tbsp. tomato purée • 1 green pepper.

Cook macaroni in boiling salt water, then drain. Heat lard in
a saucepan, add finely chopped onion, cook till golden, then
add green pepper cored and cut in four, and the herbs.
Cover and cook slowly for about 10 minutes. Sprinkle with
flour, then add the sour cream and tomato purée. Stir, bring
to the boil, remove green pepper, then add cooked macaroni. Heat up and serve.

SALADS

Lettuce Salad

Ingredients: 3 fresh, firm lettuces • 1/4 cup wine vinegar •
1 tsp. sugar • 1 tsp. French mustard • 1 tbsp. salad oil • salt •
3 hard-boiled eggs.

Mix sugar, vinegar, salad oil, salt and mustard: dilute with
1/2 cup water. Put the quartered lettuce in a porcelain or
earthenware salad bowl, cut hard-boiled eggs in four,
arrange on top. Spoon the well-mixed salad-dressing over
the lettuce 1/4 hour before serving. I always rub the inside of
the bowl with a cut piece of garlic; it definitely improves the
flavour.

Lettuce with Sour Cream Dressing

Ingredients: 3 fresh, firm lettuces • 1 1/2 gills sour cream •
pinch of salt • 1 tsp. sugar • the juice of 1 lemon.

Cut lettuce to finger-wide strips. Mix sour cream with salt,
sugar and lemon juice. Pour dressing over lettuce 1/4 hour
before serving. Turn the lettuce with a fork once or twice
during this time.

Cucumber Salad

Ingredients: 1 lb. cucumber • 1 tbsp. salt •
dressing (see lettuce salad) • a pinch of paprika •
a pinch of ground black pepper.

Slice cucumbers thinly, put in a bowl and salt. Stir, then leave to stand for 1 hour. Now press liquid out of sliced cucumbers, then place in salad-bowl. Pour salad-dressing over, add paprika and black pepper, stir and leave to stand in a cold place for at least 1 hour. Sprinkle the top just before serving with a little paprika and ground black pepper.

Cucumber Salad in Dill Dressing

Ingredients: 1 lb. cucumbers • 1 tbsp. finely chopped fresh dill • 1 gill sour cream • 2 tbsp. wine vinegar • 1 tsp. sugar • salt.

Slice, salt, then squeeze cucumbers as for cucumber salad. Mix sour cream, chopped dill, sugar and vinegar. Mix cucumbers with the dressing; leave to stand for at least 1 hour in a cold place before serving.

Green Pepper Salad

Ingredients: 1 lb. green peppers • 1 small onion • 1/2 tsp. salt • 1/4 cup wine vinegar • 1/2 cup water • 1 tsp. sugar.

Core, then cut nice, light-coloured peppers into strips. Place in a colander, pour boiling hot water over, drain. Mix vinegar and water, add a pinch of salt, the sugar and the very thinly sliced onion. Put in a saucepan and bring to the boil. Allow to cool. Place sliced peppers in a bowl, pour salad dressing over it, then leave to stand for 1 hour before serving.

Tomato Salad

Ingredients: 1 lb. nice firm tomatoes • 1/2 tsp. salt • 1 tsp. sugar • 1 tbsp. salad oil • 1/2 cup water • the juice of 1 lemon.

Dip ripe, firm tomatoes in boiling water, pull off skins. Slice, then put in a salad bowl, sprinkle with salt, sugar and salad oil. Mix water and lemon juice, pour over the tomatoes. Leave to stand for 1 hour before serving.

Radish Salad

Ingredients: About 1/2 lb. of radishes • 1 tsp. salt • 1 tsp. salad oil • pinch of ground black pepper • the juice of 1/2 lemon • 1 tsp. finely chopped chives.

Top and tail the small pink radishes, cut into slices. Put radishes into a salad bowl, sprinkle with salt, cover, and allow to stand for 10 minutes. Then add the oil, ground pepper and lemon juice, stir well, and sprinkle top with chives. Cool, then serve.

Asparagus Salad

Ingredients: 1 lb. asparagus • mayonnaise • 1/2 tsp. salt • 1 tsp. sugar.

Cut asparagus into 2-inch pieces. Cook in boiling salt water, add sugar while cooking. Drain when ready, allow to cool, then mix asparagus with mayonnaise. Chill, then serve.

Cauliflower Salad

Ingredients: 1 lb. cooked cauliflower • 1 1/2 gills sour cream • 2 egg yolks • pinch of salt • pinch of sugar • 1 1/2 tbsp. salad oil • 1/2 tsp. mustard • 2 tbsp. wine vinegar.

Pull cauliflowers into springs, place in a salad bowl. Put sour cream and egg yolks in double saucepan, add salt and sugar and cook, stirring constantly, till sauce thickens. Leave to cool. When quite cold add the oil by degrees, then the French mustard, and lastly the vinegar. Pour dressing over the cauliflower, and leave to stand for at least 2 hours before serving.

French Beans Salad

Ingredients: 1 lb. cooked beans • 1/4 pint wine vinegar • 1/2 tsp. salt • 1/2 tsp. granulated sugar • 1 small onion • 1 tbsp. salad oil.

Mix, in a small saucepan, vinegar with salt, sugar, thinly sliced onion and 1/4 pint water. Bring to the boil, then simmer for 5 minutes. Put aside to cool. Put beans into a salad-bowl, sprinkle with salad oil. Pour the cold salad–dressing over it and leave to stand for 1 hour or 2 before serving.

French Salad

Ingredients: Cooked green peas • green beans • potatoes • carrots and celeriac • 1 dill cucumber • 1 large sour apple • tartare sauce.

Cut cooked green beans to 1-inch pieces; add peas, the potatoes, carrots and celeriac to cubes. Peel and cut into cubes the cucumber and the apple. Mix well together with tartare sauce. Chill for at least 2 hours before serving.

Potato Salad

Ingredients: 1 1/2 lb. cooked potatoes • 1/4 cup wine vinegar • 1/2 tsp. salt • 1 tsp. sugar • 1 medium-sized onion • 2 tbsp. salad oil • 1/3 tsp. ground black pepper.

Cut boiled potatoes into medium-thick slices. Put into a salad-bowl, sprinkle with oil. Mix, in a small saucepan, the vinegar, salt, sugar, thinly sliced onion and about 1/4 pint or more of water. Bring to the boil, then while still hot, pour over the potatoes. Mix, then sprinkle top with a good pinch of ground black pepper. Leave to stand for at least 2 hours before serving. If you like, a few slices of cooked celeriac may be added.

Haricot Beans Salad

Ingredients: 1 lb. cooked haricot beans • 1 large onion • 1/4 pint wine vinegar • 1/2 tsp. salt • pinch of ground black pepper • 1 tsp. sugar • 2 firm tomatoes.

Rub the inside of the salad-bowl with a cut piece of garlic. Put in the cooked beans together with the thinly sliced onion, mix vinegar, sugar, salt and pepper with 1/4 pint water, pour over the beans. Skin tomatoes, cut into slices, arrange on the top of the salad. Bean salad is best prepared the day before, but 2–3 hours chilling is enough at a pinch.

Mixed Vegetable Salad

Ingredients: Cooked root vegetables left from making vegetable stock • 2 large tart apples • 1/2 lb. cooked potatoes • tartare sauce.

Use vegetable — carrots, parsnips, celeriac, kohlrabi, turnips, etc. — out of the vegetable stock pot. Cut vegetables into cubes together with peeled apples and boiled potatoes. Mix with tartare sauce, keep in a cool place for an hour before serving.

Summer Salad

Ingredients: Cooked green peas • green beans • cauliflower and potatoes • 3 fresh green peppers • 3–4 firm tomatoes • 1 tsp. salt • pinch of ground black pepper • 1 1/2 tbsp. salad oil • 1 tsp. granulated sugar • 2 hard-boiled eggs.

Cut the cooked vegetables into cubes, core and slice green peppers, skin and slice tomatoes. Mix in a salad-bowl, add salt, pepper and oil, stir and leave to stand for 1 hour. Mix vinegar and sugar with 1/4 pint water, stir till sugar dissolves then pour over the salad. Sprinkle top with coarsely chopped hardboiled eggs, decorate with thinly sliced cucumber. Chill for 1 hour, then serve.

Red Cabbage Salad

Ingredients: 1 lb. red cabbage • 1 tbsp. salt • 1/4 pint wine vinegar • 1/2 tsp. crushed caraway seeds • 1 heaped tsp. granulated sugar • 1 small onion.

Cut cabbage into very thin strips. Put in a bowl, sprinkle the salt over, stir, then stand for 1/2 hour. Pour on a sieve and drain. Then put in a saladbowl, and pour over the following salad–dressing: 1/4 pint wine vinegar, sugar, crushed caraway seeds and a little finely grated onion. Mix well, and leave to stand for 2 hours.

PASTAS, PASTRIES, SWEETS, CAKES AND CREAMS

BOILED PASTA AND NOODLE PUDDINGS

How to Prepare Pasta

Ingredients: 1 lb. flour • 1 egg • 1 tsp. salt • 1/4 cup lukewarm water.

While it is true that you can buy dried pasta of every form and size and of an excellent quality at continental grocers, the preparation of pasta is unavoidable in making ravioli, for example, or green noodles. Surplus eggs, too, could be used this way, and the pasta dried and stored for future use. It keeps for a very long time, and has a high nutritive value.

Sieve the flour into a wide bowl. Make a hole in the centre, add egg, lukewarm water and salt. Knead well together; the dough should be rather stiff and well worked. Cut the dough in two and put one part in the middle of a floured pastry-board. Cover the other piece with a cloth to prevent drying while you work with the first lot. Roll out the dough to the thickness of a matchstick, flouring the pasta every now and then to prevent sticking. Leave to dry for 20 minutes, then cut to the desired shape. Shake pasta between your hands onto a cloth. Repeat procedure with the other half. Now the pasta is ready to cook in boiling salt water, but you can leave to dry if desired, and store in airy muslin bags when completely dried.

Plum Dumplings

Ingredients: 1 lb. cooked potatoes • 1 egg • pinch of salt •
1/2 oz. butter • 1/2 lb. flour • 4 oz. coarsely chopped walnuts •
pinch of ground cinnamon • 3 oz. castor sugar •
1 lb. stoned plums.

Put hot boiled potatoes through sieve, add flour, salt, butter
and egg. Knead into a soft dough, put on a floured pastry-
board and roll out to the thickness of your finger. Cut into
palm-sized squares. Put a stoned plum in the middle of each
square. Mix the coarsely chopped walnuts with sugar and a
good pinch of ground cinnamon. Put half a teaspoonful of
this mixture into each plum, then pinching the dough together on the top, roll the squares into dumplings between your
floured palms. Put dumplings into boiling, slightly salted
water, and cook till they rise. Lift out, then roll each into the
remaining walnut and sugar mixture. Arrange dumplings in
a fireproof dish. Serve hot.

Cabbage Dumplings

Ingredients: 1/2 lb. flour • 1 oz. butter • 1 egg • a good pinch of salt •
enough water to make a soft dough • 1 lb. cabbage • 1 heaped tsp.
salt • 1 tbsp. sugar • pinch of ground black pepper • 2 oz. lard •
2 oz. grated cheese.

Make a fairly soft dough with flour, butter, pinch of salt, 1
egg and some water. Put on a floured pastry-board and roll
out to finger-thickness. Grate a firm head of cabbage, sprinkle with salt, leave to stand for 1/2 hour. Heat lard, brown
sugar in it, then add well squeezed-out grated cabbage.
Stirring constantly fry till cabbage is nicely browned. Add
ground black pepper, then spread the mixture over the
rolled-out dough, leaving a strip of the edge empty. Now roll

up the dough into a long, narrow shape, and cut to 2-inch pieces with the edge of a plate. Shape the pieces lightly between your palms into dumplings, drop them in plenty of boiling salt water. Lift dumplings out when ready, roll into grated cheese, and serve hot.

Cottage-cheese Dumplings

Ingredients: 1 1/2 oz. butter • pinch of salt • 3 eggs • 1 lb. cottage cheese • 3 tbsp. semolina • 3 oz. lard • 1 gill sour cream • 3 oz. toasted breadcrumbs.

Press cottage-cheese through sieve. Beat well together 3 egg yolks, softened butter, pinch of salt. Add cottage-cheese and semolina, mix well. Lastly fold in the stiffly whipped egg whites. Shape dumplings with hands dipped in water, drop in plenty of boiling, slightly salted water. Roll cooked dumplings in breadcrumbs browned in lard, serve in a hot dish with the sour cream sprinkled on top. Some people also sprinkle, castor sugar on top of the dumplings.

Potato Noodles

Ingredients: 1 lb. cooked potatoes • about 7 oz. flour • 1 tsp. salt • 1 egg • 3 oz. lard • 2 oz. breadcrumbs.

Press potatoes through sieve. Add salt, flour and egg and knead into a medium-soft dough, adding a little more flour if necessary. Put dough on a floured pastry-board and roll out to finger-thickness. Flour top well, cut dough first into 2-inch wide strips, then cut strip across to finger-wide noodles. Roll each noodle lightly on the pastry-board with your floured palm, then throw into plenty of boiling salt water. Heat lard in a saucepan and fry the breadcrumbs in it to a golden-brown colour. Drain cooked noodles thoroughly, then add to the fired breadcrumbs. Shake saucepan to coat noodles evenly, then serve in a heated dish.

Walnut Noodle Pudding

Ingredients: 1/2 lb. dried (or 1 lb. freshly made) noodles •
3 oz. butter • 3 oz. damson jam • 6 oz. coarsely ground walnuts •
2 oz. sugar • salt.

Cook noodles in plenty of boiling salt water, drain well, then shake in a bowl with 2 oz. of melted butter. Mix coarsely ground walnuts with sugar, add to the noodles. Butter a deep fireproof dish. Put in half of the noodles, add a good thick layer of damson jam, then cover with the other half of the noodles. Put in a hot oven and bake for 20 minutes. Serve in the casserole, first loosening sides with a knife or spatula.

Poppy Seed Noodle Pudding

Ingredients: 1 lb. freshly made (or 1/2 lb. dried) noodles •
3 oz. butter • 6 oz. finely ground poppy seeds • grated peel of
1/2 lemon • 1 oz. castor sugar • 2 tbsp. honey • 3 oz. sultanas • salt.

Poppy seed — contrary to popular belief — does not have soporific properties. It is wholesome, and its excellent flavour makes it a favourite at any table. You can buy poppy seed in continental groceries. Ask them to grind it for you; poppy seeds left whole are not palatable.

Cook noodles in plenty of slightly salted boiling water. Heat in a saucepan 2 oz. butter, mix in the cooked and well–drained noodles. Add ground poppy seed, 1 oz. of sugar, the grated peel of 1/2 lemon, and the sultanas. Mix well, pour into a deep buttered fireproof dish, and bake in a hot oven for 20 minutes. Take dish out of oven, cover and allow to stand for 4–5 minutes. Then, first loosening the sides carefully with a knife, turn out onto a flat warmed dish. Pour warmed-up honey over the top and serve.

Noodles with Egg

Ingredients: 1/4 lb. dried noodles • 6 eggs • 2 oz. lard • salt.

Cook noodles in plenty of well-salted water, then drain well. Heat 2 oz. lard in a saucepan, add cooked noodles, stir. Beat eggs well with a pinch of salt. Pour over the noodles and stirring constantly cook till eggs just begin to set. Serve immediately in a hot dish.

Layered Noodles

Ingredients: 1/2 lb. dried noodles • 2 oz. butter • 4 oz. coarsely ground walnuts • 4 oz. apricot jam • 1 oz. granulated sugar • salt.

Cook noodles in slightly salted water. Drain well, then shake in 1 oz. melted butter. Put one third in a separate bowl and mix with the apricot jam, sugar and ground walnut. Butter a fireproof dish, put half of the white noodles in the bottom. Spread the flavoured mixture on it, cover with the remaining third of the noodles. Cook in a hot oven for 15–20 minutes. Serve in the fireproof dish.

Noodles with Cottage-cheese

Ingredients: 1/2 lb. noodles • 7 oz. cottage-cheese • 1 tsp. finely chopped fresh or dried dill • 2 oz. fat bacon • 1 1/2 gills sour cream.

Cook noodles in plenty of salt water. Cut bacon into small cubes meantime, and fry on low heat till crisp. Lift out bacon, put aside. Drain the cooked noodle, then put into the bacon-fat in the saucepan. Lower heat under saucepan then add sour cream. Stir, pull aside and add the crumbled cottage-cheese and chopped dill. Put immediately into a hot dish, sprinkle the chopped, fried bacon on top and serve.

Egg Squares with Fried Cabbage

Ingredients: 1/2 lb. egg squares • 1 lb. hard white cabbage • 1 level tbsp. salt • 3 oz. lard • 1 tbsp. granulated sugar • a generous pinch of ground black pepper.

Grate the cabbage, then put in a bowl and sprinkle with salt. Allow to stand for 1/2 hour. Heat lard in a wide saucepan, add sugar and, stirring constantly, brown to a golden-brown colour. Take handfuls of the grated cabbage, press well between your hands to remove surplus moisture, then put in the lard. Stir till cabbage is nicely browned, then add pepper. Cook egg squares in boiling salt water, drain, then mix with fried cabbage. Serve hot.

Ham and Pasta Pudding

Ingredients: 1/2 lb. egg squares • 2 oz. butter • 7 oz. lean minced ham • 1 1/2 gills sour cream • yolk of 1 egg • 2 oz. grated cheese • salt.

Cook egg squares in plenty of boiling salt water. Heat 1 1/2 oz. butter in saucepan, add the cooked and well–drained egg squares. Mix in a separate bowl the minced ham, egg yolk, sour cream and grated cheese. Add this mixture to the pasta, stir well, then pour into a buttered fireproof dish. Bake in a hot oven for 20 minutes. Serve hot.

Strapachka (Shepherd's Dumplings)

Ingredients: 1 1/2 lb. potatoes • about 4–5 oz. flour • 1 tsp. salt •
2 oz. lard • 5 oz. grated or crumbled ewe's cheese • 1 tsp. finely
chopped chives.

Peel, then grate potatoes on coarse grater. Add salt and
enough flour to make a soft dough. Stir with wooden spoon
for 2–3 minutes. Have ready plenty of boiling salt water. Dip
tablespoon in the hot water and shaping the dough with it,
drop dumplings in the boiling water. Strain when cooked,
heat lard in a saucepan, and add dumplings. Shake saucepan
to prevent sticking. Turn dumplings on a hot dish, sprinkle
with plenty of ewe's cheese and 1 tsp. finely chopped chives.
Serve immediately.

FRIED DOUGH, PANCAKES
AND FRITTERS

Carnival Doughnuts

Ingredients: 1/2 pint milk • 4 lumps sugar • 1 oz. yeast • 4 egg yolks •
pinch of salt • 1 lb. flour • 4 oz. butter.

You can make feather-light doughnuts if you follow this
recipe. Put in a small bowl 4 lumps of sugar, the crumbled
yeast and 1/4 cups lukewarm milk. Cover with a piece of tis-
sue-paper, allow to rise. Take a deep bowl, put in the egg
yolks, pinch of salt, the risen yeast, lukewarm milk, flour and
nearly cool melted butter. Beat constantly with a wooden
spoon till dough is well beaten and smooth. Cover bowl with

a warmed cloth, and keep warm. After 1 hour, flour well the pastry-board, turn the dough onto it and roll out lightly to finger-thickness. Stamp out with doughnut cutter, cover with floured cloth and leave to rise for another 1/2 hour. Heat oil in deep fryer. It should be hot, but not smoking hot; regulate temperature carefully. Put a few doughnuts in the hot oil, cover with lid. Look at them after 3–4 minutes, if doughnuts are nicely browned, turn them with the help of a slicer and fry the other side, now without lid. Lift doughnuts out onto absorbent paper, and keep hot while the rest are frying. Sprinkle with castor sugar and serve hot or cold with apricot sauce.

Doughnuts Made of Rétes Pastry

Ingredients: 1 lb. flour • 1 egg • 1 1/2 oz. lard • 1 tsp. vinegar • pinch of salt.

Mix ingredients with just enough lukewarm water to make a soft dough. Beat well: it must be satin-smooth. Leave 1/2 oz. lard over. Now put pastry on a floured pastry-board and roll out, brush over with melted lard: fold like you do flaky pastry. Repeat the procedure 2 more times, then rolling it out to matchstick-thickness, stamp pastry with doughnut cutter. Fry in hot fat and, lifting out on absorbent paper when ready, sprinkle doughnuts with vanilla sugar. Serve hot with apricot sauce.

Potato Doughnuts

Ingredients: 1 lb. boiled potatoes • at least 6 oz. flour • 1/4 cup milk • 1/2 oz. yeast • 2 lumps of sugar • 4 egg yolks • 1 1/2 oz. butter • milk.

Put aside, in a cup, the sugar, the crumbled yeast and luke-warm milk, and allow to rise. Take the potatoes, pressed through sieve, and mix with the flour, and the risen yeast. Cream egg yolks with the butter, add to the pastry mixture. Add enough lukewarm milk to it by degrees to make a fairly soft dough. Work till dough is quite smooth. Heat lard, and forming small balls of the pastry, drop in the hot fat. Lift doughnuts out when ready, roll in castor sugar to which a spoonful of chocolate powder has been added. Serve hot.

Pancakes (Blintzes)

Ingredients: 1/2 lb. flour • 2 eggs • pinch of salt • 1 tsp. castor sugar • 1/2 pint milk • fat to fry.

Put the flour in a bowl; add eggs, salt and sugar. Stirring constantly, add the milk gradually; constant stirring will prevent lumpiness. Heat a little lard or cooking fat in frying-pan, pour a ladleful of the mixture into, it, and turn over with a spatula when one side is nicely browned. Turn pancakes onto a hot plate, fill with jam, etc. and roll up or fold in four, and serve with lemon juice and sugar.

Baked Cheese Pancakes

Ingredients: 7 oz. flour • 4 oz. cooked potatoes • 1 egg • 3/4 pint milk • a good pinch of salt • 3 oz. butter • 4 oz. grated cheese.

Mix pancake batter with flour, salt, 1 egg and the potatoes, pressed through a sieve. When mixture is quite smooth, fry pancakes in the usual way. Butter the inside of a deep, round fireproof dish, put in the pancakes, sprinkling a layer of grated cheese between each. Brush top thickly with sour cream and sprinkle with a little grated cheese. Bake in a hot oven for about 15–20 minutes. Cut into wedges with a sharp knife but leave in the fireproof dish. Serve hot.

Pancakes with Mushroom and Egg Filling

Ingredients: Pancake batter (see p.) • 7 oz. mushrooms • 1 small onion • 1 tsp. finely chopped parsley • 1 oz. butter • 3 eggs • 2 gills sour cream.

Fry pancakes in the usual way. Heat butter in a saucepan, add coarsely chopped mushrooms, grated onion, chopped parsley and a good pinch of salt. Cook under cover for 10 minutes. Beat well the 3 eggs with a pinch of salt. Add the hot mushroom mixture. Spread this filling over the pancakes; roll up quickly to avoid the egg running out. Put rolled-up pancakes into an oblong buttered dish. Spoon sour cream on top. Bake in a hot oven for 15–20 minutes. Serve in the fireproof dish.

Savoury Pancake Pudding

Ingredients: Pancake mixture (see p. 170) • 1 oz. butter • 3 bread-rolls soaked in milk • 1 small onion • 2 whole eggs • pinch of salt • pinch of ground black pepper • 2 oz. minced ham • 2 oz. grated cheese • 1 gill sour cream.

Prepare pancakes in the usual way. Heat butter, add grated onions, fry till golden. Add the soaked and well-squeezed rolls and, stirring constantly, cook for 5 minutes. Take saucepan away from heat and add 2 eggs, stir vigorously. Lastly add pepper, minced ham and grated cheese. Spread this mixture over the pancakes one by one, roll up and place in a buttered oblong fireproof dish. Sprinkle top with sour cream, and bake in a hot oven for about 20 minutes. Serve hot.

Pancakes with Savoury Chestnut Filling

Ingredients: Pancake mixture (see p. 170) • 1/2 lb. cooked
chestnuts • pinch of salt • 1 gill sour cream • 1 1/2 oz. butter.

Prepare pancakes in the usual way. Press cooked chestnuts
through sieve, add a pinch of salt, 1 oz. butter and 1/2 gill of
sour cream to make a creamy consistency. Spread mixture
on the pancakes, and put in a round fireproof dish. Sprinkle
top with the remaining sour cream, and bake in a hot oven
for about 20 minutes. Serve hot.

Gardener's Pancakes

Ingredients: Pancake mixture (see p. 170) • cooked vegetables •
1 oz. butter • 3 oz. grated cheese • 1 1/2 gills sour cream.

Cook different kinds of vegetables, according to season, in
boiling salt water. Drain, then chop coarsely. Make pancakes
in the usual way. Mix sour cream and grated cheese. Place a
pancake in a round buttered casserole, spread some of the
chopped vegetables over. Cover with another pancake, on
which you spread sour cream and grated cheese mixture.
Repeat till all pancakes are used up. Put in a hot oven and
bake for 20 minutes. Serve hot.

Green Pancakes

Ingredients: Pancake mixture (see p. 170) • 1/2 lb. cooked spinach •
pinch of salt • a pinch of ground black pepper •
3 oz. grated cheese • 1/2 oz. butter.

Cook spinach in salt water, drain well, then put through
sieve, add pepper. Mix this fairly dry purée into the pancake
mixture, then fry pancakes in the usual way, only they

should be a little thicker. Spread grated cheese on pancakes, roll up, then arrange in a buttered oblong fireproof dish. Put in the hot oven for 4–5 minutes before serving.

Summer Pancake Pie

Ingredients: Pancake mixture (see p. 170) • 4 oz. mushrooms •
4 oz. tomatoes • 4 oz. green peppers • 1 medium-sized onion •
1 heaped tsp. parsley • a pinch of ground black pepper • 1 oz.
butter •
1 gill sour cream • salt.

Prepare pancakes in the usual way. Heat butter in a saucepan, add grated onion, fry till golden, then add coarsely chopped mushrooms and parsley. Add a pinch of salt, cover and allow to simmer. Meantime core peppers, peel tomatoes and chop into small cubes. Add chopped pepper to the mushrooms, cook without lid on medium fire for 5–6 minutes, then add tomatoes, stir and cook on full heat for another 5 minutes. Place a pancake in a greased, round casserole, spread some of the filling on, cover with another pancake and repeat procedure till the last pancake. Cover top with last pancake and spoon sour cream over. Cook in a hot oven for 15–20 minutes. Serve in the casserole.

Cheese-and-Potato Fritters

Ingredients: 1 lb. cooked potatoes • 1 1/2 oz. butter • 3 eggs •
5 oz. grated cheese • pinch of salt.

Press potatoes through sieve. Cream the butter in a bowl, add egg yolks one at a time, the grated cheese, potatoes and lastly the stiffly whipped egg whites. Shape into small balls and fry in hot fat. Excellent with mushroom sauce or spinach purée.

Apple Fritters

Ingredients: 1 1/2 lb. sour cooking apples • 3 eggs • 1/4 pint milk •
pinch of salt • 3 tbsp. flour.

Prepare a very thick batter with flour, eggs, milk and a pinch
of salt. Peel, core and slice apples. Dip each slice in the thick
batter and fry quickly in deep fat. Serve hot with fried bacon.

Apricot Fritters

Ingredients: 1 1/2 lb. large apricots • 2 eggs • 1/4 cup milk •
1/4 cup wine • 2 tbsp. castor sugar • pinch of salt • 7 oz. flour •
pinch of ground cinnamon.

Peel, halve and stone large fresh apricots. Mix in a bowl the
eggs, milk, wine, 1 tbsp. castor sugar and salt. Add flour by
spoonfuls, beat well. Mix powdered sugar and ground cinnamon on a small plate. Heat fat in deep-fryer. Sprinkle apricot-halves with the sugar and cinnamon mixture, then dip
each separately into the batter. Fry in hot fat, lifting the basket once or twice to let surplus moisture evaporate. Serve
immediately, sprinkled with a little cinnamon-sugar.

RAISED DOUGH AND
DOUGH PIES

Jam Rolls (Bukta)

Ingredients: 2 oz. sugar • 1 oz. yeast • 3 1/2 oz. butter • 3 egg yolks •
3/4 cup lukewarm milk • 3/4 lb. flour • pinch of salt.

Put the sugar and crumbled yeast into a cup, pour about one third of the milk over it. While it is rising, melt butter in the rest of the warm milk. Add the proven yeast, 3 egg yolks, pinch of salt. Mix well, then stirring constantly, add flour gradually. Beat the dough with hand or with a wooden spoon till smooth and silky. Cover the bowl with a warmed cloth and leave the dough to rise to twice its original size. Turn out onto a floured pastry-board, sprinkle with a little flour, then roll dough out to the thickness of your finger, and cut into squares. Place 1 tsp. of jam near the edge of each square, roll up to the shape of sausage-rolls, and arrange in a greased oblong baking-tin. Covering with cloth, let rise for another 1/2 hour, then brush top with a little milk. Bake for about 20–25 minutes in a medium-hot oven.

Walnut Roll

Ingredients: 1 lb. flour • 1/2 lb. butter • 2 egg yolks • 1 whole egg • 4 oz. castor sugar • 1/4 cup milk • 1 oz. yeast • about 1/2 gill sour cream • pinch of salt.

For the filling: 1 lb. ground walnuts • 3/4 lb. granulated sugar • 7 oz. sultanas • a good pinch of ground cinnamon • 1/2 stick of vanilla.

Put in a cup a spoonful of sugar, crumbled yeast and 1/4 cup milk. Leave to rise. Put the flour in a bowl, rub butter lightly into the flour till mixture is crumbly. Add egg yolks, sugar, the risen yeast and enough sour cream to make a not too soft dough. Knead thoroughly, then cover with cloth and let dough stand for at lest 3 hours. After this time turn out onto a floured pastry-board; divide in two, shaping a ball of each part. Roll doughballs out to 1/3-inch thickness, spread generously with the filling and roll up neatly. Place rolls into a very lightly greased oblong baking tin, brush top with egg, leave to rise 1/2 hour longer. Then brush the top of the pastry again with egg, and bake in a medium oven for 20–30 minutes.

Filling: Put the sugar into a saucepan together with 2 tbsp. water. Stirring constantly, add ground walnuts as soon as sugar is melted. After 5 minutes add flavourings, put aside to cool, then stir till creamy, and use.

Poppy Seed Roll

Ingredients: yeast pastry • 1 lb. ground poppy seed • 1 lb. granulated sugar • 4 tbsp. apricot jam or 1/2 lb. grated apples.

Prepare the dough in exactly the same way as for walnut roll (above). Filling: Add 2 tbsp. water to the sugar and, stirring constantly, add the ground poppy seed as soon as the sugar has melted. Pull aside, then add either apricot jam, or grated apples. When cool, stir till creamy, then use.

Chelsea Buns

Ingredients: 3/4 lb. flour • 4 egg yolks • 3/4 cup lukewarm milk • 1 oz. yeast • 5 oz. butter • 4 oz. castor sugar flavoured with vanilla • 1 gill sweet cream.

Put the sugar, crumbled yeast and about one third of the lukewarm milk, into a cup, leave to rise. Mix the flour, risen yeast, pinch of salt and egg yolks with just enough lukewarm milk to make a medium-soft dough. Cover with floured cloth and allow to rise for 1/2 hour. Turn dough onto a floured pastry-board and roll out to an oblong shape. Cream the butter with 4 oz. of castor sugar, flavour strongly with vanilla. Spread this mixture over the rolled-out pastry, then roll up to a long narrow shape. Cut into 3-inch pieces, arrange in a lightly buttered baking tin cut side upwards, leave to rise for another 1/2 hour. Bake in a medium-hot oven for about

20–25 minutes. After 10 minutes in the oven, brush top thickly with double cream flavoured with vanilla. Serve with wine chaudeau (p. 233) or custard.

Coffee Cake

Ingredients: 1 lb. flour • 5 egg yolks • 4 oz. castor sugar •
5 oz. butter • 3/4 cup milk • 1 oz. yeast • pinch of grated nutmeg.

Crumble the yeast into a cup, add 1 tsp. sugar and the milk, leave to rise. Put the flour into a bowl, add egg yolks, sugar, butter, the risen yeast and a pinch of grated nutmeg. Beat mixture very thoroughly with a wooden spoon till smooth and silky. Pour into a thinly buttered coffee-cake tin and cover with floured warm cloth. Leave to rise to double its original size. Bake in a medium-hot oven for 1/2 hour. Turn out on a wire cake-tray, cool, then coat with chocolate-icing or dust with powdered sugar.

Rich Scones

Ingredients: 1 lb. self-raising flour • 1/2 lb. margarine •
pinch of salt • 1 1/2 gills sour cream.

Rub flour with chopped margarine till mixture is crumbly, then add salt. Add sour cream, knead dough lightly. Roll out on a floured pastry-board, stamp with scone-cutter. Place scones into a lightly greased baking-tin, brush tops with sour cream. Bake in a brisk oven for about 20 minutes.

Crackling Scones

Ingredients: 1 lb. flour • 10 oz. minced pork cracklings • 1 oz. yeast •
1 egg • 1/2 tsp. salt • about 1 1/2 gills sour cream • pinch of ground
black pepper.

Rub well together in a deep bowl the flour, minced cracklings, salt and crumbled yeast. Add egg, pepper and enough sour cream to make a not too soft dough. Cover with a warm cloth and allow to rise for 1/2 hour. Turn dough out onto a floured pastry-board and roll to finger-thickness. Score top with knife in a criss-cross pattern, then stamp out with scone-cutter. Place scones in a lightly greased baking tin and leave to rise for another 15 minutes. Brush top with milk and bake in a hot oven for 15–20 minutes.

Cabbage Scones

Ingredients: 6 oz. lard • 1/2 lb. flour • 1 egg • 1/2 lb. firm white cabbage • 1 tsp. salt • 3 lumps sugar • a pinch of ground black pepper • 1 oz. yeast.

Rub flour, 4 oz. lard, and the crumbled yeast well together. Grate the cabbage on coarse grater into a bowl, mix in the salt, and put aside for 1/2 hour. Heat 2 oz. lard in a saucepan, add sugar and, stirring constantly, brown it. Pressing tightly between your hands, squeeze all surplus moisture from grated cabbage then, adding the pepper, fry in the hot fat to a golden brown colour. Cool, mix with the dough, knead well together, then roll out to finger-thickness on a floured pastry-board. Score top in a criss-cross pattern, then stamp out scones. Place in a lightly greased baking-tin, brush top with milk, and leave to rise for 1/2 hour. Bake in a hot oven for 15–20 minutes.

Cottage-cheese Dough Pie

Ingredients: 1/2 lb. flour • 4 oz. butter • 2 egg yolks • 3 oz. castor
sugar • about 1 gill sour cream • 1 tsp. granulated sugar •
1/2 oz. yeast • 1/4 cup milk • pinch of salt.
Filling: 1/2 lb. cottage cheese • 1 egg • 4 oz. sugar • 1/2 gill sour
cream • 1 heaped tbsp. finely chopped fresh dill.

First prepare the filling: press cottage-cheese through sieve,
add egg yolks, castor sugar, sour cream, chopped dill and
the stiffly whipped egg white. Beat till creamy, then put aside.
Put granulated sugar, 1/4 cup lukewarm milk and the crumbled yeast into a cup, leave to rise well. Beat in a bowl the
sugar, egg yolk and butter, when creamy add the risen yeast,
flour, and enough sour cream to make a rather soft dough.
Pour into a greased oblong deep baking-tin. Spread filling on
thickly, and allow to stand for another 1/2 hour. Bake in a
medium oven for 30 minutes. Cut into squares. Serve either
hot or cold.

Raised Apple Pie

Ingredients: Dough according to walnut roll recipe (see p. 175) •
1 1/2 apples • pinch of ground cinnamon • 3 oz. granulated sugar •
2 oz. ground walnuts • 3 oz. sultanas.

Grate apples on coarse grater, add sugar, cinnamon, ground
walnuts and the sultanas. Divide dough in two, roll out to
oblong shapes. Line the bottom of an oblong baking tin with
one, spread the filling on it, cover with the other sheet of
dough. Brush top with milk, prick with fork. Put in a medium
oven and bake for 30 minutes. Serve hot with custard,
though it is equally good cold. In this case do not cut the pie
until quite cold.

Golden Dough Cake

Ingredients: 1 lb. flour • 3 egg yolks • 4 oz. butter • 1/2 oz. yeast •
2 tbsp. sugar • 3/4 cup milk • pinch of salt.

Put a spoonful of sugar, the crumbled yeast and one-third of
milk, lukewarm, into a cup. When yeast has risen, prepare a
soft dough with flour, egg yolks, 2 oz. softened butter, sugar,
risen yeast, pinch of salt and the rest of the milk. Beat well.
Then cover with warmed cloth and let rise for 1 1/2 hours.
Turn dough out onto a floured pastry-board, cut to pieces
with doughnut-cutter. Butter thinly a large round cake tin,
melt the remaining butter in a small saucepan. Dip each
piece of dough into the melted butter, then place pieces
tightly together in the cake tin. Leave to rise for another 1/2
hour; by this time the tin should be full. Bake in a medium
oven for about 35 minutes. Serve with wine chaudeau (see p.
233).

Walnut Pie

Ingredients: For the pastry: 10 oz. flour • 2 oz. sugar • 1 egg yolk •
1/2 oz. yeast • about 1/2 gill sour cream.
For the filling: 3 eggs • 5 oz. castor sugar flavoured with vanilla •
6 oz. ground walnuts • 2 tbsp. apricot jam.

Prepare the dough to let it stand overnight. Knead ingredients well together in a bowl. The dough should be rather stiff.
Cover with cloth and use the following day. Prepare the
filling: beat well together the egg yolks and sugar, add
ground walnuts and lastly the stiffly beaten egg whites.
Divide pastry in two, roll out to finger-thick, oblong sheets.
Place one sheet in a thinly greased, oblong baking tin.
Spread with apricot jam, then with the walnut filling. Cover
with second sheet of pastry, brush with milk and prickle the

top again with jam and walnut filling, or just walnuts. Bake in a medium oven for 20–25 minutes. Cool before cutting.

Jam Crescents I

Ingredients: 10 oz. flour • 7 oz. margarine • 3/4 pint milk •
1/2 oz. yeast • pinch of salt • 2 oz. sugar • the grated peel of 1/2
lemon •
1 oz. coarsely chopped walnuts.

Crumble the yeast into 5 oz. flour, add milk, gradually, beating all the while to obtain a batter-like substance. Cover with warm cloth, leave to rise. Meantime rub well together margarine, 5 oz. flour, sugar, grated lemon peel and pinch of salt. Add the risen yeast-mixture and knead to a fairly soft dough. Roll out on a floured pastry-board to about 1/4-inch thickness then cut rolled-out dough into triangles. Put 1 tsp. jam in the middle of each, roll up and twisting the ends, shape into crescents. Brush top with milk and sprinkle with chopped walnuts. Allow to rise for 1/2 hour, then bake in a hot oven for about 15–20 minutes. May be served hot or cold.

Salt Crescents

Ingredients: 1 lb. flour • 1 oz. yeast • 1 oz. lard • 1 tsp. salt •
1 tsp. sugar • 1 cup milk • 1/2 tsp. caraway seeds • 1 egg yolk.

Mix in a cup the sugar, about 1/4 of the milk, lukewarm, and crumbled yeast. Rub the lard in the flour, then add the risen yeast, salt and enough lukewarm milk to make a soft dough. Turn onto a floured pastry-board and divide into 4 round balls. Cover with floured cloth and leave to rise for 30 minutes. Roll each piece of dough to matchstick thickness, cut to triangles and roll up to crescent shapes. Brush tops with egg yolk and sprinkle with caraway seed. Bake crescents in a medium oven for 15–20 minutes.

STRUDELS

Rétes (Strudel)

A really Hungarian speciality, rétes (strudel) is a firm favourite even with people who do not like pastry or sweets as a rule. It is no wonder, because its dominant flavour is given by the various filling, savoury or sweet, while the pastry itself — light and crisp — only underlines their delicacy.

Ingredients: 1 lb. flour • 1 egg • 1/2 oz. lard or cooking fat • 1 tsp. vinegar • pinch of salt.

Work ingredients well together, adding enough lukewarm water to make a soft dough. Knead the dough till absolutely smooth. This is very important. When pastry is smooth and silky, divide in two and, first brushing the tops with a little melted fat, cover the pastry with a warm dish and leave to stand for 20 minutes. Cover the kitchen-table with a table-cloth, and flour well. Put one of the pastry-rolls in the middle of the cloth. Do not knead or flour; just brush the top again with melted fat then flatten the pastry to finger-thickness with a rolling pin. Now comes the most important part. Flour your hands and placing them palms downwards underneath the pastry, pull it towards the edge of the table all around. You will find that the pastry gives easily to your hand and you can pull it out to paper-thinness, the pastry reaching the edges of the table, even overlapping it. The edges will remain somewhat thick. This should not be used for rétes, but tear off carefully and use as suggested further below. Leave the pulled-out pastry for 10–15 minutes to dry a little. First sprin-kle with melted fat, then with the desired filling. Pulling and lifting the table-cloth towards yourself, roll the rétes up into a roly-poly and put in an oblong, slightly greased baking-tin. Bake in medium-hot oven for 15–20 minutes. Excellent either hot or cold.

Way to Use Left-over Strudel Pastry

I. Knead the pastry together and, first dipping into flour, tear into small pieces by pinching a small bit between your finger and thumb. Cooked in boiling salt water, it is an excellent garnish for gulash or pörkölt.

II. Roll pastry out to the thickness of a matchstick, sprinkle with a mixture of 2 oz. lard or butter, 1 oz. flour and a good pinch of salt, worked well together. Roll up to a loose roly-poly, flatten with your hand a little, then roll out again to fin-ger-thickness. Brush top with milk, sprinkle with some cara-way seeds and bake in a hot oven for 15–20 minutes. For variety you can use grated cheese instead of fat, but in this case omit the flour and use 4 oz. grated cheese.

Strudel Made with Fresh Fruits

You can use sliced or coarsely grated apples, stoned cher-ries, or morello cherries. Sprinkle the pastry with melted fat, then with a mixture of 2 oz. sugar and 2 oz. coarsely ground walnuts. Spread a finger-thick layer of fruit all over the pas-try, and roll up as directed in the rétes pastry recipe (see p. 182). Brush top with a little melted fat, and bake.

Semolina Strudel

Soak 1/2 lb. semolina in 1/2 pint milk. Cream well together 5 oz. butter, 5 oz. sugar flavoured with vanilla, and 5 egg yolks, add to the semolina. Lastly add the stiffly-whipped whites of 5 eggs. Use this filling as in recipe above.

Poppy Seed Strudel

Melt 1/2 lb. sugar in 1/4 pint milk on slow heat, add 1/2 lb. ground poppy seed and, stirring constantly, cook for five or six minutes. Add the grated peel of 1/2 lemon and 2 oz. sultanas. Cool before use.

Cottage Cheese Strudel

Press 1/2 lb. cottage cheese through sieve. Beat well together 3 egg yolks and 5 oz. sugar, add to the creamed cheese. Add 2 oz. sultanas, and lastly fold in the stiffly whipped egg whites. A spoonful of cream may be added if the cheese is too dry.

BISCUITS, PASTRIES
AND SWEETS

Walnut Biscuits

Ingredients: 3/4 lb. flour • 5 oz. ground walnuts • 4 oz. granulated sugar • 7 oz. butter • the juice and grated peel of 1/2 lemon • 1 tbsp. rum • 1 egg.

Knead all ingredients well together. If the pastry is crumbly, add a spoonful of cream. Roll out on floured pastry-board to finger-thickness, stamp with fancy biscuit-cutters. Sprinkle top with coarse sugar and bake in a moderate oven for about 15–20 minutes.

Vanilla Biscuits

Ingredients: 1 1/4 lb. flour • 5 oz. butter • 10 oz. sugar • 3 eggs • 1 gill cream • a few drops of vanilla essence • pinch of bicarbonate of soda.

Cream the butter and eggs, add sugar and cream, the bicarbonate of soda, and lastly the flour. Knead very thoroughly, then roll out on a floured pastryboard and stamp with biscuit-cutter. Place on a lightly floured baking-sheet and bake in a slow oven for 15–20 minutes. Do not allow the biscuits to get too brown.

Tea Biscuits I

Ingredients: 1 1/4 lb. flour • 1/2 lb. sugar • 7 oz. butter • 4 whole eggs • a few drops of vanilla essence.

Cream the sugar, egg and butter, then knead all ingredients well together till pastry is smooth. Divide into balls, then roll out on a floured pastry-board to the thickness of a matchstick. Cut into biscuits and bake in a slow oven for 10–15 minutes. Do not brown the biscuits. This amount will make over 2 lb. of biscuits.

Tea Biscuits II

Ingredients: 1 lb. flour • 5 oz. castor sugar • 1/2 lb. butter • pinch of salt • 1 egg • 6 tbsp. water.

Knead ingredients well together, then roll pastry out on a floured board. Cut to fancy shapes and bake in a slow oven for 10–15 minutes.

Cottage Cheese Biscuits

Ingredients: 1 lb. flour • 5 oz. lard • 7 oz. cottage cheese • 1 tsp. salt • about 2 tbsp. sour cream.

Knead ingredients well together. Roll out to the thickness of a matchstick, and cut into 3-inch squares with fluted pastry-cutter. Cut a slit in the middle of each with a sharp knife. Bake on baking sheet in a medium oven for 8–12 minutes.

Coconut Pyramids

Ingredients: 1/2 lb. castor sugar • 3 oz. flour • 4 oz. shredded coconut • the whites of 4 eggs.

Add the stiffly whipped egg whites to the coconut and sugar mixture. Beat over steam till mixture thickens. Put aside and keep on beating, adding the flour by degrees. Put the luke-warm mixture into an icing-bag with starnozzle, and press small mounds of the mixture onto the lightly buttered baking sheet. Bake in a slow oven till pyramids are easily detachable from the baking sheet (10–14 minutes).

Linzer Kisses

Ingredients: 5 oz. flour • 5 oz. ground almonds • 5 oz. castor sugar • 5 oz. butter • 1/3 tsp. ground cinnamon • 1/3 tsp. ground cloves • 2 egg yolks • 4 oz. grated chocolate • the grated peel of 1/2 lemon • 1 oz. blanched almonds • 1 oz. vanilla-flavoured castor sugar.

Knead all ingredients well together. Roll out on a floured pastry-board to the thickness of your little finger, cut out with small, round cutter. Put kisses on a baking-sheet, brush top with egg white and press half a blanched almond on each. Bake in a moderate oven for 12–25 minutes. Sprinkle with vanilla sugar while still hot.

Walnut Crunchies

Ingredients: 5 oz. flour • 5 oz. butter • 5 oz. sugar • 5 oz. ground walnuts • 2 egg yolks • 1 tsp. lemon juice • walnut halves • apricot jam.

Knead all ingredients well together with the exception of walnut halves and apricot jam. Roll out the mixture on a floured pastry-board to the thickness of a matchstick. Cut into 3-inch rounds. Arrange on a lightly greased baking-sheet, put half a walnut on top of every second round. Bake in a moderate oven for about 12–15 minutes. When cold, stick together with jam, placing those with walnuts on top.

Fruit Roll

Ingredients: For the filling: 1/2 lb. mixed peel • 1/2 lb. best prunes • 1/2 lb. figs • 1/2 lb. stoned dates • 4 oz. coarsely chopped walnuts • 4 oz. sultanas • 4 oz. ground hazelnuts • the grated peel of 1 lemon • pinch of ground cinnamon • pinch of ground cloves • 1/4 pint rum. For the pastry: 1/2 oz. yeast • 1/4 pint milk • 4 oz. flour • 1 tbsp. wine vinegar • pinch of salt. Lastly 3/4 lb. light yeast dough made according to Jam Roll recipe (see p. 174).

Chop coarsely the mixed peel, stoned prunes, figs, stoned dates, mix well in a porcelain dish together with chopped walnuts, ground hazelnuts, sultanas, grated lemon peel, cinnamon, cloves and rum. Cover dish and leave mixture to stand overnight. Put the crumbled yeast in a cup together with lukewarm milk and leave to rise. Sift the flour into a basin, add the risen yeast, a pinch of salt, the white wine vinegar, beat well, then add the fruit-mixture. Work well together with a wooden spoon. Now roll out the already prepared yeast-dough on a floured pastry-board, and spread the fruit-mixture thickly over. Roll up neatly, taking care that the filling should not peep out at the edges. Place the roll in a greased baking-tin, brush top with beaten egg or top milk, and bake in medium-hot oven, reducing the heat to moderate after 20 minutes. It should be ready in about 40 minutes. Slice when cold, cutting off only as much as you need. This is a very rich cake which will keep for quite a long time in a cake-tin.

Salt Biscuits

Ingredients: 10 oz. flour • 1 egg • 2 tbsp. goose-fat or lard • 1 heaped tbsp. grated Parmesan cheese • 1/2 tsp. salt • 1 egg yolk.

Knead ingredients, with the exception of egg yolk, well together, add just enough water (1 or 2 tbsp.) to make a fairly soft dough. It needs a very thorough kneading. Place on a floured pastry-board and roll out to the thickness of a matchstick. Stamp out with doughnut-cutter, place on a lightly greased baking-sheet, brush tops with a little water and bake in a brisk oven for 5–8 minutes. Serve hot. Any left over can be re-heated again when needed.

Baked Apple Dumplings

Ingredients: 6 even-sized apples • 2 oz. ground walnuts • 2 oz. granulated sugar • 2 oz. sultanas, or seedless raisins • 1 tbsp. rum.
For the pastry: 3/4 lb. self-raising flour • 1/2 lb. margarine • 4 oz. castor sugar • milk.

Peel and core apples. Mix ground walnuts, granulated sugar and the raisins soaked in rum previously, stuff apples with the mixture. Put the flour in a basin and rub in the margarine very thoroughly, mix in the castor sugar, and lastly add just enough cold milk to bind. Roll pastry out on a floured board to 1/4 inch thickness, and cut into squares large enough to wrap the apples. Place an apple in the middle of each square and folding the corners over, pinch the ends of the pastry together. Place on a greased baking tin and bake in a moderately hot oven for about 20–25 minutes. Serve hot with custard.

Jam Pockets

Ingredients: 1/2 lb. flour • 3 oz. butter • 1/4 pint milk • 3 egg yolks • 1 tbsp. granulated sugar • pinch of salt • 1/3 tsp. bicarbonate of soda • jam.

Beat well together melted butter, egg yolks, sugar, milk, salt and bicarbonate of soda. Lastly add the flour; beat dough till quite smooth. Roll out to finger-thickness, cut to small squares. Place 1/2 tsp. jam on each square, then fold diagonally making triangles, finger-pressing the edge to stick. Place on a lightly greased baking sheet and bake in a medium oven for 12–16 minutes.

Cocoa Slices

Ingredients: 1/2 lb. self-raising flour • 1/2 lb. sugar • 2 eggs • 1/4 pint milk • 2 level tbsp. cocoa • vanilla essence • chocolate glaze.

Cream butter and sugar, gradually add the eggs, cocoa, vanilla essence, milk, and lastly the flour. Pour into a lightly greased and floured oblong baking tin, bake in a medium oven for about 18–20 minutes. Cool, cover with chocolate glaze, then cut into squares or fingers.

Wonder Jam Rolls

Ingredients: 7 oz. flour • 4 oz. butter • pinch of salt • 1 tbsp. castor sugar • 2 tbsp. milk • 1/2 oz. yeast • 2 oz. coarsely chopped walnuts.

Put the crumbled yeast, 1 tsp. sugar and milk in a cup. Leave to rise. Rub the butter into the flour, add risen yeast, and knead into a dough. Roll out thinly, then cut to squares, add a teaspoonful of jam on each square and roll up. Place the rolls on a greased cake-sheet and leave to rise in a cool place for 2 hours. Brush with milk, sprinkle with coarsely chopped walnuts, and bake in a medium oven for about 15 minutes. Serve either hot or cold.

Fine Walnut Pie

Ingredients: 1/2 lb. flour • 7 oz. butter • 2 egg yolks • 1 tbsp. rum • pinch of salt.
Filling: 8 eggs • 1/2 lb. sugar • 1/2 lb. ground walnuts • grated peel of 1 lemon • 2 oz. mixed chopped peel • 1 oz. sultanas • grated rind of 1/2 orange • 1/2 gill cream • 2 tbsp. rum.

Knead well together the ingredients for the crust. Roll out on a floured pastry board to two rounds, larger than the usual pie, to the thickness of your little finger. Prepare the cream. Cream the sugar and egg yolks, then add gradually the other ingredients, lastly fold in the stiffly whipped egg whites. Put one round of the pastry in a large round pie-tin, spread the filling on it thickly, cover with the other half of the pastry. Prick the top, then bake in a medium oven for about 30–35 minutes. Cut when cold.

Quick Walnut Squares

Ingredients: 1 cup self-raising flour • 1 cup sugar • 1 cup milk •
1 cup ground walnuts • grated peel of 1/2 lemon • 1 egg.

Cream the sugar and egg. Add the other ingredients gradually. Bake in a buttered and floured oblong tin in a medium oven for about 15–20 minutes. Cut when cold.

Walnut Tart

Ingredients: 7 oz. flour • 4 oz. butter • 2 oz. sugar • 2 egg yolks •
grated peel of 1 lemon • juice of 1/2 lemon •
about 2 tbsp. apricot jam.
Filling: 7 oz. castor sugar • a few drops of vanilla essence • 3 egg whites • 4 oz. coarsely chopped walnuts • a few drops of lemon juice.

Work the ingredients for the pastry well together, kneading into a rather stiff paste. Roll out on a floured pastry-board to the thickness of your little finger. Line the bottom of an oblong baking tin with it. Mix in a saucepan the sugar, egg whites, and lemon juice, beat vigorously over steam till thick, then fold in the walnuts. Spread the pastry thinly with apricot jam, then spread the walnut-mixture evenly over it. Bake in a medium oven for 18–20 minutes. Reduce heat after the first 10 minutes. Serve hot, cut into neat squares.

Cocoa Squares

Ingredients: 1/2 lb. flour • 1/2 lb. granulated sugar • 6 oz. butter •
2 eggs • 1 tbsp. cocoa • 1/2 tsp. bicarbonate of soda • 3/4 cup milk •
melted chocolate.

Cream sugar, butter and egg yolks. Gradually add the flour, milk, cocoa, bicarbonate of soda and lastly fold in the stiffly beaten egg whites. Pour into a greased and floured oblong baking tin and bake in a moderate oven for about 18–20 minutes. Cut into neat squares when cold, and dip each square into melted chocolate.

Jam Tart

Ingredients: 1/2 lb. flour • 8 oz. butter, or margarine • 4 oz. castor sugar • 4 oz. ground walnuts • 3 oz. coarsely chopped walnuts • about 3–4 oz. apricot jam • pinch of salt.

Knead well together the butter, sugar, flour and ground walnuts, add a pinch of salt as well. Leave to stand in a cool place for at least 1 hour. Roll two thirds out on a floured pastry-board to a finger-thick oblong, and line a baking tin with it. Spread thickly with apricot jam, sprinkle with coarsely chopped walnuts. Cut the remaining pastry into narrow strips, roll to size, then place on the tart in a criss-cross pattern. Bake in a medium oven for 18–20 minutes. Serve hot or cold, cut to squares.

Strawberry Rings

Ingredients: 3/4 lb. flour • 1/2 lb. butter • 4 oz. castor sugar • 2 egg yolks • pinch of salt • 1 tbsp. strawberry jam • candied strawberries.

Rub butter into the flour. Add sugar, salt and egg yolks. Knead well, then chill for 3 hours. Roll out on floured pastry-board to 1/2-inch thickness, then stamp one half to plain rounds, the other half to rings. Bake in a brisk oven for 10–12 minutes. Spread the rounds with strawberry jam, put a pastry-ring on the top of each, and put a candied strawberry in the middle of each. Sprinkle with vanilla sugar.

Evening Flower

Ingredients: 6 oz. butter • 1/2 lb. flour • 1/2 lb. castor sugar • a few drops of vanilla essence • 2 whole eggs • the yolk of 1 egg • 2 oz. glacé cherries.

Prepare in the evening, let it stand overnight. Beat well together the sugar, butter and eggs. The mixture should be stiff and creamy when ready. Now add the flour by degrees, stirring constantly. Grease and flour a bakingsheet, put walnut-sized heaps of the mixture on it. Space them well apart; they will spread. Put a glacé cherry on each and leave to stand overnight in a cool place. Bake in a moderate oven for 12–15 minutes.

Double Drops

Ingredients: 1 heaped tbsp. fine breadcrumbs • 4 egg whites • 7 oz. castor sugar • 5 oz. ground hazelnuts.
Cream: 4 oz. castor sugar • 4 oz. butter • 2 egg yolks • 4 oz. softened chocolate.

Beat egg whites till very stiff. Gradually add the sugar, ground hazelnuts, lastly the sifted fine breadcrumbs. Put almond-sized heaps on a buttered and floured baking-sheet and bake in a slow oven for 10–12 minutes. Cool. Cream very thoroughly the sugar and butter, add gradually the egg yolks and chocolate. The cream should be quite stiff. Stick drops into pairs with 1 tsp. of the cream.

Chestnut Surprise

Ingredients: 1 1/2 lb. roast chestnuts • 3 gills cream • 4 tbsp. chunky orange marmalade • 2 tbsp. cognac or rum • 2 oz. grated chocolate.

Score chestnuts deeply, and bake in a hot oven. Peel, then chop coarsely. Fold into the stiffly whipped cream the sugar, marmalade and cognac. Lastly add the coarsely chopped chestnuts. Mix well, then heap up on a round plate. Sprinkle with coarsely grated chocolate, chill, then serve.

Chestnut Crescents

Ingredients: 10 oz. flour • 3 oz. lard or 5 oz. margarine • 1/2 oz. yeast • 2 oz. granulated sugar • 1 egg yolk • sour cream. Cream: 1 lb. cooked peeled chestnuts • 1 oz. butter • 2 heaped tbsp. sugar • 1 tbsp. rum or cognac • 2 tbsp. milk.

Put the crumbled yeast into a cup with 1 tsp. sugar and 2 tbsp. lukewarm milk. Allow to rise. Rub the fat in the flour, add risen yeast, sugar, egg yolk and enough sour cream to make a soft but workable dough. Knead well together, roll out on a floured pastry-board to matchstick thinness, and cut into squares. Put a round tsp. of the chestnut filling on each square, roll up and twist the ends, shape into crescents. Arrange on a medium oven for 15–16 minutes. Cream: Put cooked and peeled chestnuts through sieve, add butter, sugar and rum, and cream for 10 minutes.

Apple Meringue Tart

Ingredients: 1/2 lb. flour • 4 oz. butter • 2 egg yolks • 8 oz. castor sugar • 1 tsp. lemon juice • about 1 oz. apricot jam • 1/2 lb. peeled and sliced apples • 4 egg whites.

Knead well together the flour, butter, egg yolks, 4 oz. sugar and the lemon juice. Roll the pastry out to 1/2-inch thickness, bake in a medium oven for 8–10 minutes. Spread jam on thinly, then cover with sliced apples. Mix egg whites and 4 oz. sugar, beat over steam till stiff. Pour over the apples, then bake the pie in a medium oven for another 15 minutes. Serve hot.

Puff Pastry Made with Leaf-lard

Ingredients: 2 lb. flour • 1 1/2 lb. leaf-lard • 2 tbsp. rum • 1 tsp. white vinegar • 2 whole eggs • 2 egg yolks • jam.

Trim the well-soaked and chilled leaf-lard, peel off membranes, put through mincer. Take one-third of the minced leaf-lard and the flour, add rum and vinegar, knead into a dough. Take the remaining flour and make a fairly soft dough, adding the 2 whole eggs and 2 egg yolks and a pinch of salt. Now knead very thoroughly together the two kinds of dough, knead till smooth and silky. Roll this dough out on a floured pastry-board to the thickness of your little finger. Spread half of the remaining shredded leaf-lard over the rolled-out pastry, fold over the four sides to make a brick-shaped oblong, press together lightly with rolling-pin. Chill the pastry for 1/2 hour, then repeat the procedure using the remaining minced lard. Roll and chill the pastry twice more, then it is ready to use. Roll out, then cut to squares with a heated knife, or stamp out with hot scone-cutter. Fold over with a teaspoon of jam in the middle, brush tops with beaten egg taking care not to let the egg run down at the sides. Bake in a very hot oven for about 12–15 minutes.

Flaky Pastry

Ingredients: 1 lb. self-raising flour • 1/2 lb. butter or margarine • pinch of salt • about 1/2 cup cold water.

Sieve flour into a bowl, add well–chilled butter or margarine and a pinch of salt. Using two table-knives or spatulas, mix flour and shortening quickly. Add enough very cold water to make a workable paste, and roll out immediately. Bake in a hot oven.

Walnut Sticks

Ingredients: 3/4 lb. flour • 2 oz. butter • 2 oz. lard •
2 oz. granulated sugar • a few drops of vanilla essence • 2 eggs •
1/3 tsp. bicarbonate of soda •
3 oz. coarsely chopped walnuts, or any other kinds of nut.

Cream the butter, lard and sugar, add vanilla essence, 1 egg, flour and bicarbonate of soda. Leave to stand for 1/2 hour, then roll out to 1/2-inch thickness. Brush top with beaten egg, sprinkle with a mixture of coarsely chopped nuts and granulated sugar. Press top lightly with your hand, then cut pastry with a sharp knife dipped in cold water into 4-inch long and 1-inch wide strips. Place on a buttered and floured baking-sheet and bake in a moderate oven for about 12–14 minutes.

Hussar Kisses

Ingredients: 6 oz. flour • 4 1/2 oz. butter • 2 oz. sugar • 2 egg yolks •
1 egg white • 1 oz. coarsely chopped almonds •
candied morello cherries.

Mix flour and sugar, rub in the butter, then add egg yolks, knead well together. Shape into walnut-sized balls and put onto a greased baking sheet. Press your thumb in the middle of each ball to make a dimple. Brush with egg white, then scatter coarsely chopped almonds over. Bake in a medium oven for about 12–14 minutes. Place candied morello cherries in the dimples.

Ischler Rings

Ingredients: 7 oz. flour • 7 oz. butter • 3 oz. sugar •
3 oz. ground almonds • the grated peel of 1/2 lemon • raspberry
jam.

Knead all ingredients well together. Success depends on thorough kneading, so do not hurry. Roll out to the thickness of your little finger and stamp out with doughnut cutter. Place rounds on a lightly buttered and floured baking sheet, and bake in a moderate oven for 10–14 minutes. When cold, stick pairs together with raspberry jam, and cover with chocolate icing.

Walnut-cream Charlotte

Ingredients: 1/2 lb. sponge fingers • 1/2 pint milk • 1 tbsp. rum •
1/2 pint cream.
For the cream: 5 oz. butter • 2 egg yolks • 4 oz. castor sugar •
4 oz. ground walnuts • 1 tbsp. rum.

Have at hand a square, flat glass dish. Mix milk and rum, dip sponge fingers in and arrange in a row on the dish. Spread a layer of the walnut cream on, then repeat procedure till you finish up all the cream. Spread 1 gill whipped cream all over. Chill, then serve. The cream: cream the butter with egg yolks and sugar, stir in the ground walnuts, 1 tbsp. rum and 1 gill stiffly whipped cream.

Cream Buns

Ingredients: 7 oz. flour • 1/4 pint milk • 1/4 pint water •
2 1/2 oz. butter • 2 1/2 oz. lard • 1 tsp. sugar • pinch of salt • 6 eggs.

Put in a saucepan the milk, water, butter, lard, sugar and salt. Stirring constantly, bring to the boil, then add the flour in a thin trickle. When mixture is stiff enough to leave the sides of the pan, and adhering as a stiff ball to the spoon, remove from heat, and add the eggs one by one, working them well into the paste. Put aside for at least 1 hour. Place in walnut-sized mounds on a baking sheet well apart, then bake in a medium oven for about 1/2 hour. Do not open the door of the oven for the first 15 minutes. Allow the buns to cool, then dip the top of each in light caramel and sprinkle with coarsely chopped walnuts. Then open the bottom of the buns and fill with vanilla cream. This amount will make about 35–40 buns.

Chocolate Rusks

Ingredients: 4 oz. flour • 4 oz. castor sugar • 2 oz. grated chocolate • 8 eggs.

Cream eggs, sugar, and grated chocolate. Add flour and beat the mixture for another 1/2 hour. Pour into a buttered and floured baking tin and bake in a moderate oven for about 14–16 minutes. Cool, then cut into slices or fingers and dry in very slow oven till crisp.

Quickie

Ingredients: 1 lb. self-raising flour • 4 eggs • 7 oz. sugar • 5 tbsp. goose-fat • vanilla essence.

Cream eggs yolks and sugar, add the goose-fat, flour, and lastly the stiffly whipped eggs whites. Pour the mixture into a greased and floured baking tin and bake in a medium oven for about 15–20 minutes. Serve with stewed or tinned fruit.

Brown Jam Tart

Ingredients: 7 oz. flour • 4 oz. sugar • 4 oz. butter • 1 egg •
4 oz. chocolate • the grated peel of 1/2 lemon • jam •
1 tbsp. coarsely chopped nuts.

Knead the ingredients well together, with the exception of jam and chopped nuts. Roll the pastry out into two rounds, put each into tart-tins. Bake in a medium oven for about 15 minutes. Spread jam on one round, cover with the other, then brush top thinly with jam and sprinkle with chopped nuts.

Kossuth Crescents

Ingredients: 4 oz. flour • 2 oz. butter • 3 eggs • 5 oz. sugar •
1/2 oz. yeast • 1 tbsp. coarsely chopped almonds.

Cream well the butter with egg yolks, sugar and crumbled yeast. Add the flour, and lastly, the stiffly whipped egg whites. Pour into a buttered, floured baking tin, sprinkle chopped almonds on top, and bake in a medium oven for about 18–20 minutes. Sprinkle top with vanilla sugar, then cut into halfmoons with the help of a cutter.

Baked Vanilla Dumplings

Ingredients: 3 oz. flour • 3 oz. butter • 5 eggs • 1 pint milk • 1 heaped
tbsp. sugar • 1/2 stick of vanilla.

Beat well together 4 egg yolks, 2 oz. butter, 1 tbsp. sugar, then add the stiffly whipped egg whites. Bring milk to the boil, add 1 oz. butter and 1/2 stick of vanilla, then, using a tablespoon, cut dumplings out of the cake-mixture and crop them one by one into the slowly boiling milk. When dumplings have risen, lift out with a perforated spoon, put in a deep, round fireproof dish. Pull the milk aside, take out the vanilla, then mix in one egg yolk. Pour the milk and egg yolk mixture over the dumplings, and bake for 1/2 hour in a medium oven. Serve hot.

Vanilla Cream Slices

Ingredients: Puff pastry (see p. 195) • 1 3/4 pints milk • 4 egg yolks • 4 level tbsp. flour • 4 level tbsp. sugar • 1/2 tsp. vanilla essence • 2 sheets of gelatine.

Roll out 2 oblong sheets of pastry to 1/3-inch thickness, and bake in a very hot oven for 18–22 minutes. Reduce heat to medium after the first 15 minutes. Cool, then cut one of the sheets to neat squares. Prepare the cream: beat egg yolks, sugar and vanilla essence till creamy, add flour, mix well. Heat the milk. When at boiling point, pour milk into the cream, stirring constantly to avoid lumpiness. Lastly add the gelatine, stir mixture till absolutely smooth. Spread this cream very thickly over the pastry-sheet, and arrange the cut-up pieces over it. Sprinkle top with vanilla sugar, then cut right through along the squares.

Linzer Slices

Ingredients: 10 oz. flour • 6 oz. butter • 4 oz. sugar • 5 egg yolks • vanilla essence • 1 tbsp. coarsely chopped nuts • 1 level tbsp. granulated sugar.

Cream 4 and 1/2 egg yolks with 4 oz. sugar and a few drops of vanilla essence. Using another bowl, rub the butter into the flour, add the creamed egg yolks. Knead the pastry thoroughly, then chill for 1/2 hour. Roll the pastry out to an oblong shape on a lightly floured pastry-board, then put into an oblong baking-tin. Brush the top with the remaining 1/2 egg yolk, sprinkle with chopped nuts and granulated sugar. Bake in a moderate oven for about 12–15 minutes.

Maine Rings

Ingredients: 3/4 lb. flour • 7 oz. butter • 7 oz. castor sugar • 2 egg yolks • 1/3 tsp. vanilla essence • melted chocolate.

Using a blunt knife or spatula, mix flour, sugar, butter and egg yolks well together. Chill, then roll the pastry out on a floured pastry-board to the thickness of a matchstick. Stamp out with a doughnut cutter, then cut into rings, using a smaller sized cutter. Place rings on a lightly floured baking-sheet, and bake in a moderate oven for about 8–12 minutes. Let rings cool, then dip in melted chocolate.

Almond Slices

Ingredients: 7 oz. flour • 6 oz. butter • 2 egg yolks • the juice of 1 lemon • the whites of 3 eggs • 5 oz. castor sugar • 4 oz. finely chopped almonds • 2 tbsp. jam.

Knead well together the flour, egg yolks, butter and lemon juice. Flour a baking-sheet, then roll the pastry out on it as thinly as possible. Bake in a medium oven for 5–6 minutes, then take sheet out and let the pastry cool. Beat egg whites and sugar till stiff and peaky, then fold in the chopped almonds. Spread a thin layer of jam on the pastry, and cover with the whipped egg whites. Dry in a slow oven till top is crisp and nicely browned.

Hazelnut Crescents

Ingredients: 4 oz. fine breadcrumbs • 4 oz. butter •
4 oz. ground hazelnuts • 2 eggs • 4 oz. castor sugar •
2 oz. coarsely chopped hazelnuts • rice-paper.

Knead the breadcrumbs, butter, ground hazelnuts, 2 egg yolks and sugar well together, then add the stiffly whipped egg whites. Shape into small crescents and place on rice-paper. Since the mixture is rather soft, do not roll on the pastry-board, but shape the crescents between your palms. Sprinkle top with coarsely chopped hazelnuts and bake in a slow oven for about 10–14 minutes. The crescents will keep for a long time.

Morello Cherry Tart

Ingredients: 1/2 lb. flour • 5 oz. margarine • 1/2 gill sour cream or
cream • 2 tbsp. castor sugar • 1/3 tsp. bicarbonate of soda •
2 tbsp. fine toasted breadcrumbs • stoned morello cherries.

Knead well together the flour, margarine, cream, sugar and bicarbonate of soda. Put pastry aside for 1 hour, then roll out to two oblong sheets. Place one into an oblong pastry-tin, sprinkle with breadcrumbs, then add a layer of stoned morello cherries and some sugar. Cover with the second sheet of pastry, prick the top and brush with milk. Bake in a medium oven for 12–15 minutes.

Hazelnut Balls

Ingredients: 5 oz. castor sugar • 4 oz. chocolate • 4 oz. ground
hazelnuts • 1 oz. whole hazelnuts • 1 tbsp. granulated sugar •
a few drops of vanilla essence.

Knead together the castor sugar, softened chocolate and ground hazelnuts with a few drops of vanilla essence to a stiff but pliable paste. Form small balls of it, pressing a whole hazelnut in the middle of each. Roll the little balls in granulated sugar, then put aside for an hour or more to set.

Melba Slices

Ingredients: 2 oz. fine toasted breadcrumbs • 6 eggs • 1/2 castor sugar • 1/2 lb. ground hazelnuts.

Cream egg yolks and sugar. Add gradually the breadcrumbs, the lightly roasted and finely ground hazelnuts, lastly fold in the stiffly whipped egg whites. Pour into a buttered loaf-tin and bake in a medium oven for about 20–25 minutes. Cool, then cut into very thin slices using a sharp, narrow knife. Dry slices in a moderate oven, then store in a cake-tin.

Mylady's Whim

Ingredients: 1 lb. flour • 3/4 lb. butter • 3 egg yolks •
1 1/2 gills sour cream • 1/2 oz. yeast • pinch of salt • 1 tbsp. rum •
1 tbsp. coarsely chopped walnuts • 4 oz. granulated sugar •
1 oz. castor sugar • a few drops of vanilla essence • apricot jam.

Rub butter, flour and crumbled yeast well together, add salt, egg yolks, sour cream, rum and granulated sugar. Knead well together, then roll pastry on a floured board to 1/2-inch thick oblong. Place in a thinly buttered and floured baking-tin, cover with cloth and put aside for 1/2 hour. Bake in a moderate oven for about 16–20 minutes. Leaving the pastry in the tin, brush top with apricot jam. Beat egg whites till stiff, add a few drops of vanilla essence, then fold in the castor sugar. Spread this over the jam, sprinkle with coarsely chopped walnuts and put in a medium oven for about 5–6 minutes, to brown the top lightly. The whipped egg whites should remain soft inside.

Damson Tart

Ingredients: 3/4 lb. flour • 1 egg yolk • 1/4 pint olive oil • 5 oz. castor sugar • 1/2 tsp. bicarbonate of soda • 1 lb. stoned damsons • 3 oz. granulated sugar.

Knead well together the flour, egg yolk, oil, castor sugar and bicarbonate of soda. Roll pastry out into two oblong sheets, place onto a floured oblong baking tin. Arrange a thick layer of stoned damsons over it, and sprinkle with granulated sugar. Cover with the other sheet of pastry, prick top, and brush with milk or sugar syrup. Bake in a medium oven for about 25–30 minutes. Serve hot with custard or cream.

Water Biscuits

Ingredients: 1 lb. self-raising flour • 5 oz. granulated sugar • 3 oz. margarine • 1 egg.

Knead well together the flour, sugar, margarine and egg, adding enough cold water to make a rather stiff dough. Roll out on a floured pastry-board, stamp out with biscuit-cutter. Place on a baking sheet, and bake in a medium oven for about 8–10 minutes.

Butter Scones

Ingredients: 5 1/2 oz. flour • 5 1/2 oz. butter • 1/2 oz. yeast • 1 egg yolk • pinch of salt • milk • gooseberry or damson jam.

Knead together all ingredients other than the jam, adding the crumbled yeast and enough milk to make a stiff dough. Roll out on a floured pastry-board to about 1-inch thickness, score top with knife, then cut out scones with a small round pastry cutter. Place on a baking-sheet, brush tops with a little milk or beaten egg, then leave to stand in a cool place for about 3 hours. Bake in a moderately hot oven for about 15–20 minutes. Serve either hot or cold, with gooseberry or damson jam.

Quick Tart

Ingredients: 9 oz. self-raising flour • 7 oz. mashed potatoes • 1 egg • 7 oz. castor sugar • 6 oz. margarine or 5 oz. lard • grated peel of 1 lemon • 2 oz. ground walnuts • jam.

Press potatoes through sieve, then mix all ingredients, adding the egg last. Knead well, then cut the pastry in two oblongs, and line the bottom of a slightly greased and floured baking-tin with one. Spread jam on it and sprinkle with ground walnuts, indeed, any kind of ground nuts will do. Cover with the other half of rolled-out pastry. Prick top, then brush with a little milk. Bake in a moderate oven for about 20–25 minutes. When ready, cut into squares and sprinkle with castor sugar. It is best when fresh.

Plum Slices

Ingredients: 4 1/2 oz. butter • 3 oz. flour • 4 egg yolks • 2 oz. granulated sugar • 2 oz. sultanas • 2 oz. seedless raising • 2 oz. chopped mixed peel • 1 tbsp. rum.

Cream butter, sugar and egg yolks. Add rum and mixed fruit, fold in the flour last. Pour in a grassed and floured oblong sandwich tin, and bake in a moderate oven for about 20–25 minutes. Cool, then slice.

Plain Fruit Cake

Ingredients: 1 lb. self-raising flour • 1 1/2 gills sour cream •
4 oz. granulated sugar • 2 oz. lard • 4 oz. mixed peel • 2 oz. sultanas.

Rub lard into flour and sugar. Add mixed fruits, then, adding the sour cream, knead the mixture well together. Put the mixture into a greased, floured cake tin and bake in a medium oven for about 1 hour. Reduce heat to low after 1/2 hour.

Styrian Noodles

Ingredients: 1/2 lb. flour • 5 eggs • 2 gills sour cream •
1/2 lb. cottage cheese • 3 oz. sugar • 3 oz. butter • 1 gill cream •
the grated rind of 1/2 lemon • 2 oz. sultanas • salt •
vanilla sugar.

Knead into a stiff dough the flour, 2 eggs, sour cream, the cottage cheese (pressed through sieve previously), 1 oz. sugar and a pinch of salt. It needs a very thorough kneading. Roll the pastry out to the thickness of your finger, on a floured pastry-board. Cut first into 3-inch wide strips, then cut the strips into thick, finger-wide noodles. Cook these noodles in boiling water, lifting them out of the water with a perforated spoon or a slicer as soon as they rise and place into a colander to strain. Now prepare the following cream: cream the sugar and butter, add 3 egg yolks one by one, 1 gill cream, grated lemon-rind and sultanas; lastly fold in the 5 egg whites, stiffly whipped. Mix this cream with the cooked noodles, and pour the mixture into a deep fireproof dish. Bake in a moderate oven for about 20–30 minutes. Serve hot in the casserole, sprinkle top with vanilla sugar.

Love Letters

Ingredients: 5 oz. flour • 5 oz. butter • 4 eggs • 6 oz. castor sugar •
6 oz. ground nuts • grated peel of 1/2 lemon • vanilla essence •
icing sugar.

Prepare the pastry the previous night. Knead well together the butter, flour, egg yolks and a pinch of salt. Next day roll pastry out thinly on a floured pastry-board to the shape of a five-inch wide strip. Now prepare the filling: beat egg whites with sugar till stiff, add ground walnuts, grated lemon peel and vanilla essence. Spread the filling on one side of the pastry, then fold the other side over it. Press edges with your finger and place pastry on a bakingsheet. Bake in a medium hot oven for about 15–20 minutes. Cut into oblongs and sprinkle with castor sugar.

Jam Crescents II

Ingredients: 10 oz. flour • 3 oz. granulated sugar • 7 oz. butter •
1 1/2 oz. finely chopped almonds • 1 egg yolk • jam.

Mix sugar and flour, rub in butter. Add 1 oz. finely chopped almonds and egg yolk. Knead mixture well together, then roll out on a floured pastry-board to 1/3-inch thickness. Cut into squares, and put a spoonful jam in the middle of each square. Roll up into small crescents. Arrange crescents on a lightly buttered and floured baking-sheet and bake in a moderately hot oven for about 15–20 minutes. Dust crescents with vanilla sugar while still hot.

Tyrolese Strudel

Ingredients: For the pastry: 1/2 lb. flour • 5 oz. butter • 6 eggs •
1/2 oz. yeast • 1/2 gill sour cream.
Filling: 4 eggs • 4 oz. castor sugar • vanilla essence • 3 oz. finely
chopped mixed peel • 7 oz. ground almonds • 4 oz. sultanas.

Rub well together the flour, crumbled yeast, and butter. Add egg yolks and sour cream, knead till pastry is smooth. Roll pastry out on a floured board to 3/4-inch thickness, and spread thickly with the following mixture: beat 4 egg yolks and sugar till creamy, add vanilla essence, mixed peel, sultanas and ground almonds. Fold in the stiffly whipped egg whites. Spread this mixture evenly on the pastry, then roll it up, place roll on a baking-sheet and bake in a hot oven for about 20–25 minutes. slice and serve while hot. Hot wine chaudeau (see p. 233) may be served with it.

Cottage Cheese Jam Tart

Ingredients: 1/2 lb. flour • 1/2 lb. cottage cheese • 4 oz. butter •
1 egg • 1 tbsp. castor sugar • pinch of salt • 3 tbsp. gooseberry
or damson jam.

Press cottage cheese through sieve, mix with flour, butter, egg, sugar and salt: knead well. Roll pastry on a floured board to 1/3-inch thickness and line a flat tin with it. Spread over it a thick layer of damson or gooseberry jam. Roll the remaining pastry into strips and arrange them on the top of the flan in a criss-cross patter. Bake in a medium oven for about 20–25 minutes. It is equally good hot or cold.

Cottage Cheese Turnovers

Ingredients: 4 lb. flour • 1 oz. yeast • 1/2 pint milk • 4 oz. butter •
4 oz. granulated sugar • 4 egg yolks • pinch of salt.
Filling: 1/2 lb. cottage cheese • 3 oz. castor sugar • 2 egg yolks •
1 oz. butter • 2 oz. sultanas.

Prepare a thick batter from 3 oz. flour, crumbled yeast and 1/2 pint milk. When well risen, add 1 lb. flour, 4 oz. butter, 4 oz. sugar, 4 egg yolks and a pinch of salt. Beat into smooth dough, and cover with warm cloth. Prepare filling. Press cottage cheese through sieve, add 3 oz. sugar, 2 egg yolks, 1 oz. butter and 2 oz. sultanas. Stir till creamy. In 1/2 hour the dough is ready for rolling out. Turn onto a floured pastry-board, roll out to finger-thickness. Brush top thickly with melted but cool butter, sprinkle well with sugar. Now fold over the dough first left to right, then right to left, then the side nearest to you, lastly the side opposite, always only to the midline. Press lightly with rolling pin, cover the dough with floured cloth and repeat the rolling-out procedure once again after 15 minutes. Cut the rolled-out dough into squares, put a round spoonful of the filling in the middle of each square, moisten the edges with water and fold the dough over to form a triangle. Place turnovers on a grassed baking sheet, leave to rise for another 15 minutes, then brush tops with milk and bake in a moderately hot oven for about 15–20 minutes.

Cottage Cheese Scones

Ingredients: 5 oz. flour • 5 oz. cottage cheese • 5 oz butter •
2 egg yolks • 1 tsp. granulated sugar • pinch of salt.

Press cottage cheese through sieve. Cream butter and egg yolks, add flour, cheese, sugar and salt, knead well, then roll out on a floured pastry-board to 2-inch thickness. Cut into small scones and arrange on a greased baking sheet. Bake in a medium oven for about a 20–25 minutes.

Vanilla Crescents

Ingredients: 10 oz. flour • 4 oz. granulated sugar • 6 oz. butter • 2 egg yolks • vanilla essence.

Cream thoroughly the sugar, butter and egg yolks. Add the flour, then the vanilla essence and knead into a stiff paste. Cover with a bowl and leave in a cool place for 2 hours. Roll out on a floured pastry-board to 1/4-inch thickness, then cut to strips about 2 inches long and 3/4 inch wide. Twist into horseshoe shaped crescents, and place on a grassed baking sheet. Bake in a moderately hot oven for about 12–15 minutes. Dust thickly with vanilla sugar while still hot.

Apricot Surprise

Ingredients: 1 tin apricot-halves in syrup • 2 gills cream • 1/2 oz. gelatine • 4 oz. castor sugar • a few drops vanilla essence.

Drain the juice off the apricots, and place them on absorbent paper. Melt the gelatine in a little water, cool, but do not leave to set. Whip cream till stiff, fold in the sugar, add a few drops of vanilla essence, mix in the melted gelatine. When it begins to set, scoop out egg-shaped pieces of the jelly with a tablespoon, and arrange on a round flat dish. Push half apricots into the middle of each, to make it resemble a halved hard-boiled egg, then chill. This is a great favourite in the nursery.

Almond Tips

Ingredients: 3 oz. flour • 2 oz. sugar • 4 oz. ground almonds •
6 eggs • 4 oz. butter • 3 oz. grated chocolate • 4 oz. butter •
melted chocolate.

Cream egg yolks, sugar and ground almonds. Put the butter and grated chocolate in a bowl, place over hot water, and stir till butter and chocolate have melted. Add it to the almond and egg yolk mixture, stir well, then fold in the stiffly whipped egg whites and spoon to it the flour. Pour into a small floured and buttered oblong baking tin and bake in a moderate oven. Slice to triangles and dip the tips of the triangles into melted chocolate.

Glazed Prunes

Ingredients: 1 lb. best prunes • 3/4 cup white wine • 2 oz. blanched
almonds • 5 oz. granulated sugar.

Stone the prunes, soak them in the wine for 2 hours. Strain the wine into a wide saucepan, add sugar, bring to the boil slowly. Press and almond into each prune, then place prunes in the syrup. Boil gently, turning over the fruit carefully every now and then, till all moisture is absorbed. Place the fruit on greaseproof paper and keep in a well aired place for 24 hours, after which the fruit can be stored in boxes.

Chocolate Disks

Ingredients: 3/4 lb. flour • 4 oz. granulated sugar • 2 tbsp. cocoa •
7 oz. butter • 2 egg yolks • melted chocolate.

Cream butter and sugar, then add other ingredients with the exception of chocolate. Knead lightly, then roll the pastry on a floured board to matchstick-thickness. Stamp into rounds with doughnut-cutter, place the rounds on a slightly greased baking-sheet and bake in a moderate oven for about 8–10 minutes. Leave to cool, then dip in melted chocolate. Store in a greaseproof-paper lined tin, put greaseproof-paper between each row of disks. They will keep for weeks.

Grillage

Ingredients: 1/2 lb. almonds • 1/2 lb. castor sugar •
1 tsp. lemon juice • 1 tsp. rum • a pinch of grated lemon peel.

Scald, then remove skin of almonds. Dry in the oven but take care not to brown them. Chop almonds coarsely. Melt the sugar in a heavy saucepan over moderate heat, then add lemon juice, rum and a pinch of grated lemon peel. Add chopped almonds last. Keep on stirring till the mixture turns light brown, then pour out onto a lightly oiled marble-slab or thick glass. Using an oiled rolling-pin, roll the mixture into a thin sheet, working quickly, while the grillage is hot. Cut into 1-inch wide and 3-inch long strips, twisting each into a spiral. Leave to cool, then store in a greaseproof-paper lined tin.

Almond Toffee

Ingredients: 1/2 lb. sugar • 1/2 lb. almonds •
a few drops of vanilla essence. .

Prepare exactly the same way as grillage (see above), using vanilla essence instead of lemon juice. Roll to finger-thickness and cut into small squares while still hot. Leave to cool, then wrap each square first into greaseproof-paper, then in fancy tinfoil.

Devil's Pills

Ingredients: 1/2 lb. granulated sugar • 1/2 lb. ground almonds •
about 1/4 pint water • coarsely grated chocolate.

Place sugar and water in a thick saucepan and, stirring constantly, melt sugar on low heat. Add ground almonds, stir for another 5 minutes, then put mixture aside and continue stirring till cool enough to handle. Shape balls between your palms and roll them in the coarsely grated chocolate.

Baked Chestnuts in Wine

Ingredients: 1 lb. chestnuts • 1/2 lb. granulated sugar •
juice of 1 lemon • 1/4 cup white wine • 1/4 cup water.

Score chestnuts deeply and bake in a hot oven for 10 minutes. Remove skins. Mix in a saucepan the sugar lemon juice and water, and, stirring constantly, bring to the boil over medium heat. Add chestnuts, cover and allow to simmer for about 15 minutes. Add wine, boil up again and serve.

PUDDINGS AND SOUFFLÉS

Glacé Fruit Pudding

Ingredients: 10 oz. mixed glacé fruits • 7 oz. mixed peel • 4 eggs •
4 tbsp. flour • 4 tbsp. sugar • 3/4 cup milk • 3 oz. butter.

Beat egg yolks, flour, sugar, milk and melted butter well together. The longer you stir, the lighter the pudding will be. Chop mixed glacé fruits and mix with the chopped peel, fold in whipped egg whites. Turn mixture into a buttered and floured pudding basin. Keep in mind that the pudding will rise during cooking, therefore choose the basin accordingly. Cover tightly and boil slowly for about 1 hour. Leave the pudding to rest 5 minutes before you open and turn it out. Serve with raspberry syrup or wine chaudeau (see p. 233).

Pied Pudding

Ingredients: 1 lb. sponge cake • 2 tbsp. vanilla liqueur or cherry brandy • 2 tbsp. green chartreuse • 1 1/2 oz. melted chocolate • 2 oz. butter • 4 eggs • 3 tbsp. castor sugar.

Cut the sponge cake into 1-inch cubes. Divide into four on separate plates. Sprinkle one with the green chartreuse, another with vanilla liqueur or cherry brandy, and mix the third with melted chocolate. Now cream butter, egg yolks and sugar, add all the sponge-cake cubes (the chocolate-flavoured ones last), then fold in the stiffly whipped egg whites. Butter and flour a deep round fireproof dish, turn the mixture into it and bake in a medium oven for about 20–25 minutes. Pour rum on top and light just before serving.

Sponge Cake Pudding

Ingredients: 1/2 lb. sponge cake • 4 eggs • 3 tbsp. castor sugar • 1/2 tsp. vanilla essence • 3/4 cup milk • 1 tbsp. rum.

Cream egg yolks and sugar. Gradually add the milk, coarsely broken sponge cake, vanilla essence, 1 tbsp. rum. Fold in the stiffly whipped egg whites. Turn into a buttered pudding basin, cover tightly and steam for 1 hour. Leave to stand for 5 minutes before removing the cover. Serve with vanilla custard sauce. This pudding will rise while cooking, therefore choose a basin accordingly.

Christmas Pudding

Ingredients: 1/2 lb. flour • 1/2 lb. butter • 1/2 lb. castor sugar •
5 eggs • 1/2 lb. currants • 1/4 lb. raisins • 2 oz. mixed peel •
3 1/2 oz. ground walnuts • 3 1/2 oz. ground almonds •
half a tsp. each of grated lemon peel • ground cinnamon and
ground cloves •
1/4 cup rum.

First prepare the fruit: stone raisins, chop mixed peel, rub and dry currants, ground the almonds and walnuts, grate lemon peel. Cream the butter in a large basin till fluffy. Add egg yolks one by one, then the flour, the fruits, ground almonds and walnuts, and lastly the stiffly whipped egg whites. Pour the mixture into a buttered and floured pudding basin and cover tightly. Steam for 2 hours. Leave to stand for 5–6 minutes before opening the top. Serve with brandy butter or thick wine chaudeau (see p. 233).

Boiled Apple and Rice Pudding

Ingredients: 4 oz. rice • 1/2 pint milk • 5 eggs • 3 1/2 oz. butter •
4 oz. castor sugar • 1 1/2 oz. white breadcrumbs • 1/2 lb. apples •
half a stick of vanilla pod.

Cook the rice in the milk with a spoonful of sugar and vanilla added. Put aside to cool and remove vanilla pod. Cream egg yolks, butter and sugar thoroughly, mix in the cooked rice, breadcrumbs and the thinly sliced, peeled apples. Fold in the stiffly whipped egg whites. Turn the mixture into a buttered pudding basin, cover tightly and steam for 1 hour. Leave to stand for 5 minutes before taking off the cover. Serve with custard or wine chaudeau (see p. 233).

Lemon Pudding

Ingredients: 4 oz. flour • 8 oz. sugar • the juice and grated peel of
1 lemon • 6 egg whites.

Adding egg whites to the sugar one by one, stir till the mixture is white and creamy. Add the juice and grated peel of one lemon, add flour spoon by spoon. Pour into a buttered pudding basin, cover tightly and steam for 3/4 hour. Serve with lemon custard.

Walnut Soufflé

Ingredients: 6 eggs • 5 oz. ground walnuts •
2 oz. castor sugar flavoured with vanilla • 2 1/2 oz. butter.

Cream sugar, egg yolks and butter, till stiff and fluffy. Fold in the ground walnuts, add stiffly whipped egg whites last. Pour the mixture into a buttered soufflé-dish and bake in a medium oven for about 1/2 hour. Serve immediately with custard.

Mousse Pudding

Ingredients: 6 egg whites • 2 tbsp. flour • 4 oz. castor sugar •
juice of 1 lemon.

Whip well together one egg white, sugar, flour and lemon juice. Fold in the stiffly whipped egg whites and pour the mixture into a buttered and floured pudding basin. Cover tightly and steam for about 25 minutes. Serve with wine chaudeau (see p. 233).

Almond Pudding

Ingredients: 3 bread-rolls soaked in milk • 3 1/2 oz. butter •
3 oz. granulated sugar • 6 eggs • 3 oz. ground almonds.

Cream sugar, egg yolks, and butter, add well-squeezed rolls
and ground almonds. Stir till mixture is stiff, then fold in the
well-beaten egg whites. Butter and flour a pudding basin,
pour in the mixture and cover tightly. Steam for about 25
minutes. Serve with chocolate sauce or wine chaudeau (see
p. 233).

Brown sugar in a heavy saucepan, stir in flour, then add cold
milk. Stir constantly till it thickens, then put aside to cool.
When mixture is cold, stir in 6 egg yolks and softened butter,
then add a few drops of vanilla essence. Fold in the stiffly
beaten egg whites last. Pour the mixture into a buttered pudding basin, cover tightly and steam for 1 hour. Leave to stand
for 5 minutes before taking off cover. Serve with custard.

Rice Soufflé

Ingredients: 7 oz. rice • 1 3/4 pints milk • 4 eggs •
3 1/2 oz. granulated sugar • the grated peel of 1/2 lemon •
1/2 stick of vanilla pod.

Put the milk, together with the vanilla, into a saucepan, add
rice and, stirring frequently, cook till rice is tender. Put aside
to cool. Meantime beat egg whites till stiff, add yolks, sugar
and grated lemon peel. Stir till creamy, then add the cooled
rice. Turn into a buttered, floured soufflé-dish and bake in a
medium oven for about 35–40 minutes. Serve with raspberry
syrup or tinned fruit.

Meringue Rice Soufflé

Ingredients: 8 oz. rice • 1 3/4 pints milk • 3 eggs • 3 oz. apricot jam •
a few drops of vanilla essence • 1 oz. blanched almonds •
4 oz. castor sugar.

Cook rice in milk, add vanilla essence and 2 oz. sugar. Leave to cool. When rice is lukewarm, stir in the egg yolks one by one, then pour the mixture into a buttered fireproof dish. Beat egg whites till stiff, fold in the rest of the sugar and the apricot jam. Cover the rice with this mixture stick, then peeled almond all over the top. Bake in a medium oven for about 30–35 minutes, reducing heat to slow for the last 10 minutes. Serve with apricots in heavy syrup.

CAKES AND GATEAUX

Basic Cake Mixture

Ingredients: 4 whole eggs • 2 egg yolks • 1/2 oz. sugar •
3 1/2 oz. flour • 2 oz. butter.

Put the eggs and egg yolks, together with the sugar, into a bowl. Place over boiling water and, beating constantly, heat up the eggs, but do not allow to boil. Take off heat as soon as hot and continue beating till mixture is cool. Add flour and softened butter, continue beating till mixture is stiff and creamy. Turn it into a thinly buttered cake-tin, bake in a moderate oven for about 30 minutes.

Water Sponge

Ingredients: 3 eggs • 6 tbsp. granulated sugar • 6 tbsp. water •
1/2 lb. flour.

This is an inexpensive basic cake mixture. Cream egg yolks and sugar, adding 4 tbsp. water one at a time. Add flour. Mix 2 tbsp. water with egg whites, beat till stiff and peaky. Fold this into the mixture. Butter and flour a cake-tin, line bottom with paper. Pour in the cake mixture and bake in a moderate oven for about 30 minutes.

Dobos Cake

Ingredients: 2 oz. flour • 2 oz. granulated sugar • 3 eggs.
Cream: 6 oz. castor sugar • 6 oz. butter • 6 oz. chocolate.

Cream egg yolks and sugar, add stiffly whipped egg whites, stir, then fold in the flour. Now butter and flour a sandwich tin and spread a sixth of the cake mixture on it very thinly. Bake in a moderate oven for about 5–8 minutes. Remove from tin with the help of a spatula. Place the round on a flat surface, to cool. Meanwhile butter and flour another baking tin and repeat the above procedure until you obtain 6 rounds of thin wafer-like layers. (Of course, if you have several sandwich tins of equal size, you can bake several layers at once.) Now prepare the filling. Cream the sugar and butter. Melt the chocolate on low heat adding 3 tbsp. water. Take off heat and stir till cool, then stir into it the creamed butter and sugar. Spread one fifth of filling on first layer, cover with second layer and repeat, finishing with a layer of sponge. Chill it. Prepare the top as follows: Melt 3 oz. sugar, stir till golden brown. Pour thick caramel on the top round, even it with a wide-bladed knife dipped in oil. Mark the slices while the caramel is still hot, cutting the glaze right through.

Walnut Cake

Ingredients: 8 eggs • 1/2 lb. castor sugar • 2 tbsp. white breadcrumbs • 1/2 lb. ground walnuts • grated peel of 1/2 lemon • 1 tbsp. rum.
Cream: 3 bars of chocolate • 4 oz. butter • 3 1/2 oz. sugar • 1 egg.

Cream egg yolks and sugar; add breadcrumbs, ground walnuts, grated lemon peel, and 1 tbsp. rum. Mix well, then fold in the stiffly whipped egg whites. Turn into two buttered sandwich tins and bake in a moderate oven for about 20–25 minutes. Do not open the oven door for the first 15 minutes. Let cool, and prepare filling. Cream melted chocolate with butter, sugar and whole raw egg until smooth. Spread a thick layer of filling on one of the cakes, and cover with the other. Spread evenly the remaining chocolate cream on the top of the cake, then sprinkle with coarsely chopped walnuts. Chill, then serve.

Walnut Layer Cake

Ingredients: 7 eggs • 7 oz. castor sugar • 1 1/2 oz. chocolate • 3 oz. fine breadcrumbs.
Filling: 5 oz. ground walnuts • 1/4 pint milk • 5 oz. butter • 5 oz. sugar • chocolate icing.

Cream egg yolks and sugar. Stir in softened chocolate, add sifted crumbs and the stiffly whipped egg whites. Bake in four layers, using buttered and floured sandwich tins for the purpose. Cool it. Cream: place ground walnuts in a bowl, pour 1/4 pint boiling milk over. Leave to cool. Cream sugar and butter, add to the scalded walnuts, and beat till stiff and creamy. Spread filling between the layers, cover the cake with chocolate icing.

Hazelnut Cake

Ingredients: 8 egg whites • 1/2 lb. castor sugar • 4 oz. ground
hazelnuts • 3 1/2 oz. finely chopped mixed peel • 1 tbsp. flour.

Beat egg whites and sugar till very stiff. This is the basic procedure on which success depends; do not grudge the time
spent on it. Fold in the flour, ground hazelnuts and the finely
chopped mixed peel. Pour mixture into a buttered cake tin
and bake in a moderate oven for about 25–30 minutes. Let
cool, then cover with lemon icing.

Hazelnut Cream Cake

Ingredients: 3 oz. ground hazelnuts • 6 eggs • 7 oz. granulated
sugar • 3 tbsp. white breadcrumbs.
Cream: 5 oz. butter • 7 oz. castor sugar • 1 egg • 4 oz. grated
hazelnuts • 1 1/2 gills cream.

Cream egg yolks and sugar, add 3 oz. grated hazelnuts and
2 tbsp. white breadcrumbs. Fold in the stiffly whipped egg
whites. Turn into a buttered and floured cake tin and bake in
a moderate oven for 30 minutes. Prepare the filling. Cream
5 oz. butter, 7 oz. castor sugar and 1 whole raw egg. Add 4
oz. ground hazelnuts, mix well with the stiffly whipped
cream. Split the cooled cake in two, spread one-third of the
filling on the bottom half, cover with top half and spread the
remaining cream-filling on the top and sides of the cake.
Decorate with roasted hazelnuts and chocolate drops.

My Favourite

Ingredients: For the cake: 4 oz. fine toasted breadcrumbs • 6 eggs •
4 oz. castor sugar • 4 oz. ground walnuts • 4 oz. butter.
Cream: 4 oz. ground walnuts • 4 oz. castor sugar • 1 tbsp. cognac •
1 gill cream • chocolate icing.

Cream egg yolks, sugar and butter. Stir in the ground walnuts and breadcrumbs, fold in the stiffly whipped egg whites. Pour the mixture into a thinly greased oblong cake-tin, bake in a moderate oven for about 20–22 minutes. Cool it, then cut in two lengthwise. Now prepare the filling. Mix ground walnuts and castor sugar with the cognac, stir in the stiffly whipped cream. Spread the cream in a thick layer over the lower half of the cake, cover with other half, press gently. Glaze with chocolate icing.

Almond Wedges

Ingredients: 4 eggs • 5 oz. granulated sugar • 5 oz. ground almonds •
2 1/2 oz. white breadcrumbs.
Cream: 3 eggs • 5 oz. castor sugar • 3 oz. chocolate • 5 oz. butter •
coffee icing.

Cream egg yolks, sugar and ground almonds. Add breadcrumbs spoon by spoon, then fold in the stiffly whipped egg whites. Turn mixture into a buttered and floured oblong tin and bake in a moderate oven for about 20–25 minutes. Cool it, then cut cake in two lengthwise, to obtain two long pieces. Cream: mix eggs, sugar and grated chocolate in a bowl. Place over boiling water and, stirring constantly, cook till mixture thickens. Put aside and when lukewarm add the butter and stir till stiff and fluffy. Spread this filling thickly between two layers of cake. Cut into triangle-shaped pieces, cover each wedge with coffee icing.

Chocolate Cake (Plain)

Ingredients: 8 egg whites • 7 oz. castor sugar • 7 oz. chocolate •
3 1/2 oz. butter • 3 1/2 oz. flour.

Beat egg whites with sugar till stiff and peaky. Add softened
chocolate, softened butter, and fold in the flour. Turn into a
buttered and floured round cake tin and bake in a moderate
oven for 30 minutes.

Chocolate Wedges

Ingredients: 4 oz. flour • 6 oz. butter or margarine • 6 oz. castor
sugar • 6 eggs • 4 oz. chocolate • 1 tbsp. chopped nuts.

Cream egg yolks, sugar and butter. Add the softened chocolate and flour, then fold in the stiffly whipped egg whites.
Turn the mixture into a buttered, floured, oblong baking tin,
sprinkle top with chopped nuts. Bake in a moderate oven for
about 25–30 minutes. Cool, then cut into triangles. Serve
with a round spoonful of whipped cream on top of each
wedge.

Chocolate Log

Ingredients: 6 tbsp. flour • 6 level tbsp. sugar • 6 eggs • 3 tbsp. strong
black coffee.
Cream: 6 oz. butter • 2 oz. icing sugar • 3 oz. chocolate • 1 egg yolk;
For decoration: 1 oz. pistachio nuts or almonds.

Cream sugar, egg yolks and cold black coffee. Add flour in
spoonfuls, then fold in the stiffly whipped egg whites. Turn
into a paper-lined oblong tin and bake in a moderate oven
for about 15–20 minutes. Turn the cake out onto a cloth or
napkin and, first pulling off the paper, roll it up together with

the cloth. Prepare the filling. Beat the butter, sugar, softened chocolate and egg yolk till creamy and stiff. Chill it, then beat cream again till smooth and fluffy. Spread half of this filling on the sponge which you unroll and then roll up again. Spread the rest of the cream on the outside of the log, so as to suggest the rough bark of a tree. May be sprinkled with sliced pistachio nuts or chopped almonds.

Sacher Cake

Ingredients: 5 oz. butter • 5 oz. sugar • 6 eggs • 5 oz. melted chocolate • 4 oz. flour • 1/2 pint cream • chocolate glaze.

Cream sugar and butter. Add egg yolks one by one, add melted chocolate, then flour, lastly fold in the stiffly whipped egg whites. Turn into a buttered cake-tin and bake in a moderate oven for 1/2 hour. Cool it, then cover with chocolate glaze. Serve whipped cream in a separate dish.

Cocoa Cake

Ingredients: 6 eggs • 2 oz. butter • 7 oz. castor sugar • 2 1/2 oz. flour • 1 1/2 oz. cocoa.
Cream: 3 1/2 oz. butter • 3 oz. castor sugar • 3 1/2 oz. ground hazel-nuts • 1 tbsp. rum • lemon icing.

Cream egg yolks, butter and sugar, add flour and cocoa, fold in the stiffly whipped egg whites. Turn into a buttered and floured cake-tin and bake in a moderate oven for 30 minutes. Let cool. Cream butter and sugar, add ground hazel-nuts, and rum. Split the cake in two, spread the filling in a thick layer on the lower half of the cake, and cover with top half. Spread top with lemon icing.

Coffee Cream Cake

Ingredients: 8 eggs • 9 oz. castor sugar • 5 oz. chopped almonds •
5 oz. flour.
Cream: 6 egg yolks • 9 oz. sugar • 1/2 cup strong black coffee •
5 oz. butter • few drops of vanilla essence • 1/2 oz. chocolate coffee
beans.

Cream egg yolks and sugar. Add finely chopped almonds, flour, the stiffly whipped egg whites. Turn into a buttered and floured cake-tin and bake in a moderate oven for 1/2 hour. Let it cool. Cream: beat together the egg yolks, sugar and strong black coffee. Place the bowl containing the mixture over boiling water and continue beating till it thickens, remove from heat and stir boiling water and continue beating till it thickens, remove from heat and stir mixture till cool. Cream butter and stir into the mixture, add a few drops of vanilla essence. Split cake in two, spread half of the cream on bottom half and the rest evenly on top of the cake. Decorate with chocolate coffee beans.

Caramel Cake

Ingredients: 10 circular-shaped wafers • 1/2 lb. hazelnuts •
1/2 lb. castor sugar • 3 egg yolks • 2 1/2 oz. butter • 3 oz. lump
sugar •
2 tbsp. cream.

To make cream, lightly roast hazelnuts in oven, then rub off skins between cloth. Chop coarsely. Mix sugar and chopped hazelnuts in a thick saucepan, and, stirring constantly, melt sugar over medium heat till mixture is golden-brown. Take aside and, stirring constantly, pour over 1/4 cup of cold water. Now beat well together egg yolks and cream, cook over steam till thick, then add it to the grillage, together with butter. Stir till mixture is creamy. Spread this cream on wafers, placing them on top of each other. Melt lump sugar to a light brown caramel, pour over the top, smooth with oiled knife. Mark slices with knife before caramel hardens, to facilitate cutting.

Orange Cream Cake

Ingredients: 6 eggs • 5 oz. granulated sugar • 7 oz. ground almonds • the grated rind of 2 oranges • the juice of 1 orange • 2 tbsp. fine breadcrumbs.
Cream: 1/2 lb. butter • 5 oz. castor sugar • juice and grated rind of 1 orange • 2 egg yolks.

Cream sugar and egg yolks. Stir in the ground almonds, orange juice, grated peel, crumbs and the stiffly whipped egg whites. Bake the mixture in three layers, using circular sandwich tins for the purpose. Turn them on cakerack and cool. Filling: cream butter and sugar, stir in the egg yolks, orange juice and grated rind. Beat till mixture is stiff and hard. Spread between the layers and cover the top of the cake as well. Decorate with orange jelly and skinned orange-slices. Chill well before serving.

Pineapple Gateau

Ingredients: A four-egg sponge cake • 2 gills cream • 10 oz. fresh pineapple • 7 oz. castor sugar.

Cut sponge-cake in two, obtaining two rounds. Whip cream till stiff, fold in the coarsely chopped pineapple. Spread a thick layer of it on the bottom round, cover with the other piece of sponge, then top with the remaining whipped cream and pineapple mixture. Chill, then serve.

Strawberry Jam Cake

Ingredients: 10 oz. granulated sugar • 6 eggs • 1 oz. cocoa •
5 oz. flour • strawberry jam • 2 gills cream.

Mix 2 oz. sugar, 1 oz. cocoa, and 3 tbsp. cold water in a small
saucepan, cook on low heat for 5–6 minutes, then put aside
to cool. Cream egg yolks with 8 oz. sugar, adding 8 tbsp. cold
water, one at a time. Pour the cooled cocoa mixture into the
creamed egg yolks, add flour and the stiffly whipped egg
whites. Turn into a buttered and floured cake-tin and bake in
a moderate oven for about 30 minutes. Cool, then split cake
in two. Sandwich with a thick layer of strawberry jam, then
pile stiffly whipped cream on top. Chill before serving.

Cherry Cake

Ingredients: 1/2 lb. butter • 1/2 lb. chocolate • 1/2 lb. granulated
sugar • 8 eggs • 5 oz. ground almonds • 1 tbsp. flour • bottled
morello cherries • chocolate glaze.

Cream butter, sugar and egg yolks. Add softened chocolate.
Add ground almonds, flour and the stiffly whipped egg
whites. Spread 1-inch-thick layers of the mixture in two buttered and floured cake tins. Bake in a moderate oven for
about 14–16 minutes, then turn them out onto a pastry-
board or any flat surface. Repeat the procedure twice more
to obtain 6 cake layers. Filling: drain, stone then chop bottled
morello cherries, mix with 1 oz. ground almonds. Spread this
mixture between cake layers, press top of the cake gently
with your palm. Cover with chocolate glaze, and serve with
the syrup from the fruit separately.

Chestnut Cream Cake

Ingredients: 2 lb. cooked and peeled chestnuts • 6 eggs •
6 tbsp. granulated sugar • 1 tbsp. flour. Cream: 3 1/2 oz. butter •
3 1/2 oz. castor sugar • some of the chestnut purée • 3 tbsp. rum.
Butter glaze: 2 tbsp. milk • 4 oz. chocolate • 1 oz. butter.

Press cooked and peeled chestnuts through sieve. Cream in
a bowl the egg yolks and sugar. Stir in 9 tbsp. chestnut purée,
1 tbsp. flour, add stiffly whipped egg whites. Blend well; then
turn the mixture into a buttered and floured cake-tin and
bake in a moderate oven for about 30–35 minutes. Turn out
to cool, then carefully split in two. Cream: cream butter and
sugar, stir in the remaining chestnut purée, add 3 tbsp. rum
and beat into a smooth cream. Spread this filling thickly
between the layers of cake. Butter icing: add chopped
chocolate to milk and, stirring constantly, heat till chocolate
melts. Take off heat, add butter and stir till lukewarm. Spread
over the cake. Chill.

Punch Cake

Ingredients: 6 eggs • 6 tbsp. granulated sugar • 6 tbsp. flour • a few
drops of cochineal • 1/2 oz. chocolate.
Cream: 6 egg yolks • 1/2 lb. castor sugar • 2 gills cream • 5 sheets
gelatine • 1/4 pint rum • some pink icing.

Cream sugar and egg yolks. Add stiffly whipped egg whites
and stir in the flour. Spoon half of the mixture into two separate bowls (1/4 into each), mix the cochineal in one, add
chocolate powder to the other. Bake in buttered and floured
sandwich-tins first the two coloured ones, and then the
remaining plain mixture, divided in two. Bake in a moderate
oven for 12–15 minutes, then turn the layers onto a flat sur-

face. Cool, then sprinkle the coloured layers and one plain layer with 3 tbsp. rum.

Cream: cream egg yolks and sugar. Add 1 gill cream and gelatine, place the bowl over boiling water and, stirring constantly, cook till mixture thickens. Take it off heat and stir till cool, add rum and the stiffly-whipped cream left. Chill for 15–20 minutes, then spread thickly between the cake-layers. Top cake with the layer which was not sprinkled with rum. Chill again, then spread top with pink icing.

Cottage Cheese Cake

Ingredients: 2 oz. butter • 3 1/2 oz. flour • 1 egg yolk • 1 tsp. castor sugar • about 1/2 gill sour cream.
Cream: 10 oz. cottage cheese • 8 eggs • 3/4 lb. castor sugar • vanilla essence.

Knead butter, flour, sugar, egg yolk, and sour cream into a rather stiff dough. Divide in three, roll out, and line the bottom of a cake-tin with one of the rounds. Prepare the cream: press cottage cheese through sieve. Add egg yolks and sugar, stir thoroughly, then fold in the stiffly beaten egg whites. Spread one-half of the mixture on the pastry, placed in the bottom of the cake-tin. Cover with pastry, then spread all the remaining cream over it. Cover with third piece of pastry. Flatten lightly with your palm. Bake in a moderate oven for 1 hour. Remove from cake-tin, sprinkle top with castor sugar and serve while still warm.

SWEET SAUCES, GLAZES, CHAUDEAUX

Vanilla Custard

Ingredients: 3 eggs • 2 1/2 oz. sugar • 1/2 pint milk • vanilla essence.

Cream eggs and sugar in a bowl, add cold milk gradually. Cook mixture in top of a double saucepan, till it thickens. Flavour with vanilla essence. Serve chilled.

Chocolate Glaze

Ingredients: 1/2 lb. icing sugar • 3 oz. chocolate • 1 tsp. butter.

Place sugar into a porcelain bowl. Add 2 tbsp. water and softened chocolate. Stir with wooden spoon till mixture is shiny and smooth. Add the butter and after 5 minutes further stirring it is ready for use.

Chocolate Sauce

Ingredients: 1/2 pint milk • 1 egg yolk • 4 oz. grated chocolate • 1 tbsp. vanilla-flavoured castor sugar.

Beat egg yolk and milk, add chocolate and sugar. Cook over boiling water, stirring constantly till it thickens. Can be served either hot or cold.

Chocolate Chaudeau

Ingredients: 5 eggs • 1 tbsp. granulated sugar • 5 oz. grated chocolate • 1 3/4 cups milk.

Cream eggs, sugar and grated chocolate. Add hot milk and, placing the bowl over boiling water, beat the mixture till it thickens. Pull off heat and keep on beating 10 minutes longer. Serve hot or cold.

Punch Glaze

Ingredients: 1/2 lb. icing sugar • 1 tbsp. rum • a few drops of cochineal.

Place sugar into a porcelain bowl. Add 2 tbsp. water and 1 tbsp. rum. Stir with wooden spoon till mixture is shiny and smooth. Stir in the cochineal and use.

Coffee Glaze

Ingredients: 1/2 lb. icing sugar • 3 tbsp. strong black coffee.

Stir sugar and cold black coffee till the mixture is shiny and smooth.

Coffee Chaudeau

Ingredients: 5 eggs • 1 1/4 cups milk • 1/2 cup strong black coffee • 3 tbsp. castor sugar.

Cream eggs and sugar. Add milk and black coffee. Place the bowl over boiling water and, stirring constantly, stir the mixture till it thickens. On no account allow to boil. Serve hot or cold as an accompaniment to plain cakes or sponge cakes.

Chestnut Chaudeau

Ingredients: 5 eggs • 1 3/4 cups milk • 2 tbsp. chestnut purée •
3 tbsp. castor sugar • 1 tsp. rum.

Cream sugar and eggs. Add chestnut purée and milk. Place the bowl over boiling water and, stirring constantly, cook till mixture thickens. Add 1 tsp. rum just before serving.

Strawberry Sauce

Ingredients: 1 lb. fresh strawberries • 1 1/2 gills cream •
4 tbsp. castor sugar.

Press fresh strawberries through sieve. Place the purée, together with the sugar and cream in a bowl and whip the mixture with an egg-whisk for 15 minutes. Serve cold.

Raspberry Sauce

Ingredients: 1 lb. fresh raspberries • 1/2 lb. castor sugar.

Press fresh raspberries through sieve. Add sugar to the juice and placing the bowl over boiling water, stir till mixture is well heated up but does not boil. Serve hot or just cooled; it turns to jelly if chilled.

Orange Chaudeau

Ingredients: 5 eggs • the juice of 3 oranges • grated rind
of 1 orange • 4 tbsp. castor sugar.

Cream eggs and sugar. Add orange juice and 2 tbsp. water, place the bowl over boiling water and, beating the mixture

SWEET SAUCES, GLAZES, CHAUDEAUX •

constantly, cook till thick and fluffy. Stir in the grated orange rind.

Lemon Glaze

Ingredients: 1/2 lb. icing sugar • the juice of 1 lemon.

Place the sugar in a porcelain bowl, add lemon juice and 2 tbsp. water. Stir with wooden spoon till mixture is smooth and shiny, then it is ready to use.

Wine Chaudeau

Ingredients: 1/2 pint white wine • 2 eggs • 2 oz. castor sugar • 1 tsp. corn-flour.

Cream castor sugar, eggs and corn-flour, add wine gradually, then beat mixture over steam till thick and fluffy. Serve hot.

Punch Chaudeau

Ingredients: 4 egg yolks • 4 tbsp. castor sugar • the juice of 1 lemon and 1 orange • grated peel of 1/2 orange and 1/2 lemon • 1/4 pint strong tea • 2 tbsp. rum.

Cream egg yolks and sugar. Add lemon and orange juice and grated peel. Place the bowl over boiling water and, beating constantly, add the tea. Continue beating till mixture thickens, then add rum and serve hot.

CREAMS
AND CREAM MOULDS

Chocolate Cream Mould

Ingredients: 3 1/2 oz. castor sugar • 5 oz. chocolate • 3 sheets of gelatine • 3 1/2 gills cream • vanilla essence.

Mix in a small saucepan the sugar with 1/3 cup water. Stirring constantly, cook over medium heat till sugar is dissolved, add chocolate, then put aside to cool. Meantime melt gelatine in 1/4 cup water, add it to the syrup. When the mixture is cold, fold into the stiffly whipped cream. Pour into a rinsed blancmange mould and chill for at least 3 hours. Turn out and serve with sponge fingers.

Cocoa Cream Mould

Ingredients: 6 eggs • 1/2 lb. castor sugar • 1 1/2 oz. cocoa • 3 gills cream • 2 sheets of gelatine.

Cream sugar and egg yolks. Add cocoa and the cream. Place the bowl over boiling water and, whipping constantly, cook the mixture till it thickens. Remove from heat, add gelatine dissolved in 1/2 cup water. Mix well. Add stiffly beaten egg whites. Turn into a rinsed fancy mould, and chill for at least 3 hours.

Coffee Cream Mould

Ingredients: 1/2 cup very string black coffee • 1 sheet of gelatine •
3 oz. castor sugar • 1 oz. chopped roasted hazelnuts •
3 1/2 gills cream • vanilla essence.

Melt gelatine in the coffee. Add sugar and stir till mixture is cool. Fold in the stiffly whipped cream, then the chopped hazelnuts. Turn into a rinsed fancy mould and chill. Serve with whipped cream flavoured with a little sugar and a drop or two of vanilla essence.

Vanilla Cream Mould

Ingredients: 4 egg yolks • 2 oz. castor sugar • 1 pint cream •
2 sticks of vanilla pod • 3 sheets of gelatine.

Cream egg yolks and sugar, vanilla pods and 1/2 pint cream. Place bowl over boiling water and stir mixture till it thickens. Remove vanilla pods, add gelatine melted previously in a spoonful of hot water, stir well, then put aside to cool. Fold in rest of the stiffly whipped cream. Pour mixture into a rinsed mould and chill for at least 3 hours.

Almond Cream Mould

Ingredients: 5 oz. castor sugar • 4 egg yolks •
5 oz. ground almonds • 1/4 pint milk • 3 1/2 gills cream.

Mix ground almonds and milk in a small saucepan. Place over low heat and stirring constantly, bring to the boil. Put aside to cool. Cream egg yolks and sugar, mix with the cooked almonds, fold in the stiffly whipped cream. Pour the mixture into a rinsed mould and chill for at least 4 hours.

Turn mould onto a glass dish, place small rolled wafers all around.

Chestnut Cream Mould

Ingredients: 1 lb. cooked chestnuts • 1/2 pint milk • 3 egg yolks • 1/2 lb. castor sugar • 1 stick of vanilla pod • 3 sheets of gelatine • 3 tbsp. rum • 2 oz. finely chopped candied fruits.

Peel boiled chestnuts. Put aside five whole chestnuts, put the rest through sieve. Beat well together 2 oz. sugar, egg yolks and milk. Place the bowl over boiling water and, stirring, cook mixture till it thickens. Put aside to cool, then add chestnut purée. Prepare a thick syrup with 6 oz. sugar and 2 tbsp. water. Melt gelatine in 1/4 pint hot water. Add syrup and melted gelatine to the chestnut mixture, stir well then add rum, coarsely chopped chestnuts and candied fruits, fold in stiffly whipped cream last. Pour into a rinsed mould and chill for at least 4 hours.

Pineapple Cream Mould

Ingredients: 1 lb. fresh pineapple • 4 oz. granulated sugar • 1 oz. gelatine • 4 gills cream.

Place the pineapple on a plate or shallow dish, and chop the fruit coarsely. Strain off the juice into a small saucepan, add 1/4 pint water, 4 oz. sugar and the gelatine. Cook on low heat till gelatine melts then pour it over the chopped pineapple. Cool it. Just before the point of setting, fold in the stiffly whipped cream and pour the mixture into a rinsed mould. Chill. Dip mould in hot water just before serving and turn contents onto a flat dish.

Cantaloupe Cream Mould

Ingredients: 1 medium-sized cantaloupe melon •
3 oz. castor sugar • 4 sheets of gelatine • 1 1/2 gills cream •
vanilla essence.

Cut out a palm-sized, round piece at the stalk end of the melon. Remove seeds through this opening, then scrape the meat out, leaving the rind whole. Press the scraped-out fruit through sieve, add sugar and a few drops of vanilla essence. Melt gelatine in 2–3 tbsp. water, add to the purée. Cool the mixture, then fold in the stiffly whipped cream. Fill the scooped-out rind with the mixture, replace stalk end. Chill for at least 4 hours. Cut melon on table.

Strawberry Cream Mould

Ingredients: 1 lb. strawberries • 4 oz. granulated sugar •
4 egg yolks • 1 large cupful milk • 3 1/2 oz. castor sugar •
2 1/2 sheets of gelatine • 1 1/2 gills cream.

Leave the washed fruit on a sieve to dry. Mix half a pound strawberries with 4 oz. sugar and cook in a saucepan for 15 minutes. Add gelatine. Cream egg yolks with castor sugar, stir in the strawberry and gelatine mixture, add milk. Place in a bowl over boiling water and, beating vigorously, cook the mixture till it thickens. Cool, then fold in the stiffly whipped cream and the uncooked strawberries. Pour into a rinsed mould and chill for at least 3–4 hours. Turn out and decorate with whipped cream.

Raspberry Cream Mould

Ingredients: 5 eggs • 5 tbsp. castor sugar • 5 tsp. flour • 1 pint milk •
1 sheet gelatine • a few drops of cochineal • 2 oz. butter •
1/2 lb. raspberries • 2 tbsp. coarsely chopped hazelnuts.

Cream egg yolks, sugar and flour. Stirring constantly, add milk spoon by spoon. Place the bowl over boiling water and cook the mixture till it thickens. Put aside and add gelatine, stirring till gelatine melts. Now work in well the creamed butter and leave mixture to cool. Fold in the fruit, chopped hazelnuts and the stiffly whipped egg whites. Pour mixture into a rinsed mould and chill for at least 3–4 hours. Serve decorated with sponge fingers.

Fruit Cream Mould

Ingredients: 4 oz. sugar • 3 gills cream • 4 oz. candied fruit •
2 oz. mixed peel • 6 egg yolks • vanilla essence.

Mix sugar with 1/4 pint water, bring to the boil, then cool. Add egg yolks and, placing the bowl over boiling water, cook the mixture till thick and creamy. Add few drops of vanilla essence, chopped peel and candied fruit. Cool, then fold in the stiffly whipped cream. Pour the mixture into a rinsed mould and chill for at least 3–4 hours. Turn onto a glass dish and decorate with maraschino cherries.

Peach Cream Mould

Ingredients: 1 lb. peaches • 4 oz. granulated sugar • 3 egg yolks •
2 oz. castor sugar • 3 1/2 gills cream • vanilla essence •
chopped walnuts or hazelnuts • 3 sheets gelatine.

Peel and halve the fruit, then put 1/2 lb. into a saucepan, together with 4 oz. granulated sugar. Bring to the boil and cook gently for 15 minutes, put aside to cool. Cream egg yolks and sugar, add 2 gills cream and placing the bowl over boiling water, cook the mixture till thick and creamy. Add a few drops of vanilla essence. Put aside, stir in the gelatine, add the peach and sugar syrup. Cool, then add 1 1/2 gills stiffly whipped cream. Pour one-third of the mixture into the bottom of a rinsed mould. Cover with a layer of halved peaches, repeat the procedure and top with mixture. Chill for at least 3–4 hours, dip the mould into hot water and turn contents out carefully. Brush top with a little cream and sprinkle chopped nuts over.

Apricot Cream Mould

Prepare exactly as the peach cream mould, using apricots instead of peaches. Decorate with whipped cream.

Tutti-frutti

Ingredients: 1 lb. mixed bottled fruit • 2 oz. candied orange peel • 6 egg yolks • 5 oz. castor sugar • 5 oz. flour • 1 3/4 cups milk • 1 oz. gelatine • 1 3/4 cups cream • 2 tbsp. orange marmalade • 1 tbsp. rum.

Drain bottled fruit, then chop into neat cubes. Cream sugar and egg yolks, mix into the flour, add milk and stir well. Add gelatine and marmalade. Place bowl over boiling water and stir contents briskly, till thick and smooth. Put aside and add fruit, chopped peel and rum. Cool, then fold in the stiffly whipped cream. Pour the mixture into a rinsed mould and chill for 4 hours. Turn out onto a glass dish, decorate with whipped cream.

Punch Cream Mould

Ingredients: 3/4 pint strong tea • 5 sheets of gelatine • 1/2 lb. castor sugar • the juice of 1 lemon • 1/4 cup rum • 1 1/2 gills cream.

Place gelatine into a bowl, pour the hot tea over and stir till gelatine melts. Add castor sugar, lemon juice, and rum; leave to cool. when mixture is cold but still runny, fold in the stiffly whipped cream. Pour into a rinsed mould and chill very thoroughly for at least 4 hours. Do not use a very deep mould for this.

FRUIT DISHES

Banana Salad

Ingredients: 1 lb. peeled bananas • 1 gill maraschino
(or chartreuse) • 2 1/2 oz. castor sugar.

Slice bananas and arrange in a glass dish in layers. Sprinkle
each layer with sugar and liqueur. Leave to stand for at least
2 hours before serving. Chill thoroughly.

Orange Salad

Ingredients: About 6 Jaffa oranges • 1/4 pint rum (or cognac) •
2 1/2 oz. castor sugar.

Peel juicy oranges carefully, scraping all the pith off the fruit.
Slice oranges, remove pips if there are any, and arrange
slices in a glass bowl. Sprinkle each layer of fruit with sugar
and cognac or rum. Chill for at least 2 hours before serving.

Strawberry Salad

Ingredients: 2 lb. fresh strawberries • 2 1/2 oz. castor sugar •
2 gills sour cream.

Sprinkle sugar on cleaned strawberries. Add sour cream and
stir carefully to avoid breaking the fruit. Chill for at least
1 hour before serving.

Iced Orange Cream I

Ingredients: 6 large • juicy oranges • 6 egg yolks • 6 tbsp. castor sugar • 1 tbsp. rum • 2 sheets of gelatine • 1 1/2 gills cream • 2 tbsp. milk.

Cut out a shilling-sized piece from the bottom side of the oranges. Scoop out inside carefully into a bowl. Add the grated rind of one orange to the fruit pulp and press through sieve. Cream egg yolks and sugar in another bowl, add orange-purée, rum or cognac and the gelatine melted in 2 tbsp. hot milk, fold in the stiffly whipped cream. Fill the orange skins with the mixture, top with the cut-off pieces of peel and chill for 2 hours before serving.

Iced Orange Cream II

Ingredients: 6 oranges • 2 tbsp. cognac • 2 tbsp. granulated sugar • 3 sheets gelatine • 4 tbsp. castor sugar • 4 eggs • 4 tbsp. coarsely ground hazelnuts • a few drops of vanilla essence.

Cut oranges in two, scoop out insides carefully, and press the fruit-pulp through sieve. Pour the purée into a saucepan, add cognac, 2 tbsp. granulated sugar, and gelatine. Heat the mixture till gelatine melts. Put aside. Cream egg yolks and 4 tbsp. castor sugar, add ground hazelnuts and the stiffly whipped egg whites. Stir the jelly into it, spoon the mixture into the empty orange skins and chill for about 2 hours. Pile whipped cream on top of each just before serving, and sprinkle with a very little grated orange rind.

Orange Jelly

Ingredients: 6 oranges • 1 lb. apples • 2 oz. roasted almonds • sugar.

Cut oranges in two. Scoop out insides, and place the pulp into a saucepan together with quartered, unpeeled apples. Add just enough water to cover, bring to the boil, then reduce heat and simmer till apples are soft. Pour the mixture into a jelly-bag, and leave to drip overnight. Next day measure the resulting juice and add the same weight of sugar. Cook till a spoonful of the liquid jellies within a few minutes on a porcelain plate. Now add the coarsely ground almonds and fill the orange skins with the mixture. Chill, then serve on a flat glass dish.

Fruit Jelly

Ingredients: 2 lb. fruit (strawberries, raspberries or red currants) •
1 1/2 lb. granulated sugar.

Place the sugar into a saucepan, add about 3/4 cup water. Stirring constantly, cook till sugar has melted and begins to bubble. Pour this syrup over the crushed fruit, stir, then leave to stand till lukewarm. Pour the mixture into a jelly-bag and allow to drip overnight. Melt the resultant jelly next day and pour into a jelly-mould or — if you wish to keep for a longer time — into jars. In the latter case the jars should be closed tightly and steamed.

Cantaloupe Melon Salad

Ingredients: 2 lb. melon • 3 oz. castor sugar • 1/4 cup rum.

Peel 1 or 2 melons, according to size, and scrape out the seeds. Cut the fruit into 1-inch thick slices and arrange in a glass bowl. Sprinkle the sugar over and put aside till sugar melts. Sprinkle the rum over the fruit, cover the dish with a plate, and chill for 1 hour before serving.

Honeydew and Cantaloupe Melon Salad

Ingredients: 2 melons • 3 oz. sugar • 1/4 cup cognac.

Cut the fruit into small balls with a gouger. Sprinkle with sugar. When sugar is melted add the cognac, stir carefully, then chill. Serve in individual glass dishes.

Steamed Figs

Ingredients: 1 lb. best-quality dried figs •
a pinch of grated lemon and orange peel • 1 1/2 cups white wine •
1 oz. granulated sugar.

Wash figs in warm water. Add sugar and grated peel to the wine, bring to the boil. Place the figs into the wine and simmer for about 10–15 minutes. Put aside to cool, then pour into a glass dish and chill for 1 hour before serving.

Tipsy Figs

Ingredients: 1 lb. fresh figs • 1 oz. granulated sugar • 1 1/4 cups white wine.

Place the ripe fresh figs into a bowl and pour the warmed-up wine over. Cover and leave to stand for at least 2–3 hours. Pour the wine of the fruit into a small saucepan, add sugar and bring to the boil. Pour the hot wine over the figs again. Cool, then chill for at least 2–3 hours before serving.

Salted Almonds

Place almonds into a bowl and pour boiling water over them. Strain off the water in 10 minutes' time, rub almonds between cloth to remove skins. Place almonds with a handful of salt into a baking tin, and, shaking occasionally, roast till pale brown colour. Turn into a colander and shake to remove surplus salt.

Roasted Hazelnuts

Place hazelnuts together with a handful of salt into a baking tin and, shaking occasionally, roast till pale brown and the skin comes off. Pour onto a cloth and rub off skin. this is best freshly roasted.

INDEX